Lafland
June, 1979

Ideology in America

Change and Response in a City,
a Suburb, and a Small Town

IDEOLOGY IN AMERICA

Change and Response in a City, a Suburb, and a Small Town

Everett Carll Ladd, Jr.

Cornell University Press
Ithaca and London

First published 1969

Library of Congress Catalog Card Number: 69-18214

PRINTED IN THE UNITED STATES OF AMERICA
BY THE COLONIAL PRESS INC.

To my mother and father

Acknowledgments

The research for this volume was generously supported by the National Science Foundation, the Social Science Research Council, and the University of Connecticut Research Foundation. The principal support was Grant GS-1174 from the National Science Foundation. An award from the Committee on Faculty Research Grants of the Social Science Research Council in 1966–67 permitted me to undertake an important phase of the research which would not otherwise have been possible. The University of Connecticut Research Foundation provided the grant which allowed me to begin the study in the spring of 1965 and continued to provide valuable assistance throughout. I gratefully acknowledge this support.

Many citizens of Hartford, Bloomfield, and Putnam helped me in this study, many more than I can personally acknowledge here. I am especially indebted to three: Mr. Louis Edman, of the Edman Agency in Putnam; Mr. Preston King, town manager of Bloomfield; and Mr. Jack Zaiman, of the Hartford *Courant*. They were valued sources of information and assistance and gave generously of their time.

Andrew Hacker of Cornell University, Theodore Lowi of the University of Chicago, and Lowell Field, my colleague here at the University of Connecticut, read all or large portions of the manuscript, and I benefited from their wise advice. I want to thank, too, for professional assistance and understanding far beyond the call of duty, the staff of Cornell University Press and Hugh Clark, Associate Dean of the Graduate School, for Research, at the University of Connecticut.

A number of my students here, both graduate and undergraduate, helped me in the collection of data. The efforts of three—

Morris Shepard, now of Pennsylvania State University, Lauriston King, and William Zenon—played an especially large part in the completion of this study.

I owe a special debt to Mrs. Eleanor Wilcox. She typed several drafts of the manuscript with care and met the demands of a somewhat hectic schedule.

Finally, I want to thank my family: my wife Cynthia for her advice and criticism and for her willingness to take on some extra responsibilities; and my children, Carll and Corina, for patiently enduring the many little disruptions a project like this necessarily requires.

EVERETT CARLL LADD, JR.

Storrs, Connecticut
June 1968

Contents

Maps

Figures

Tables

Ideology in America

Change and Response in a City,
a Suburb, and a Small Town

Introduction: Scope and Orientation

This is a study of political ideas and ideology in three American communities—of three community ideational systems. It is also a study of American political ideology, of what is happening to it in the face of massive social and economic change, of the response and adaptation in political ideas and ideology at a stage in this country's development that has variously been called postcivilized, overdeveloped, affluent, postindustrial, a *civilisation technicienne*. The approach is to compare community ideational systems in three quite different settings—a central city, a white-collar suburb, and a small mill town—each of which appears to have been affected differently by the continuing transformations of American society.

It is not hard to demonstrate the extent of continuing change in American society. Our nation was built on change, and it is one of the few constants in our experience. Born as it was at the juncture of two great revolutions—technological-industrial and egalitarian—the country really could have taken no other course. At its birth the United States was a farming nation of four million. Now we are two hundred million, increasingly metropolitanized, and one in fifteen in our work force grows ample foodstuff for the rest.

Yet the transformation of American socioeconomic structure has never been more rapid or profound than in the two decades since World War II. The social and economic order emergent in this period departs sharply from the old: new residential patterns, with the movement of "the center of gravity" from small towns and older core cities to the metropolitan sprawl around the cities; new employment patterns, as white-collar workers outnumber those wearing blue collars by seven million and as the number of self-employed persons declines precipitously; a new affluence, not extended to all but impressive in its general outlines and bringing new patterns in consumption and leisure; a new interdependence, summoned by a complexly integrated national economy, by metropolitanization, and by nationalized culture, with this interdependence defining a new and expanded role for government; and a new status as the leader of the "overdeveloped nations," the select few no longer operating from an economics of scarcity and no longer preoccupied with the problems of scarcity.

So much that is important in contemporary sociopolitical change in the United States appears to organize itself around changes in cities, suburbs, and towns. Observers note that each type has fared very differently. The position of urban America is painted in the most somber tones. Commentary on our cities stresses problems and crisis, and this crisis is increasingly discussed in terms of black and white. Bayard Rustin has written of the "dangerous convergence of race and class" in contemporary America, and our big cities more and more are the home of the black lower class. Between 1960 and 1966 alone, the major cities of the United States lost 2.5 per cent of their white residents while their Negro population increased by 25 per cent. The flight of the successful, physical deterioration, crime and violence, air pollution, a demand for services that collides with available resources—all are part of the crisis of the city.

There is also a crisis of the old small towns. Decline is as much their legacy, although it is a different kind of decline that often is seen through glasses deeply tinted with nostalgia. We live in an America run by metropolitan residents who were born on the farm or in the village or town. But there is more than nostalgia.

American political history really is a history of the ascendancy of small towns: they were the political center of gravity, their elites dominant nationally and their ideas and ideology controlling. The present decline of the small town is more than a relative loss of population by a certain category of community.

It is a decline of certain forms of small and independent business and the ascendancy of the large corporation; it is the decline of the old entrepreneurial middle class and the rise of a new corporate middle class; it is the decline of a personalized and localized society and politics and the development of a more impersonal, complex, bureaucratized, and nationalized society. Although early expectations apparently overstated the significance of state legislative reapportionment, there can be no doubt that reapportionment followed a massive metropolitanization of the population and that it took representation from rural and small town America, thus sealing its loss of political power.

The small town is our lost innocence, our lost boyhood; the city, a slightly disreputable past and the encapsulation of the big public problems of the present and future. The suburbs, in contrast, are quintessentially the new America, children of the new affluence and the new technology. They harbor the new ruling class—the white-collar managers whose working hours are spent in the interstices of big bureaucracies, whether government, business, or academia. As varied as suburbs are, and as inadequate as are some of the simplistic model descriptions (not all suburbs are like Westport, Shaker Heights, or Grosse Pointe, and not all suburban males depart each morning on the 8:02), it is still clear that we are building on a massive scale a type of community that is neither town nor city, that these metropolitan-places-outside-central-cities are absorbing the lion's share of population growth, and that they are an important response to change in our social and economic structure.

We need not belabor the obvious: much of the discussion of change and its political implications in contemporary America pivots on the urban–suburban–small town distinction. Our troubled central cities, bulging suburbs, and declining towns are described here as three Americas—affected differently by the central features of socioeconomic change, confronting different political problems with different resources, and evidencing markedly different social structures.

We would expect other kinds of variation to contribute to

divergent responses in ideas and ideology. We could, for example, inquire about responses organized regionally—Northeast, Midwest, Southeast, and so on. But no categories have been treated as fully as the ones we explore here, and none are discussed as frequently in the context of sociopolitical change. This is a study of political ideas and ideology in three communities, but we expect the selection made will afford us some insights into the ideational responses to broader currents in American sociopolitical life.

The more specific questions, areas of interest, assumptions, and formally drawn hypotheses on which this study was predicated all relate to one or more of three subject areas. First, we wanted to examine from an immediate focus the views of public life of the contending elites in each community. What differences on public policy separate the leadership of the Democratic party organization in the city (Hartford, Connecticut) from the leadership of the large corporations based there? What differences distinguish the "old families" of our suburb—those who were there when Bloomfield (Connecticut) was not a suburb but a small town—and the young professionals who have moved to ascendancy in both the political parties and in the various civic organizations of Bloomfield? We wanted, too, to describe the *perception of conflict* of contending community elites. The area is large and filled with analytic dangers. But it seemed important to compare how the various elites of our three communities perceive their political differences with other elites. These data permitted construction of a kind of ideational profile of the town, the suburb, and the city.

The second area encompassed an assessment of the political meaning of metropolitanization through a comparison of political ideas and ideology in the small town and the metropolitan region. In what ways, if any, do the community elites and the rank and file of small-town and metropolitan America see political life differently? The importance of this to a country in rapid and continuing metropolitanization is obvious. A literature beginning with Alexis de Tocqueville's *Democracy in America* and extending through such varied treatments as Granville Hicks' *Small Town* and Joseph Bensman's and Arthur Vidich's *Small Town in Mass Society* describes small-town politics as dealing with the immediate and the close-up, dwelling on personalities and on matters of patronage or direct self-interest. There has been little or no ideological conflict. The public sector is depicted as narrow and typically not extending beyond such matters as road repair and the property tax rate. We hypothesized that the view of conflict acquired through continued exposure to narrow interests, limited governmental activity, immediate self-interest, and the dominance of the personal characteristics of the actors—the "friends-and-neighbors" politics of the small town—cannot readily be dropped upon moving to a situation where conflict is broad and systematic. To put it differently, this way of viewing conflict becomes part of the intellectual equipment of small-town elites and helps shape their response to national and international politics.

But in the 1960's two out of every three Americans lived not in small town and country but in metropolitan areas. And the metropolitan political setting appears to differ sharply. It is far more impersonal, is marked by broader and more systematic conflict, and has a far larger public sector. The more interdependent a society becomes, the more it requires some vehicle to maintain delicate balances, and that vehicle is government. The metropolitan region is the microcosm of the interdependent society. Metropolitan elites cannot avoid—though their responses may be inadequate—the demands of interdependence; they cannot be oblivious to—as their small town counterparts still can–the big domestic concerns of the day. It was hypothesized that the political problems facing the elites of the metropolitan region are qualitatively different from those confronting small-town leaders and produce vastly different patterns of ideational conflict. The political problems of the small town cannot be "packaged." Those of metropolitan America admit matters often essentially remote and abstract, generate conflict that is systematic, and thus encourage ideological speculation.

Finally, at the broadest level, we wanted to contribute to a clarification of the principal ideological axes in contemporary America. This subject area—ideology in the United States or in the West generally—is filled with confusion, in part because the term *ideology* has known so many different constructions since it was introduced around 1800. With magnificent understatement, David Minar has said that "ideology appears to have lost some of its cutting edge as a tool for social science." [1]

This is no better shown than in the argument over whether the United States and Europe are experiencing an "end" or a "decline" of ideology.[2] Those who write of its demise typically construe *ideology* as a "secular religion," a dogmatic set of beliefs passionately held and proclaimed: orthodox Marxism, fascism, Maoism, a virulent nationalism. These great "secular religions" emerged in a revolutionary epoch in which old forms of social, economic, and political organization were swept away by unparalleled technological and industrial change and new forms competed for ascendancy. They were—and today are—products of unreconciled societies and thus speak to individuals seeking identity in the midst of change, to polities seeking stability while experiencing instability, to social systems seeking solidarity while sharply divided by class, ethnicity, and the varying stages of development of their populations.

Is politics in most Western nations less ideological today

[1] Minar, "Ideology and Political Behavior," *Midwest Journal of Political Science,* V (November, 1961), 319. Minar's treatment of the intellectual history of *ideology* is excellent.

[2] Daniel Bell and Seymour Martin Lipset have written extensively on the "end of ideology" theme. See, by Bell, *The End of Ideology* (2nd rev. ed.; New York: Collier Books, 1962); "Ideology and the Beau Geste," *Dissent,* VIII (Winter, 1961), 75–77; and his commentary in a debate with Henry David Aiken, "The End of Ideology: A Debate," *Commentary,* XXXVIII (October, 1964), 69–76. By Lipset, *Political Man* (Garden City, N.Y.: Doubleday, 1960), pp. 403–417; and "The Changing Class Structure and Contemporary European Politics," *Daedalus,* Winter, 1964, 271–303.

than three decades ago? Yes, if you mean, as Daniel Bell does, that political conflict is more pragmatic, less rent by "apocalyptic beliefs that refuse to specify the costs and consequences of the changes they envision"; yes, in the sense Raymond Aron understands it, that a handful of great historical idea systems like Marxism have run out of steam and no longer dominate Western political debate; yes, in that, as S. M. Lipset observes, Western Europe has moved a long way toward a political consensus, with Left and Right no longer intensely divided over core institutions and processes.

But we take issue with the effort to conceptualize these developments as an "end of ideology." By this construction, American politics—in contrast to European—has never been ideological: New Deal liberalism, for instance, never had the qualities of a "secular religion." But how do we describe the competing positions of liberals and conservatives in the 1930's if not in terms of ideology? We see little justification for insisting that one variety of political idea system, such as messianic Marxism, which arose in certain countries under conditions that were in no sense permanent, is the genus ideology. It is easier to describe dogmatic, rigid, codified, highly programmatic idea systems than it is those of the American variety, which are flexible, nondogmatic, and diffuse, with shifting sets of policy prescriptions. But the latter are as important as the former to an understanding of political behavior. They are simply two species of the same genus. There are different ideologies for different systems, and by understanding more fully the nature and characteristics of the various species of ideology we will be better able to understand the dynamics of different political systems.

We cannot finally resolve, of course, the variation in constructions of *ideology,* but we can be precise as to how it is construed here. *Ideology* refers to a set of prescriptive positions on matters of government and public policy that are seen as forming a logically or quasi-logically interrelated system, with the system treating an area of political life that is both broad and significant. This area of political life typically includes such things as the structure of government and the distribution of power, the political objectives that the society should try to realize and how it should go about it, the distribution of the resources of the system, and the manner and bases for their allocation. An ideology is like a quilt, with individual policy items the patches. Like a quilt, an ideology is more than the sum of its patches; it is the patches firmly bound together in a specified and ordered arrangement. A person sees politics ideologically when he applies some overarching conceptual dimension to the myriad of policy choices, when he organizes remote and abstract matters into what for him is a logical or quasi-logical system.

A given individual may or may not apply such an overarching dimension, may or may not, that is, comprehend or share in any ideology. Philip Converse has convincingly demonstrated that the vast majority of the American (and presumably of any other) population lacks a contextual grasp of the standard ideologies.[3] We frequently fall into the confusion of assuming that support of a "liberal" policy requires comprehension of and commitment to "liberalism."

When we describe conflict in a particular political setting as ideological, we call attention to two interrelated features of it: that a significant segment of at least the participating elites sees politics ideologically, that is, that they apply some overarching conceptual dimension to order a wide array of policy choices; and that the constraints of ideology fit the conflict found, that the divisions are broad, abstract, wide-ranging, and categoric.[4]

We located in Hartford competing ideological positions, but

[3] Philip Converse, "The Nature of Belief Systems in Mass Publics," in David Apter (ed.), *Ideology and Discontent* (New York: Free Press of Glencoe, 1964), p. 213.

[4] It is essential to distinguish *ideology* thus understood from the more informal and less comprehensive collections of political ideas and attitudes which groups of people share in. If *ideology* is attached to all clusters of political ideas held by groups, it is effectively destroyed as an analytic tool. A number of community leaders may have opinions or attitudes treating some element of social change which are not part of any wide-ranging idea system but which are so generally held as to affect the func-

not the ones we expected. Most descriptions of ideological divisions in the United States have revolved around *liberal* vs. *conservative*—what we call the "Conventional Dichotomy" (C.D.) —and we began a pilot study in Greater Hartford in the summer of 1965 working with the hypothesis that the C.D. was the most enduring and comprehensive ideological dichotomy. But this study demonstrated that its economies did not closely fit the conflict found.

Any ideological category, of course, is nothing more than a form of shorthand, an intellectual yardstick for measuring, simplifying, and organizing a multitude of political idea elements. Both participants and analysts have a natural interest in describing political events as economically, as parsimoniously, as possible. A conflict situation comes into existence, and labels are attached to the competing positions. As long as this conflict situation persists, the use of these labels to describe a component of it efficiently conveys extensive information about the component. But let the conflict situation be substantially altered and the continued application of the old categories only distorts. This is what we found in Hartford with reference to the Conventional Dichotomy—not that there no longer is any conflict of the type it envisions, but that many of the assumptions about the conflict situation that this shorthand embodies are to a significant degree incorrect.

Samuel Beer has observed that *liberal* and *conservative* were rarely used by contemporary commentators on ideological divisions in the United States prior to the 1930's; then, suddenly,

---

tioning of the polity. In such a situation, we prefer to speak simply of their political ideas on change or of their *ideational response* to change. Similarly, it is not at all clear that there is any prescriptive system sufficiently rigorous and thoroughgoing to permit reference to the *ideology of organized labor*. But many labor leaders appear to share views on such matters as what constitutes the proper relationship among business, labor, and government. *Ideational* becomes a general term permitting reference to any set of idea responses without further specification as to their characteristics, and *ideology* is "saved" for more comprehensive and far-reaching systems.

they were "in the air." He concludes that these terms came into currency then as the shorthand for a new conflict situation.[5] Not unrelated to this, a number of historians have warned against the hasty application to a particular period of descriptions of ideological conflict drawn from another period: the shape of conflict in the 1830's is badly distorted, for example, if the Jacksonian Democrats are called "liberals" and the Whigs "conservatives." [6] The point is, of course, that distinct sociopolitical settings generate distinctive patterns of ideological conflict, and that the problem in utilizing labels to describe a conflict situation sharply different from the one for which they were originally developed is not merely semantic: they conceptualize the conflict in a way that has become invalid.

Chapter 1 generally and Chapter 5 more specifically develop our argument as to how and why the ideological disagreements among elites in Greater Hartford are not adequately accounted for by the economies of the Conventional Dichotomy. Chapter 5 then outlines the ideological conflict we did find. In brief, we locate a new ideological polarity of substantial comprehensiveness and describe it as *Cosmopolitanism-Parochialism.* Chapters 7 and 8 provide extensive empirical data on this conflict.

As our study led us toward this formulation, a number of other studies using quite disparate materials were being completed that, by different routes, were approaching the same conclusion—that the important changes in American society are producing new patterns of conflict and that the Conventional Dichotomy does not adequately account for these. The present study is part of a now rather substantial effort to reconceptualize conflict in a changed and changing society.

As we have said, our data come principally from a study in depth of ideas and ideology in three communities. Hartford,

[5] Samuel H. Beer, "Liberalism and the National Idea," *The Public Interest,* Fall, 1966, 70–82.

[6] See Lee Benson, *The Concept of Jacksonian Democracy* (Princeton, N.J.: Princeton University Press, 1961).

the Connecticut capital and a city of 155,000, was selected as the core city. Bloomfield, a suburb to the north and west of Hartford which has tripled its population in the last decade and a half, became the suburb. And Putnam—a town of 8,400 in the sparsely populated northeastern corner of Connecticut, well set off from the urban areas of southern New England, its population static for a half century—was picked as the independent small town. Any use of the community study as a vehicle to explore developments which are seen as national is fraught with danger, even though it offers distinct advantages. How "representative" are the communities chosen? What are they representative of?

Here, the chain of assumptions that sustained the selections made and the approach adopted went like this: As varied as the experiences of our central cities are, the category *central city* is not a meaningless one. Hartford appears representative in social structure, political problems, resources, and in its position as the troubled center of a metropolitan region. Like that of so many of our older core cities, Hartford's size has remained essentially static. Like so many other cities, Hartford has lost massive numbers of whites over the last decade and a half as "older" ethnic groups have fled to the suburbs. We would expect to find basic common elements in the ideational responses of the elites who govern Hartford and those commanding other core cities around the country.

The case of the small town is similar. Putnam in many ways is not a "typical New England small town." There is no handsome, newly painted Congregational Church resting on the edge of a green. Putnam is a sweaty mill town. Its inhabitants are predominantly of French Canadian rather than Yankee ancestry. Its population is heavily Roman Catholic and its politics Democratic. But it was precisely because Putnam is not the stereotyped small town that we chose it.

We assumed the key variables distinguishing the small town from other types of communities to be these: that it is not part of any metropolitan region and so does not share in either the problems or the assets of such a region; that it has experienced a set of developments that spell decline, including an economic life dominated by small and relatively marginal industries, the exodus of younger and often more productive people to metropolitan regions, and a failure to grow, with a concomitant drop in relative political power; and its social interactions generally and its politics specifically are based on the face-to-face contact of the actors and on their knowledge of one another extending back over some time—interactions are more personalized and immediate, less categoric. Putnam satisfies these criteria as well as any Yankee small town. If the factors here identified are indeed controlling, in most fundamental regards the ideational life of Putnam should not differ sharply from that of a Yankee town in northern Maine or a German-American town in the Midwest.

It is the same, too, with our suburb. There are, of course, suburbs and suburbs. Bloomfield is a white-collar suburb, and the income of its inhabitants is in the middle range for white-collar suburbs in Connecticut. There can be no doubt that a white-collar suburb like Bloomfield differs in rather fundamental ways from a blue-collar suburb, and the differences are not limited to occupation. But Bloomfield appears to share a set of characteristics that set the suburb off from the other two categories of communities. It is part of a metropolitan region. It cannot successfully avoid regional problems, and they intrude on its internal politics. It has shared in the explosive growth of the metropolitan region, and the "old-timers" have been inundated by a flood of newcomers. Above all, perhaps, it looks two ways—it still has the green grass, the low population density, the size of a small town, but its metropolitan location makes it part of a new interdependence.

The limitations in an attempt to generalize about the ideational life of city, suburb, and small town from data on three communities cannot be avoided. But there are practical considerations which cannot be avoided either. We are not able to examine every community in the country or anything approaching that number. And there are great advantages in being able to explore the subject in detail, over time, and in a rigorous and systematic manner. Hartford, Bloomfield, and Putnam seem to be reasonably representative in the variables that distinguish city, suburb, and town.

Research was begun in the three communities in the spring of 1965, and data were collected over the next thirty months. The selection of the leadership and mass interview samples, interview schedules, and related matters of method are treated in the Appendix. Here we need only outline the approach followed.

Detailed background information on each community was collected, including community histories, basic demographic data, and a "blow by blow" account of recent (the fifteen years preceding the study) political developments. In the summer and fall of 1965 mass surveys were conducted in each community that, when "weighted," produced a sample of 1,561 respondents. Three hundred and fifty-five community influentials were interviewed between October, 1965, and December, 1967—210 in Hartford, 90 in Bloomfield, 55 in Putnam. Selection procedures —described in the Appendix—were designed to include a large cross section of those persons in each municipality who, through their position in some institution prominently involved in the public life of the community (elective office, "good government" groups, and the like) or through their high prestige, were in a position to influence the community's response to the various public policy questions coming before it. We say "large cross section" because no effort was made to include all of the "top leaders" of each community. This is not a study of community power. It seemed important only to represent broadly all contending positions and groups in local public life. The leadership interviews were semistructured.

A much smaller number of interviews were conducted to gain background information from long-time residents, newspaper reporters, and others with detailed knowledge of the public life of each community. In addition, the author and his assistants were present at numerous meetings of organizations and governmental bodies in Hartford, Bloomfield, and Putnam.

Close attention was paid to three distinct facets of the context for community ideational life. Part of this context is American society itself. The ideational life of any American community is different now from what it was a hundred, or fifty, or thirty years ago because American society is different. So in Chapter 1, an effort is made to locate a number of historical contexts for American political ideas and ideology, each defined by underlying social and economic conditions. Changes in historical setting are better understood as changes in the *agenda of politics,* and we want to suggest the bold type on the agenda being worked out in the American sociopolitical experience of the 1960's.

The context changes over time. But it also varies from community to community at a given time, and some of this variation can be organized. Distinguishing cities, suburbs, and small towns is one effort to organize varying community experience, and Chapter 2 suggests both the confusion and utility of this trichotomy. Does the trichotomy point to significant differences in community setting? What do we know about town, suburb, and city as contrasting sociopolitical settings?

Finally, every community has in some sense its own peculiar mix of historical experience, personalities, economic structure, political institutions, interest groupings, and political demands. Chapter 3 treats this mix for Hartford, Bloomfield, and Putnam. Here, our attention to the context for community ideational life assumes its most immediate focus.

The ideational system of any American community, then, is shaped partly by national experience, partly by constraints peculiar to a type of place, and partly by the community in its idiosyncratic self. The first three chapters try to underline this, to describe with some precision and detail the setting for the community ideational life which the remainder of this volume treats.

PART I

SETTING

is right and wrong, what needs to be changed and how for what objectives, what the *summum bonum* is. Put an- r way, the agenda of politics is defined by the controlling ctations about the shape of political life: those expectations h dictate the response of the system to the major policy tions of the day. A given agenda does not arise in a vacuum, ourse. It is summoned by the stage and structure of economic elopment, the organization of social institutions and proc- s, and the framework of political institutions.

pecifically, I wish to suggest that the American sociopolitical erience has generated four great agendas of politics: the t agenda beginning with the founding of the regime and ting approximately to the Civil War; the second bred of vil War and post-Civil War industrialization and extending ough the 1920's; the third delivered by the midwifery of e New Deal; and a new agenda first outlined after World War and assuming clear form in the 1960's. This type of break- wn is not unusual, but our focus perhaps is: on the distinctive eational components of each. I will be at pains to demonstrate ow each agenda reflects the major social and economic reali- es of its period. This exercise is related, of course, to the roader concerns of this study. I want to suggest changes in the ourse of American ideology with the evolving of American ociety, to indicate with some detail the distinctive attributes f the contemporary setting, and thereby to invite the reader o consider early a central underlying theme of this volume: hat ideological divisions in the 1960's and 1970's have and will differ in some substantial ways from those most of us were breast-fed on.

I

America was born at the juncture of two great revolutions: egalitarian, the attack on ascriptive class society, dramatically expanding the segment of the population that "counts," de- manding new and popular governmental structures; and in-

1. The Course of A
Political Ideology

There have been many efforts to chart the
American political ideas and ideology, and a
ganizing principles" have been identified a
century and a quarter ago, Tocqueville locate
principle in egalitarianism: America is the ega
its ideas and ideology are distinguished by a n
of egalitarianism.[1] In an influential piece of rec
Louis Hartz finds the organizing principle
specifically in the settlement of the United State
fragment severed from Europe at the height of
eral thought, a fragment which in the virgin terr
America became the whole.[2] Still others have foun
ing principle in mass-extended abundance.[3]

Here, I wish to use a somewhat different app
American macroideological order, working aroun
of *agendas of politics*. An agenda of politics points t
aries of political argument in a system at a poi
Broader than any single ideology, it is the sum tot
cant concerns and conflict over the operations of

[1] Alexis de Tocqueville, *Democracy in America*. The edi
this work is that of Vintage Books (New York, 1959), in 2 volun

[2] Louis Hartz, *The Liberal Tradition in America* (New Yor
Brace & World, 1955); and *The Founding of New Societies*
Harcourt, Brace & World, 1964). Throughout this book, I dis
tween classical or eighteenth-century Liberalism, the ideolog
on aristocratic society; and liberalism as the term is commo
contemporary political arguments in the United States, the a
certain types of popular social reform.

[3] See, for example, David M. Potter, *People of Plenty* (Chicag
sity of Chicago Press, 1954).

dustrial-technological, destroying the old agrarian and feudal economic order and precipitating conflict as to the shape of the new. These two revolutions might better be described as sides or facets of a single revolution, and the effect of this great revolution was nothing less than to alter fundamentally the agenda of political life, ushering in modern politics in the West.

American ideology owes much of what has been distinctive in it to the working out of this revolution on virgin territory. Tocqueville was thinking of this when he described as a great advantage our having arrived at "a state of democracy without having to endure a democratic revolution; [having been] born equal, instead of becoming so." So was Hartz when he wrote that the United States was "born Liberal." Some aristocratic institutions were set up in the colonial period; but they were established precisely when aristocracy was being taken apart in Europe itself. They clashed with raw physical necessities of life in the Colonies, and floundered on the *petit-bourgeois* impulses of most of the population. John Adams described *"this radical change in the principles, opinions, sentiments, and affections of the people"* as the *"real American Revolution."* [4] So the aristocratic transplants were weak, never really took root, and were swept completely away after 1776.

It is hard to overemphasize the importance of American society's being established *de nouveau,* cut off from the social, economic and political institutions—and the ideological defenses—of ascriptive class societies. This is central to the much-acclaimed American consensus. Those who rode the crest of the egalitarian and industrial revolution in Europe continued throughout the nineteenth century to confront residues—in varying strength–of the old order. A French middle class faced in Church and aristocracy the still powerful defenders of the monarchical tradition.

European political life after 1790 has often been called "ide-

[4] "Letter to Hezekiah Niles," February 13, 1818; in Charles Francis Adams (ed.), *The Works of John Adams* (Boston: Little, Brown, 1856), X, 282–289.

ological" in contrast to a "nonideological" American politics. This description makes sense only if understood to mean that European societies after the revolution were unreconciled, battlegrounds for competing positions on questions most vital to the polity: the organization of government, who should rule, what objectives the society should try to achieve, the arrangement of the economy, and the distribution of economic values. Ideological conflict on the continent extended to the core institutions and processes of the system, while in the United States it was and has remained largely *within* acceptance of a set of institutions and processes. Hartz incisively pointed to this: "It is only because history had already accomplished the ending of the old European order in America that its 'social revolution,' instead of tearing the soul of the nation apart, integrated it further." [5]

Conflicts within a Liberal tradition assume a different proportion when the tradition becomes the whole. Thus Hamilton, spokesman for middle-class mercantile capitalists, is excoriated as an aristocrat.[6] For their part, the Hamiltonians branded the acquisitive agrarian capitalists "the mob." Still, the importance of these descriptive distortions can easily be overdrawn. The Jeffersonians may have *called* their opponents aristocrats, but they didn't *act* as though they were at war with opponents who wanted to establish an entirely different kind of (aristocratic) political order. They acted as though they were agrarian capitalists contending with mercantile capitalists.

[5] Hartz, *The Liberal Tradition in America*, p. 71.

[6] Hamilton described his political creed as "attached to the republican theory. I desire above all things to see the equality of political rights, exclusive of all hereditary distinction, firmly established by a practical demonstration of its being consistent with the order and happiness of society. As to State governments, the prevailing bias of my judgment is that if they can be circumscribed within bounds, consistent with the preservation of the national government, they will prove useful and salutary" ("Letter to Edward Carrington," May 26, 1792; in Henry Cabot Lodge [ed.], *The Works of Alexander Hamilton* [New York: G. P. Putnam's Sons, 1885], IX, 533). We can take Hamilton at his word.

American Liberal society—capitalistic, achievement-oriented, egalitarian, individualistic, committed to secular progress—did not confront viable aristocratic institutions and ideology, and thus it came to possess a singular ideological unity. Maintenance of this unity was not inevitable. We cannot agree that "the escape from the past leads inevitably to an escape from future enemies . . . [with] socialism fading in America because feudalism has been left behind . . . radicalism [dying] as a result of the flight from feudalism." [7] Ideologies are responses to the political needs of substantial groups in societies, and there is no necessary reason why a society without an aristocratic tradition cannot develop the base for a flourishing socialist movement—that is, a large, class-conscious, "deprived" proletariat. The United States avoided successful assaults on a more individualistic capitalism because the capitalism was seen as broadly successful. This success can better be described as a rapid growth of economic resources and their sufficiently popular distribution to convince controlling majorities of lower economic groups that they had enough to gain within existing economic arrangements to make rejection of these unwarranted. Prior to the Civil War, enlargement or growth was secured through resources in arable land so enormous that even with mammoth land grabs by such interests as railroads, the people could be cut in; and after the war, as millions of immigrants streamed into the country, by an industrialization which for all its crass exploitations gave much to many—more than any of its competitors—and thus laid claim to legitimacy. It was the comparative success of industrialization that precluded socialist assaults, or rather, denied them success.

Born Liberal, the United States buttressed liberalism with success, and maintained broad agreement on the principal institutions and processes of the polity. And derivatives of classical Liberalism retain a greater force, have submitted to less drastic revisions in the United States than in any other nation.

[7] Hartz, *The Founding of New Societies*, pp. 6–7, 36.

Understanding of the past and present currents in American ideology demands recognition of this.

Certain identifying features of our ideational life, chiseled by the completeness and success of the egalitarian-industrial revolution, have remained remarkably unchanged through our history. Tocqueville was writing of Americans in the age of Jackson when he observed that "they love change, but they dread revolution,"[8] yet it is as true of Americans in the 1960's. His *Democracy* is a virtual treatise on American individualism:

> Aristocracy had made a chain of all the members of the community, from the peasant to the king; democracy breaks that chain and severs every link of it. As social conditions become more equal, the number of persons increases who, although they are neither rich nor powerful enough to exercise any great influence over their fellows, have nevertheless acquired or retained sufficient education and fortune to satisfy their own wants. They owe nothing to any man, they expect nothing from any man; they acquire the habit of always considering themselves as standing alone, and they are apt to imagine that their whole destiny is in their own hands. Thus not only does democracy make every man forget his ancestors, but it hides his descendants and separates his contemporaries from him; it throws him back forever upon himself alone and threatens in the end to confine him entirely within the solitude of his own heart.[9]

American ideas and ideology are scarcely less influenced by so massive a dose of individualism today. Hartz described Jeffersonian and Jacksonian America as periods when "virtually everyone . . . has the mentality of an independent entrepreneur," and thus "two national impulses [were] bound to make themselves felt: the impulse toward democracy and the impulse toward capitalism."[10] Though capitalism has been transformed, material acquisitiveness and the appeal of democratic capitalism are undiminished. Francis Grund, one of the many traveler-

[8] Tocqueville, *op. cit.,* II, 270.

[9] *Ibid.,* II, 105–106.

[10] Hartz, *The Liberal Tradition in America,* p. 89.

commentators in the 1830's, observed that "man, in America, is not despised for being poor at the outset . . . but every year which passes without adding to his property is a reproach to his understanding or industry. . . ."[11] This orientation toward achievement, placing responsibility for status squarely on the shoulders of the individual, continues to provide an important contour to American ideational life.

Within this broad unity, Americans have fought out their ideational battles. Treatment of the various specific divisions obviously lies beyond our scope and interests, and any general attempt to run a plow over such a well-cultivated field would be fruitless. But I do wish to call attention to the utility of seeing several periods in American sociopolitical history, each necessarily blurred as to beginning and end, but still distinct, with each period producing its distinctive and distinguishing pattern of ideational conflict. Again, I urge the reader to be aware of where I propose to lead him: to a view of political ideas as products of larger sociopolitical settings and as windows through which to view these settings; and to a recognition that the United States has had few such basic settings, of how momentous a move from one setting to another is, how the setting into which we are now moving departs from its predecessors, and thus that we must take off New Deal–tinted glasses to see clearly ideas and ideology in the 1960's.

II

History does not oblige the analyst by abruptly stopping and starting eras, and the dividing lines between agendas of politics are not nearly so sharp as we will at times seem to suggest. But if beginnings and endings are blurred, the outlines of each are clear. The first great period took the United States from birth to the tumultuous transition of the 1850's and 1860's. America was a rural nation, and most of its labor force was in ag-

[11] Grund, *The Americans in Their Moral, Social and Political Relations* (Boston: March, Caren and Lyon, 1837), p. 204.

riculture. But though the preponderance of social and political power rested with a class of landowning agrarians, a counter-persuasion challenged throughout in the name of a more urban, money-based order. By the end of the era, this challenge was led by industrial rather than mercantile capitalists and had become irresistible.

The Federalist party of Hamilton and Adams spoke to the needs of mercantile capitalism, and by doing so in an agrarian capitalist society ordained their (short-run) defeat. Of the slightly more than five million inhabitants of the United States when Jefferson was elected President, fewer than one in sixteen (322,271) lived in urban places (of more than 2,500 persons). And in 1830, when "Old Hickory" occupied the White House, the United States was still 90 percent rural. Table 1 shows the

Table 1. Population of the United States urban-rural (and urban of 100,000 or more), 1790–1860

	Urban		Rural		Urban over 100,000	
Year	Number (in thousands)	Percentage of total	Number (in thousands)	Percentage of total	Number (in thousands)	Percentage of total
1790	202	5.2	3,728	94.8		
1800	322	6.1	4,986	93.9		
1810	525	7.3	6,714	92.7		
1820	693	7.2	8,945	92.8	124	1.2
1830	1,127	8.8	11,739	91.2	203	1.5
1840	1,845	10.9	15,224	89.1	517	3.0
1850	3,544	15.3	19,648	84.7	1,175	5.0
1860	6,217	19.8	25,227	80.2	2,639	8.3

Source: U.S. Bureau of the Census, *Historical Statistics of the United States, Colonial Times to 1957* (Washington, D.C.: Government Printing Office, 1960).

slow gain in the urban population of the United States during this period.

This was a farming nation. Indeed, in 1820, the first year for which we have data, three out of four Americans were farmers.

Table 2 underlines the clear ascendancy of agriculture in the pre-Civil War period.

Table 2. Labor force in agricultural pursuits, 1820–1860

Year	Total labor force (in thousands)	Total in agriculture (in thousands)	Percentage in agriculture
1820	2,881	2,069	71.8
1830	3,932	2,772	70.4
1840	5,420	3,720	68.6
1850	7,697	4,902	63.6
1860	10,533	6,208	58.9

Source: U.S. Bureau of the Census, *Historical Statistics of the United States, Colonial Times to 1957.*

The defeat, then, of the Federalists as mercantile capitalists in an agrarian society is not surprising; that they did so much is. Before Washington left office, Congress had enacted in virtual entirety Hamilton's program for the establishment of capitalist enterprising in America. The Continental debt was funded at its face value, and state debts from the Revolutionary period were assumed. A national bank was chartered and invested with the right of issuing notes. A mint was established, a tariff enacted, a sinking fund set up. Public lands were to be sold in large minimum lots, to obtain revenue. "Large property was now secure against any assaults by misguided *sans-culotte* legislators in the states; and its interests commanded the ever-watchful regard of the central government." [12]

Hamilton's "Report on the Subject of Manufactures," one of a series of state papers which he released as Secretary of the Treasury, is an extraordinary issuance in an agricultural society. Hamilton deplored the exclusive preoccupation with agriculture and called for greater support for domestic manufactures. He asked that government encourage the immigration of arti-

[12] Louis Hacker, *The Triumph of American Capitalism* (New York: Simon and Schuster, 1940), p. 189.

sans, aid inventors, and impose duties and grant bounties in industry's behalf. To a scattered, localized, farming nation he evoked the image of factories, smokestacks, and cities. And he urged the new state not to be squeamish in going about the job of industrial nation-building. Women and children, for example, should be put to work in factories.[13]

The Federalists left power in 1801, not to return again. The struggle between the Jeffersonians and the Hamiltonians did not pit liberals against conservatives and certainly was not between monarchists and republicans. The mansion of American Liberalism was large, and this struggle was fought out within it. The Jeffersonians were Liberals who saw the good society in an unfettered agrarianism, while the Federalists favored measures to achieve a mercantile and indeed, with Hamilton, an industrial system.

In the Age of Jackson, the United States was still an equalitarian, preindustrial society. Great concentrations of property had not developed. Indeed, Louis Hacker points out that as late as the 1850's, after generations of striving, a respectable merchant-capitalist fortune was in the neighborhood of a few hundred thousand dollars, and he contrasts this to the fortunes of the Carnegies, the Rockefellers, and the Fricks of the next epoch.[14] Richard Hofstadter's description of Jackson's America is instructive.

> To understand Jacksonian democracy it is necessary to recreate the social complexion of the United States in the 1830's. Although industrialism had begun to take root, this was still a nation of farms and small towns, which in 1830 found only one of every fifteen citizens living in cities of over 8,000. Outside the South, a sweeping majority of the people were independent property-owners. Factories had been growing in some areas, but industry was not yet concentrated in the factory system; much production was carried

[13] *Works,* III, 207–208.

[14] Hacker, *op. cit.,* p. 323.

out in little units in which the employer was like a master craftsman supervising his apprentices.[15]

But though still clearly ascendant in the 1830's, the rural, agricultural society was increasingly challenged by forces of change—that conspiracy of technology and economics which before the end of the century was to utterly transform this into an industrial system. And the most persistent and far-reaching ideational conflict arose around these various pressures to alter some phase of the old and familiar order. William Chambers described this conflict as between "enterprise" and "arcadia," typically pitting agrarian against mercantile (not industrial) capitalists.[16] Such a description can easily be overstated. Unless carefully construed, it raises pictures of a class of tillers of the soil constantly at odds with businessmen, trying to save their society from uniformly repugnant changes. Such was never the case. Certain developments in transportation, for example, were welcomed by some agricultural and some business interests and were resisted by others in both camps. What we are arguing is simply that this society through the middle of the nineteenth century was primarly agricultural, rural, localized, fragmented, and that in its basic outlines it was valued by many of its inhabitants.

Movement throughout this period was away from this, however, toward a money-based economy, a more integrated, urbanized, commercial, and, as the period drew to a close, industrial society. Many of the hot disputes of the Jacksonian period—involving opposition to special corporate charters, hostility to paper money, suspicion of public enterprise and public debt—can readily be understood in these terms. Conflict over the "Monster Bank" (the Second Bank of the United States) caught on and assumed its intensity as a revolt of agrarians against pressures to transform a familiar and valued world. Van Buren

[15] Hofstadter, *The American Political Tradition* (New York: Vintage Books, 1958), pp. 56–57.

[16] Chambers, *Old Bullion Benton: Senator From the New West* (Boston: Little, Brown, 1956).

was striking this note of concern when he blamed the banks for the crisis of 1837: "Proneness to excessive issues has ever been the vice of the banking system," and banking necessarily serves "to stimulate extravagance of enterprise by improvidence of credit." Far too much labor that should have been expended in agriculture went into speculation, and the economy experienced "overaction in all departments of business."[17] The parties of the Hamiltonian tradition (the Federalists and Whigs), he lamented elsewhere, were dominated by the heads of banks, insurance companies, and manufacturing and transportation corporations, enterprises marked by "possession of special and, in some of these cases, of exclusive privileges." But he rejoiced that the Hamiltonian parties were doomed to defeat in the United States because they could not get the support of "the most numerous and consequently the most powerful class of our citizens—those engaged in agriculture." He prophesied that "it can only be when agriculturists abandon the implements and the field of their labor and become, with those who now assist them, shopkeepers, manufacturers, carriers, and traders, that the Republic will be brought in danger of the influences of the money power. But this can never happen."[8]

[17] James D. Richardson (ed.), *Messages and Papers of the Presidents, 1789–1897* (Washington, D.C.: Government Printing Office, 1896), III, 325–334.

[18] Martin Van Buren, *An Inquiry Into the Origin and Course of Political Parties in the United States* (New York: Hurd and Houghton, 1867), pp. 230–231. Lee Benson argues that historians have badly erred in accepting Van Buren's claim that the Jackson party championed the "producers" against the "special interests." Without wishing to get into the debate over the nature of Jacksonian democracy, we would agree that Van Buren's polemical exercise exaggerates in much the same way as a description of the Republican party as the party of big business and the Democrats of the working man in 1935 exaggerates. American parties have always contained disparate groups, and interests have never been neatly polarized. The Jacksonians were not "the little guys" and certainly were not liberals doing battle with conservatives. They did in national conflict stand as the principal defenders of the "Old Republic," and the Whigs did come to

There is a strong temptation to see the ideological struggles of earlier periods through glasses colored by later experience and, as a specific example, to equate Jacksonian democracy and the New Deal. Hofstadter notes that "there is a suggestive analogy between Nicholas Biddle's political associates and the 'economic royalists' of the Liberty League, and, on the other side, between the two dynamic landed aristocrats who led the popular parties. Roosevelt himself did not fail to see the resemblance and exploit it." [19] But the differences between the two are of critical importance. The Jacksonians were a parochial party, looking back to a purer past; the New Deal saw the good society in the future, an industrial order harmonized, civilized, and regulated by government. The role of government for the Jacksonians was largely negative; the New Deal inaugurated vast positive government. The Jacksonians were ambivalent if not hostile to pressures for growth, development, and national integration; the New Deal sought "to make the nation more solidary, more cohesive, more interdependent in its growing diversity: in short, to make the nation more of a nation." [20]

The America of the first period, then, having discarded aristocratic legacies, flourished as a Liberal society. The main ideological currents of the period were generated by the basic social and economic divisions. This was a localized, rural, agricultural society, one of enormous dispersion of resources. Fear of concentrated power, and opposition to a money-based society were real and pervasive. Throughout the period a more popular agrarian tradition did battle with a somewhat more elitist, mercantile capitalist position.

---

be the principal spokesmen for a newer, more integrated, money-based and commercial society. See, for conflicting assessments of Jacksonian democracy, Lee Benson, *The Concept of Jacksonian Democracy* (Princeton, N.J.: Princeton University Press, 1961); and Marvin Meyers, *The Jacksonian Persuasion* (New York: Vintage Books, 1960).

[19] Hofstadter, *op. cit.,* p. 56.

[20] Samuel H. Beer, "Liberalism and the National Idea," *The Public Interest,* Fall, 1966, 71.

III

The Civil War gave enormous impetus to incipient American industrialization, hastening the ascendancy of an industrial order. Through war-induced measures (bond issues and greenbacks), the federal government added fully three billion dollars to the basic credit resources of the country, and high profits made possible substantial accumulations of capital. Hacker thus summarizes the effects of the Civil War on industrialization:

A vastly expanded domestic market, created by the necessity of maintaining and supplying a gigantic military establishment, and the great increase in and circulation of the capital fund, due to governmental borrowing and spending, helped in the maturing of our industrial production, and, more particularly, our heavy industry, virtually overnight. By the end of the Civil War, the industries turning out boots and shoes, men's clothing, iron, machinery, dressed meats, and woolen textiles had reached full stature. The factory system now reigned in America.[21]

Thomas Cochran also sees the Civil War as marking the transition from mercantile to industrial capitalism and, more fundamentally, from an agricultural to an industrializing society. By 1860, "the industrial revolution had come to America, and created the modern world of business." [22] An industrial labor force and the other forms and functions of an emerging industrial order made their appearance.

In the first period, the political center of gravity rested in rural America; in the second, it shifted to city and town. In the first, agrarians were ascendant; in the second, power gravitated to a class of industrialists. This second great period in American sociopolitical history, beginning with the Civil War, extended through the 1920's. As the country changed substantially between 1790 and 1850, so it did between 1865 and 1925. But the

[21] Hacker, *op. cit.*, p. 252.

[22] Cochran, "Business Organization and the Development of an Industrial Discipline," in Harold F. Williamson (ed.), *The Growth of the American Economy* (New York: Prentice-Hall, 1951), pp. 279–280.

Civil War and the Great Depression form the outer boundaries of a distinct period. The dominant impulse defining this period was the construction and maturation of an industrial society. The principal ideological conflict was generated around the movement of a developing industrial society, with an ascendant defense of the new industrial order, and continuing resistance in the name of an older, rural and agricultural society. "American Whiggery," Hartz has written, "marched into the Promised Land after the Civil War and did not really leave it until the crash of 1929." [23]

The population of the United States increased more than fivefold between 1850 and 1930 as this became an urban society. The big cities (over 100,000) held only one American in twenty in 1850, but three in ten eighty years later. The census of 1870 was the first to show a majority of workers in nonagricultural pursuits, and the agricultural labor force began a precipitous relative decline that by the end of the period had become absolute. The number of farmers reached 11,340,000 in 1910, but it was never to be that high again. Other indicators point to the transition from an agricultural to an industrial order. Capital invested in manufacturing increased by over 500 percent between 1850 and 1880, the number of wage earners tripled, and the total value added to the gross national product by manufacturing quadrupled. In the seven decades between 1860 and 1929, the gross national product of the United States increased fifteen-fold, from 6.7 billion to 104.4 billion dollars.

In the thirty-five years after Appomattox the United States opened and settled the West, established a vast railway system, and emerged as an industrial power. Hofstadter observes that "there is no other period in the nation's history when politics seems so completely dwarfed by economic changes, none in which the life of the country rests so completely in the hands of the industrial entrepreneur." [24] Industrial capitalists came into full possession of the instruments of political power, and they

[23] *The Liberal Tradition in America*, p. 203.

[24] Hofstadter, *op. cit.*, p. 164.

controlled the state as mercantile capitalists were never able to in the pre-Civil War period. The whole system was bent to the needs of industrialization, and governmental powers were committed to policies and programs on behalf of the ascendant industrial order: the protective tariff, a national banking structure, aid to Pacific railways, a program of "sound money." Profits were able to mount at the expense of labor. Wages were kept low, the industrial exploitation of women and children was the rule, and the state countenanced all this. A new class of leaders emerged as the old merchant capitalists proved incapable of making the necessary adjustments. Horatio Alger stories were not uncommon as the children of the lower middle class, from small villages and farms, became titans of industry.

Thus the system was committed to a headlong rush to industrialization, and the dominant themes in American political ideas and ideology reflected this commitment. Social Darwinism could not have flourished before the Civil War—and not because it required Darwin. It was, simply, one statement of the more general ideological defense of rapid industrialization and the men who were directing and profiting most magnificently from it. How could enormous accumulations of capital in the hands of a few be justified in the face of mass misery? Why, the rich and successful are the fittest, and the whole system benefits from their encouragement. How are low wages and long hours, opposition to minimum wage and maximum hours regulation, the impoverishment of a gigantic industrial army to be countenanced? Why, the poor are the unfit, and deserve to be eliminated. Stupidity, laziness, idleness, vice, all are weaknesses—and not natural, but moral weaknesses. "The whole effort of nature is to get rid of such, to clear the world of such, and make room for the better. . . . If they are sufficiently complete to live, they do live, and it is well they should live. If they are not sufficiently complete to live, they die, and it is best they should die." [25] In a society still operating in an economics of scarcity and committed

[25] Herbert Spencer, *Social Statics* (New York and London: D. Appleton, 1915), pp. 79–80.

to rapid industrial growth, that many would suffer and be harshly exploited was unavoidable; and the unavoidable came to be described as the desirable.

This ascendant ideological statement of industrial nation-building found its principal opposition in a popular reformism, primarily agrarian in base, which boiled over in such movements as the Greenbackers and the Populists. Populism was a joining together of western and southern agrarians in an effort to recapture national political power from proponents of an industrial society. "The railroad corporations will either own the people or the people must own the railroads," read the People's party platform of 1892. Government-supported industrialization enriches a few while impoverishing many: "From the same prolific womb of governmental injustice we breed the two great classes of tramps and millionaires." The key Populist planks spoke for agrarian-based popular reform. They backed the free and unlimited coinage of silver; urged government ownership of railroads, telegraphs and telephones; called for a graduated income tax; favored the parcel post to break the hold of the great express companies; advocated restrictions on immigration that was providing labor for the great factories and swelling the cities; and supported measures to end the control of public office by the "interests," such as the popular election of United States Senators, the Australian ballot, and the initiative and referendum. But the Populists were too late. By 1896 industrial capitalism was firmly entrenched. The aroused farmers received little support from the growing numbers of foreign-born workers of the factory towns of the East and the Middle West, who were cold to their *petit-bourgeois* strivings. After 1896 it was clear to all that farmers had become permanently a minority interest, able to bargain with the controllers of American public policy, but never to command.

Through two-thirds of the second period, popular reformism originated in rural America, and it was not until the twentieth century that an equalitarian, reformist movement developed in urban America—and then, of course, it originated in the industrial working class. Democratic reformers in the nineteenth century were fundamentally backward-looking, found the good society somewhere in a less complex, pastoral past. They were parochial and confronted opponents who, while more elitist, were the nationalizers, who carried forth the idea of national integration. Samuel Beer argues that for much of our history

> the main division of political forces consisted of the following: (1) On the one hand, a national party, tending toward elitism, *viz.*, the Federalists, the Whigs, and then the Republicans; (2) on the other hand, an anti-national or "provincial" party tending to be "democratic," *viz.*, the Jeffersonian Republican and the Democratic Party.[26]

There is much to Beer's analysis positing a "democratic idea" and a "national idea" and suggesting that throughout nineteenth-century America these were the property of two different coalitions: the democratic idea championed by rural and agricultural, and the national idea by urban and mercantile interests. Not until this century, Beer argues, did a single coalition build upon "old traditions of democratic reformism, but also [join] to them a powerful thrust toward national integration." [27] The New Deal linked the popular and the national ideas in establishing a new agenda of politics.

IV

After World War I, the United States moved into a third great setting—from an *industrializing* to an *industrialized* so-

[26] Beer, *op. cit.*, p. 72. He adds: "I take the adjective [provincial] from Albert Beveridge who, in his biography of John Marshall, described how in the 1790's the political parties arose, 'one standing for the National and the other for the Provincial idea.' "

[27] *Ibid.*, p. 71. Since 1933, we have come to think of the Democratic party as the "natural" proponent of the national idea. It is instructive to recall Herbert Croly's contention that in American history to that time no "measure of legislation expressive of a progressive national idea can be attributed to the Democratic party." That party, he concluded, "cannot become the party of national responsibility without being faithless to its own creed" (*The Promise of American Life* [New York: Macmillan, 1914], pp. 163, 171).

ciety. In the first, the principal ideological division separated a provincial, agrarian, and popular posture from a nationalizing, mercantile, and elitist persuasion; in the second, an elitist defense of rapid, harshly exploitative, but dynamic industrialization confronted the declining remnants of a more equalitarian agrarianism. Now in the third, an ideological position fusing the national idea and the democratic idea within complete acceptance of an industrialized society triumphed over an elitist persuasion which represented the dated national idea of the earlier industrializing society.

The transition from rural to urban, from agrarian to industrial, from independent and local to interdependent and national, begun with so headlong and careless a rush after the Civil War, was substantially completed by the 1920's. In the sixty years after 1869 our gross national product expanded by 1500 per cent. Agriculture, which occupied over half our labor force until 1870, employed only slightly more than 20 per cent of all workers in 1930. Farm workers declined by half a million between 1900 and 1930, while the total labor force grew by nearly twenty million. The productivity of American industry had expanded enormously.[28]

Equally important to the picture being drawn here of the economic developments which precipitated the third period is the tremendous absolute growth of big corporations after 1900. The

[28] John W. Kendrick (*Productivity Trends in the United States,* Princeton, N.J.: Princeton University Press, 1961) constructed an index of manufacturing with 1929 as the base, for bench mark years, 1869, 1879, and 1889, and annually thereafter. Kendrick's index represents the development of manufacturing as follows:

Manufacturing Output, Selected Years 1869–1929 (1929 = 100)

1869	7.1
1879	10.2
1889	18.3
1899	27.5
1909	43.4
1919	61.0
1929	100.0

number of manufacturing establishments increased by less than one per cent between 1899 and 1929, but the value added by manufacturing jumped more than 550 per cent. By 1929, the American economy was dominated by large industrial aggregates engaged in oligopolistic competition.

The United States in 1930 was an urban society. There were 191 cities with more than 50,000 persons, and 43 million Americans, 35 per cent of the total, lived in them. The 15 million Americans living in cities of over a million represents the highest percentage ever to reside in such cities.[29] For a brief time in the 1930's and 1940's, the political center of gravity in the United States appeared to rest in the great central cities, only to shift again after World War II to the metropolitan region.

By 1930, the United States was a developed, interdependent society. A revolution in communications triumphed over distance and exerted irresistible nationalizing pressures. All the mass media of communication except television were widely used by 1930. The first regularly licensed radio station began operating September 15, 1921, but by 1930 there were 618 commercial broadcasting stations and 13,750,000 families with radios. In a similar fashion, a new transportation technology tied the country more closely together. In 1900, people and goods were moved outside railroad lines by animal and foot. But by 1930 the automobile had reached mass distribution, had enormously extended individual mobility, and had fundamentally transformed the society's life styles, residence patterns, and physical mobility, contributing to the breakdown of a more localized and independent society (see Table 3).

The third great period in American sociopolitical history owes much to these advances in communication and transportation. Events in one area became instantly the concern of the entire country. Horizons and vistas were extended. The changes effected both a quantitative and a qualitative nationalizing of the society: the physical interaction of the various parts was

[29] In 1930, 12.2% of our population lived in cities of over one million. By 1960, this had declined to 9.7%.

Table 3. Motor vehicle sales and total motor vehicle registration, 1900, 1915, and 1929 (in thousands)

Motor vehicles	1900	1915	1929
Sales	4	896	4,455
Total registrations	8	2,491	26,705

Source: U.S. Bureau of the Census, *Historical Statistics of the United States, Colonial Times to 1957.*

enormously increased, and *the nation* became much more the decisional frame of reference.

The interdependent society demanded increased coordination and direction by government. The Depression, of course, dramatized the need for a bigger role by government, and speeded up the expansion of government services, but the expansion had preceded the "Great Collapse." Table 4 shows that federal expenditures in 1925 were four times higher than a decade earlier. The increase in state and local government expendi-

Table 4. Federal government expenditures, selected years, 1790–1940

Year	Amount (in thousands of dollars)
1792	5,080
1810	8,157
1850	39,543
1900	520,861
1915	760,587
1925	3,063,105
1934	6,520,966
1940	9,062,032

Source: U.S. Bureau of the Census, *Historical Statistics of the United States, Colonial Times to 1957.*

tures rivals this. More was spent for highways in 1927 than in 1940. And it was the end of the 1930's before expenditures for education regained the 1927 level. In all of the areas except welfare, the big increases were recorded between 1902 and 1927, not between 1927 and 1940 (see Table 5).

Table 5. State and local government expenditures, total and by function, selected years,1902–1940 (in millions of dollars)

Year	Total	Education	Highways	Public welfare	Hospitals	Police
1902	1,095	255	175	37	43	50
1927	7,810	2,235	1,809	151	279	270
1934	7,842	1,831	1,509	889	309	291
1940	11,240	2,638	1,573	1,156	450	365

Source: U.S. Bureau of the Census, *Historical Statistics of the United States, Colonial Times to 1957.*

The distinctive features of the third setting are a mature industrial plant, massive concentrations of resources, a dramatic new interdependence, and completion of the century-long transformation from rural and agricultural to urban and industrial. From the new interdependence arose greater demands for positive government as balancer, coordinator, and protector of the public welfare. From the maturation of the industrial plant came pressures to humanize industrialization, to assure a more equitable distribution of the economic values that the system now was able to furnish. From the concentration of resources, and especially of economic power, grew efforts to rebuild pluralism, to control the new aggregates of power, and to assure their subordination to national interests. These pressures shaped the agenda of politics of the third period.

Samuel Beer has noted that the liberal-conservative dichotomy was rarely used in American political debate prior to the New Deal. But with the New Deal, this "Conventional Dichotomy" came into wide frequency. Beer recognized that "in politics words are cheap and this striking innovation in political terminology could have been merely verbal." But he argues that it was not. "In fact, the New Deal brought into existence not only a new alignment of social forces and a new balance between the parties, but also a new outlook on public policy." [30]

Two broad ideological persuasions confronted each other after 1932. One was more elitist, and resisted change designed to distribute more equally such values as income (through social welfare programs, redistributive taxation, maximum hour and minimum wage legislation) and political power (by encouraging the growth of labor unions and the introduction of government as a "countervailing force" against business). At the same time, it insisted that national development and integration could continue to proceed with less central direction and regulation and with greater autonomy for such constituent units as corporations. The rival persuasion was more popular, favored change toward a more equitable distribution of economic values and political power, and, abandoning the provincial orientation of popular reformism in earlier periods, was firmly committed to the national idea in the context of a highly interdependent society.

The second ideological configuration made its greatest contribution in adapting the national idea to a changed society. For the further development and integration of the nation in the third period could not be achieved through such programs as internal improvements and the encouragement of trade and commerce, as in the first; nor by giving a *carte blanche* to businessmen, as in the second; but rather through (1) bringing into the system those who had been forced to live on the periphery of American life (newer ethnic groups, for example), giving them a larger share in its benefits; and by (2) centralizing governmental power and equipping government to provide the overall coordination, regulation, and direction which the exceedingly complex and interdependent economic order requires if catastrophic collapses such as the Great Depression are to be avoided and national prosperity assured.[31]

[30] Beer, *op. cit.,* pp. 70–71.

[31] Beer observes that "by these measures [the main policies of the New Deal] beneficiary groups, such as industrial labor and recent immigrants,

Both the Republican and Democratic parties had nationalizing and provincial wings. The Democrats' nationalizing wing, ascendant in the Presidental party, committed itself to a broader extension of prosperity and political power and to a vastly expanded role for government as the principal nationalizing force in the interdependent society; on this program, on this ideological posture, this group seized national power. It did battle with the provincial wings of both its own and the opposition party, with factions that looked back fondly on a more independent and localized America. But it also had to face the older business nationalism, which was equally committed to national growth and development but opposed to so broad an integrating role for government and especially hostile to the use of government to assure "the people" prosperity.

The terms *liberal* and *conservative* speak for the principal ideological division generated by the sociopolitical setting of the 1930's. Liberalism was the ideological statement of the interests of a "have-not" class of industrial workers and their allies who found the good society not in some agrarian past but in a future of more humanized industrialism and who invoked government to get there. And conservatism was the ideological defense of those of an elitist inclination opposed to the use of government on behalf of a broader extension of values. But there were two quite different groups of conservatives: a parochial elite (rural and small-town) looking back; and a nationalizing elite, quite content to move ahead to urbanism and industrialization, to large concentrations of economic and political power, but profoundly unhappy about its "fall" from a position as custodian of nationalizing impulses. This combination was fundamentally unstable, and I will argue that one characteristic of the fourth period into which we have moved is its disintegration.

---

also won a degree of acceptance in the national consciousness and in everyday social and economic intercourse that they had never previously enjoyed. . . . It was . . . 'nationalizing' in the sense that it integrated into the national community groups which had previously been marginal or excluded" (Beer, *op. cit.*, p. 75).

V

The third period does not have a specific terminal point, but by the late 1960's the outlines of a fourth setting can easily be distinguished. American societal structure now differs profoundly from that of New Deal America, with new patterns of ideological conflict. Five principal and closely related developments are ushering in the new sociopolitical setting: (1) The extension of nationalization to a new stage producing a far more complexly integrated national society, a quantitative change from the third period so great as to become qualitative. (2) A mass-extended affluence, blurring economic conflict between business and labor. (3) The rise of a new ruling class, a white-collar, corporate-based, new middle class residing in the metropolitan region, principally in the suburban fringe around the central cities; and the further decline of older ruling classes, of farmers (now only 5 per cent of the population), of the old small-business-owning middle class, of a disadvantaged industrial working class. (4) The supplanting of class politics—or more precisely of politics organized around the interests of competing economic groups—by status politics, with the result that quite different groups now find themselves threatened by demands for change. (5) Finally, a whole new set of public problems, defined in large part by the achievement of gross solutions and the subsequent preoccupation with fine adjustments, by a new technology which brings within reach of solution problems previously dismissed as the "woes of mankind," and by a scientific culture or orthodoxy which represents a new way of conceptualizing public problems. Science and technology have redrawn the public sector. This last-mentioned development will occupy us at length in the chapters which follow, especially Chapter 5, and can best be left without further comment here. But we will deal briefly with each of the others.

The United States has moved since World War II to a new interdependence and a more nationalized society, summoned by a complexly integrated national economy, by a communications system which brings the Batman into homes from Biloxi to Butte, by the growth of sprawling metropolitan regions which preclude traditional independent local government. The metropolitan region has become the representative residential setting, just as, for example, the farm was in the first and the small town in the second historical period. Developments in communications and transportation have been influential throughout our history. But present patterns in the creation, dissemination, and consumption of culture and in the mobility of people and ideas are as clear a departure from 1935 as the pattern then was from 1890. Television set usage averaged five hours and thirty-two minutes per home per day in 1966, and 53.8 million households had at least one television set (see Table 6). More than 175 mil-

Table 6. Homes with television sets, and number of sets

TV homes	1955	1959	1962	1965	1966
Total number of TV sets in TV homes (in thousands)	32,500	50,000	58,175	67,050	71,150
TV homes (in thousands)	32,106	44,000	49,000	52,600	53,800
Multi-set households (in thousands)	1,100	4,400	6,900	9,500	13,200
TV homes as percentage of total homes	64.5	85.9	90.0	93.0	94.0

Source: Data supplied by Advertising Research Foundation, Electronic Industries Association, National Association of Broadcasters, and N.B.C. Corporate Planning Estimates; and taken from *Television Factbook* (Washington, D.C.: Radio News Bureau, 1967).

lion radio sets and about 66 million television sets were produced between 1957 and 1967. Six thousand radio stations and over 700 television stations were operating in the United States in 1967. We could go on. But the point is simply that a nationalized culture manufactured in Hollywood and New York is peddled to an audience of unparalleled size—very nearly conterminous with the total population—and this audience is reached by this nationalized culture far more regularly and exposed far more pervasively than any other in history.

These are but some of the features of the interdependent society. Americans from Fort Kent to El Paso simultaneously consume the same culture, imbibing it in tremendous doses, and buy the same cereals in nearly identical supermarkets and shopping centers. Local and regional differences vanish as an entire population is continuously turned on and tuned in to national norms, consumption patterns, and life styles. Few doubt any longer that a massive responsibility for central coordination, regulation, and direction is imposed upon government by this interdependence: big business which resisted an expanded role for government in the 1930's has made its peace and shares in a general acceptance of this corporate, collectivized system.

The fourth period is ushered in as well by a mass-extended affluence, impressive despite its limitation. The American "Mr. Average" by a wide margin is the most affluent average citizen in history. Table 7 shows what happened to family income in the United States between 1947 and 1966. Even when increases in the cost of living are taken into account and the data expressed in constant rather than current dollars, the gains are impressive. Though the relative claims on aggregate personal income by the different strata of the population have not changed over the last two decades, the pie itself has become much larger.[32] The increase in the purchasing power of the median family income between 1947 and 1965 was no less than 61 per cent of the total purchasing power of the 1947 median. Values previously limited to a tiny elite have thus come within the grasp of large segments of the population. Cereals no longer suffice by being nourishing; they must excite the imagination with delightful shapes and colors. Soaps must do more than clean; they must become imaginative toys, or clean in the absence of scrubbing. Dog foods compete with extravagant claims as to which best titillates the palates of discerning dogs. And leisure,

[32] The lowest 40% of the families (in income) received 17% of the total personal income in 1947 and 17% in 1965; and the two highest quintiles received 46% of the income in 1947 and 45% in 1965.

Table 7. Percentage of families earning over $10,000 per year, and median family income, selected years, 1947–1966

Family earnings	1947	1950	1955	1959	1961	1964	1965	1966
Percentage of families earning over $10,000								
In current dollars	3	3	6	12	16	23	25	30
In 1965 dollars	8	7	10	15	18	24	25	28
Median family income								
In current dollars	$3,031	$3,319	$4,421	$5,417	$5,737	$6,569	$6,957	$7,436
In 1965 dollars	$4,275	$4,351	$5,223	$5,856	$6,054	$6,676	$6,957	$7,239

Source: U.S. Bureau of the Census, *Current Population Reports*, No. 51, January, 1967.

long a "problem" only in its absence, now becomes a problem in its use.

A description of the United States as affluent can be defended both in relation to other contemporary societies and to the United States in earlier periods. We lead the world in gross national product per capita, and no other country is a close competitor (unless the noncomparable Kuwait is included). Our gross national product stood at $100 billion in 1940 (still lower than the gross national product in 1929, indicating the severity and duration of the Depression) but by 1966 it had increased, in current dollars, sevenfold. Robert Lane argues that the United States effectively entered the "Age of Affluence" in the 1950's, after the Korean War.[33] The 1940's had been an anomalous period in which the per capita GNP hovered around $1,000 (in 1929 prices), although it increased by 250 per cent in current prices—from $761 in 1940 to $1,876 in 1950. Indeed, the per capita GNP in 1949, in constant dollars, was the same as in 1942. The rate of growth improved in the next decade: from 1950 to 1960 the annual rate of growth was about 3 per cent in constant dollars. But an explosion has come since 1960. In that year, the U.S. GNP stood (1958 prices) at $487.8 billion. It expanded by a third over the next six years. From early 1961 through 1968, there were no recessions, the longest continuous period of prosperity in American history. The recession in 1957–1958 is the last time a decline in per capita GNP—in real terms—has occurred.

Lane's description of the principal features of the "Age of Affluence" is one we can accept:

(1) A relatively high per capita national income;
(2) A relatively equalitarian distribution of income;
(3) A "favorable" rate of growth of per capita gross national product (GNP);
(4) Provisions against the hazards of life—that is, against sickness,

[33] Lane, "The Politics of Consensus in an Age of Affluence," *American Political Science Review,* LIX (December, 1965), 874–895.

penury, unemployment, dependence in old age, squalor—the features now associated with the term "welfare state"; and

(5) A "managed economy" in the sense of conscious and more or less successful governmental use of fiscal and monetary powers to smooth out the business cycle and avoid depressions, as well as to provide for the economic growth mentioned in (3) above.[34]

Government, organized interests, and individual citizens alike become occupied with "luxury" concerns in this age of affluence. We become aware that we perhaps need not always have the poor with us, so the 17 per cent of American families (in 1965) with less than $3,000 a year total income points, for some, to national failure. Serious men can begin to talk of the elimination of poverty. Corporation leaders, their firms well established and sharing in the prosperity, begin to pursue luxury interests, such as making the communities in which they are based more attractive places to live, not only through a physical renewal of the business area, but by promoting metropolitan cooperation and consolidation, slum clearance, and efforts, however halting, toward relief of the tensions of the ghetto. And "Mr. Average," unlike his counterpart of the 1930's who was often preoccupied with such basic needs as food and housing, worries about getting his son or daughter into college.[35] College and professional school enrollment, just 52,000 in 1870, less than half a million when World War I ended, less than a million and a half before the outbreak of World War II, climbed to more than two and one-half million in 1956, three and one-half million in 1960, and six million in October, 1966. The increase between 1960 and 1966—2,515,000 or 70.4 per cent—was greater than the to-

[34] Lane, *op. cit.*, p. 874.

[35] Chester Bowles, vacationing in the United States in the spring of 1967 for the first extended period in two years, was struck by the meaning of the new affluence: "America is changing very rapidly. It is going from issues of scarcity to issues of affluence. In the Thirties and Forties, the big questions were how to get more schools, jobs, security. Those are still questions, but the big issue now is how to distribute the enormous wealth the country has" (quoted in the Hartford *Times*, June 14, 1967).

tal enrollment up to the end of World War II. Some census projections of college enrollment show nearly twelve million enrolled in 1985.[36]

Historic economic conflicts like that between business and labor fade in this mass-extended prosperity. Observers comment on the transformation of the American labor movement, concluding that "the fire has gone out in labor's belly," and so it has, because we no longer have a large, coherent class of "have-not" wage workers. Stewart Alsop has written of Franklin Roosevelt's packing Cadillac Square in Detroit with a half million cheering workers at the Labor Day rallies, contrasting this to the mere 30,000 who turned out for Lyndon Johnson in 1964, when Johnson was his most popular and his opponent, Barry Goldwater, was dressed as a genuine bogeyman—the clearest target given labor in many moons. Why then the poor turnout? "The workers who crowded shoulder to shoulder into Cadillac Square to hear Franklin Roosevelt regarded themselves as 'little guys' or 'working stiffs.' . . . The poor, and those who regarded themselves as poor, were in those days a clear majority of the population." [37] Alsop goes on to point out that the Mr. Average in Detroit in 1964 was in a far different position—much more prosperous, drawn to the warm and inviting bosom of the middle class, the owner of a motor car or two, with substantial equity in a private home, not at all an exploited and forgotten man.

Michael Harrington, among others, has referred to the old poverty as general, a prominent part of the society. "It was the condition of life of an entire society, or at least of that huge majority who were without special skills or the luck of birth." Today's poor are the first minority poor in history, the first poor not to be seen.

[36] The data are from the U.S. Bureau of the Census, *Historical Statistics of the United States; Current Population Reports,* No. 161, February, 1967; and *Current Population Reports,* No. 365, May, 1967.

[37] Alsop, "Can Anyone Beat LBJ?" *Saturday Evening Post,* May, 1967. p. 28.

In the past, when poverty was general in the unskilled and semi-skilled work force, the poor were all mixed together. The bright and the dull, those who were going to escape into the great society and those who were to stay behind, all of them lived on the same street. When the middle third rose, this community was destroyed. And the entire invisible land of the other Americans became a ghetto, a modern poor farm for the rejects of society and of the economy.[38]

Thus, the affluent society, by reducing dramatically the number of poor, transforms the poor and the meaning of poverty.

The United States is not alone in blurring the economic conflict of earlier industrialization. Throughout the West, class conflict has declined, and with this has come a restructuring of ideological conflict sometimes described as "the end of ideology." Seymour Martin Lipset is one who has discussed this:

This change in western political life reflects the fact that the fundamental political problems of the industrial revolution have been solved: the workers have achieved industrial and political citizenship; the conservatives have accepted the welfare state; and the democratic left has recognized that an increase in overall state power carries with it more dangers to freedom than solutions for economic problems.[39]

The new prosperity has not alone calmed intense and bitter ideological conflict in the West, but it has helped draw the venom from the old economically-derived ideologies.

The new agenda of politics into which the United States has plunged in the 1960's is defined, too, by a new ruling class. "Ruling class" is used loosely here. It does not connote some tight-knit ruling elite. Rather it suggests that in any period the bal-

[38] Harrington, *The Other America: Poverty in the United States* (Baltimore, Md.: Penguin Books, 1963), pp. 17–18.

[39] Seymour Martin Lipset, *Political Man* (Garden City, N.Y.: Doubleday, 1959), p. 406. Daniel Bell also has prominently associated himself with the "end of ideology" position. Note 2 in the Introduction to the present study gives further references.

ance of political power has as its fulcrum some socioeconomic grouping. In Jackson's America it was a class of small land-owning farmers; in McKinley's America, the old middle class, the small business elite of the small town and the industrial entrepreneurs. Today's ruling class is the new middle class: white-collar workers, their careers committed to the interstices of large bureaucratic structures—business corporations, governments, universities, foundations—their residential base the suburban and exurban fringes of our major cities. The white-collar work force increased by 600 per cent between 1900 and 1965, a period in which the number of blue-collar workers did not quite manage to double. White collars outnumbered blue by more than six and a half million in 1965.

More revealing than aggregate figures on blue- and white-collar employment is the extraordinary expansion of certain categories of technical and bureaucratic skill positions between 1900 and 1960 (see Table 8). A category like engineers, which increased by 2,300 per cent while the labor force was little more than doubling, points both to the growth of the new class and to its principal features: college-educated, affluent by any historical standard, employed by large corporate structures, its status assured by its command of the new orthodoxy of science.

The substitution of status politics for class politics is still another development shaping the contemporary agenda. Status politics calls attention to a situation in which people project their anxieties about social status onto political objects. Status concerns presumably have always been present, but they become especially acute in an egalitarian society—which continually invites invidious comparisons with the status of others—as the majority of the population, indeed today the vast majority, is liberated from the more pressing economic worries. Our technology has made possible the reduction of the deepest economic tensions, giving more to many without taking from any through an unparalleled increase of productivity. But still in the age of

Table 8. Growth of selected white-collar occupational categories, 1900–1960 (in thousands)

Category	1900	1910	1920	1930	1940	1950	1960
Total labor force	29,030	37,291	42,206	48,686	51,742	58,999	64,639
Accountants and auditors	23	39	118	192	238	390	471
Engineers	38	77	134	217	297	543	861
Chemists	9	16	28	45	57	77	83
Natural and social scientists*	12	20	32	73	153	302	671

Source: U.S. Bureau of the Census, *Historical Statistics of the United States, from Colonial Times to 1957;* and *U.S. Census of Population, 1960.*

* Includes dietitians and nutritionists, foresters and conservationists, natural scientists (not elsewhere classified), personnel and labor relations workers, social scientists, professional, technical, and kindred workers not elsewhere classified.

affluence, status remains in seriously short supply and many perplexing domestic problems come to hinge on status concerns.

The common man was an economic "have-not" in the earlier periods, and demands for popular change were demands for a more equitable distribution of economic values. The economic "haves"—typically businessmen—saw threats in these demands, and their resistance we commonly call conservatism. But in an era of status politics, quite different collections of individuals are threatened by demands for popular change, because the demands are vastly different. Specifically what has happened is this: the American common man is now a have albeit a marginal have; he values the system which has made him a have, and frequently resists and resents pressures for change. Where, then, is the pressure for popular change? It comes from *uncommon* men, minority have-nots such as Negroes, who are seeking both dollars and recognition as whole men—status. The economic system appears far better able to meet the material needs of our have-nots than the social system to meet their status needs, for marginal haves, especially, feel threatened by the status demands of potentially ascendant have-nots and greater prosperity is not likely to remedy this. Many of the really vexing political conflicts in metropolitan America today pivot on status anxieties: those surrounding segregation in housing and schools are primary examples. Put simply, instead of Mr. Average as have-not making economic demands which are resisted by the more prosperous, political cleavage more commonly pits minority have-nots against the common man with status the value at issue.

The dimensions of status politics are broader than this, however. We are an egalitarian society, one that has involved the mass of people in status concerns far more than aristocratic societies ever did. Weber observed that "modern democracy is devoid of any expressly ordered status privileges." Birth has counted in America in many subtle ways, but it has not been finally determinative of status. Now a series of interrelated developments in contemporary America serve to make status and status concerns even more consuming. (1) There is increased physical mobility, putting more and more Americans in a situation where they must convince those who have not known them over time of their worth. (2) Technology has made new occupational demands, emphasizing the manipulation of people rather than the manipulation of things; and the new middle-class worker typically lacks the tangible testimony to his worth that the skilled artisan had. The standard of his success is the judgment of others that he is doing well. (3) There is a decline in the value of experience, as technology and life styles unfold so rapidly that the experience of two decades ago frequently is an accumulation to be unlearned. Few can be certain that by assiduously building up a store of certain forms of experiential knowledge they will be assured social recognition. (4) Finally, the new affluence frees increasing numbers from preoccupation with economics, permitting them a preoccupation with status. Conflict in the United States of the fourth agenda commonly involves status groups, while that of the past more often saw economic groups at odds.

I have suggested four distinct socioeconomic settings in the United States from the founding of the regime to the present, each defining its distinctive agenda of politics. The massive transformations of American society since World War II have ushered in the fourth agenda. This study of the ideational life of an American city, a suburb, and a small town in the 1960's is one effort to chart more clearly and completely the shape of conflict in the new agenda, the changing dimensions of American ideational life.

2. Cities, Suburbs, Small Towns: Contrasting Sociopolitical Settings

The city-suburb-town trichotomy is a common one, frequently encountered in both casual and scholarly discussion of local communities as sociopolitical settings. The differences in local community experience which it appears to bespeak make its incorporation in this study of community ideational systems mandatory.

The chapters which follow will treat comparatively and in some detail community ideational systems in one central city, one suburb, and one small town. Here, I propose to explore what we know and don't know about cities, suburbs, and towns as contrasting settings. Beyond the obvious differences of scale and relationship to other communities, what distinguishes the community settings of the trichotomy? What categoric differences in problems, resources, scope and activities of local government, in the impact of social change and the response to it, can be located? I will necessarily be guided in this by the principal concerns and themes of the literature on the trichotomy.

I. THE PROBLEM OF CATEGORIES

At the outset, something must be said about the technical boundaries of the categories. Here, the question "What is a suburb?" is the hardest. In a sense, this is strange because an avalanche of cartoons, jokes, novels, and popularized social commentary have fixed in our mind's eye a picture of suburbia seemingly clearer and more complete than of urban or rural America. It is a picture of places with lawns and trees and single-family houses near big cities, occupied by white-collar professionals and managers who depart each morning for work in Gotham City, who are affluent and college-educated and drivers of station wagons. As we stare more intently, however, our picture of suburbia becomes a double vision. In the first, we see New Canaan, Connecticut or Shaker Heights, Ohio or Grosse Point, Michigan or at least Park Forest, Illinois: expensive houses, corporation executives at the top or moving toward the top. The second image is of a Levittown: row upon row of mass-produced houses, each identical to the others around it, as far as the eye can see across the potato field. Clearly, most of these people will never command IBM or General Motors. Yet as we look harder, the two visions again merge to one and we see conformity and frantic socializing and rapid social mobility and transience and cultural homogeneity. We have, in a small way, been tyrannized by these ideal type depictions to the point of not recognizing the variety in suburbs, and, perhaps as well, what is essential to the genus.[1]

Most definitions of *suburb* blend two or more ecological and social characteristics: (1) location in close proximity to a central city; (2) orientation toward the city, part of metropolitan life; (3) land use that is largely residential and consistently nonfarm; (4) a labor force engaged in urban-type occupations, with a far higher than normal number of commuters. But the combina-

[1] In a commentary on the tyranny of the ideal type, a number of my students concluded that Bloomfield—the suburb intensively examined in this study—wasn't a "real" suburb, or was at least a poor selection. When asked why they invariably replied it was because they found blue-collar workers there, or many families in which both husband and wife work to get the family income up to $9,500, or because many of the white-collar workers were clerical and sales people, not fast-rising young executives. Also, Bloomfield just didn't look like William Whyte's Park Forest. Neither did it look like Levittown. And I found many Bloomfield residents half reluctant to call their community—contiguous though it is to Hartford—a suburb. Of course, they knew that by any ecological definition Bloomfield was a suburban place. But even for these suburbanites, *suburb* connoted something else, the something else that Shaker Heights and the Levittowns have, that Bloomfield does not.

tions of social and ecological criteria vary, and the conceptual disagreements and confusions are substantial.

There are many different kinds of metropolitan-places-outside-central-cities, and unless one begins with a restrictive construction, arbitrarily limiting *suburb* to only one variety such as prosperous white-collar commuter towns, it is imperative to explore the relationship of type of suburb to the characteristic(s) under investigation. A serious weakness of much of the popular literature is a failure to recognize the variety of suburban experience. Park Forest is a suburb, but many suburbs are unlike Park Forest in important ways. This has not always been explicit—Whyte did not make it so in his Park Forest study—and we have come to expect *suburb* to say too much.

There are residential suburbs and industrial suburbs; suburbs created *de nouveau,* like the Levittowns of New York, New Jersey and Pennsylvania, as the builder plows up virgin land, and others conceived as rural villages and only late in life reached by the spreading metropolis. Most definitions of suburbia yield great variations in size, from places under a thousand to those well over 100,000. And suburbs vary widely in the SES (socioeconomic status) composition of their inhabitants. There are middle-class and working-class suburbs, of course, but this distinction is too crude. If a lower-middle-class community like "Willingboro" (Levittown), New Jersey, which Herbert Gans dissected, and an upper-middle-class place like Winnetka, Illinois—a north-shore Chicago suburb where in 1959 the median income was $20,166, where nearly half the population over 25 were college graduates, and over half of those employed were professionals and managers—are lumped together as "middle-class suburbs," the category becomes too diffuse.

Connecticut's suburbs (see Table 9) show an enormous range when ranked by an index of socioeconomic status.[2] The differ-

[2] The five variables which form the index in Table 9 are: median years of school completed (by those 25 years and older); percentage with four or more years of college; median family income; percentage of families earning over $10,000 per year; and percentage (of the labor force) in

Table 9. Connecticut suburbs, ranked in a five-variable index of socioeconomic status, and by income alone

Suburb	SES index	Community income as a ratio to state income (1959 figures)
New Canaan	219	192
Darien	215	189
Westport	197	161
West Hartford	173	141
Greenwich	168	139
Wethersfield	137	127
Bloomfield	135	115
Glastonbury	133	117
Fairfield	133	116
North Haven	127	115
Middlebury	126	115
Hamden	125	112
Trumbull	124	119
Newington	120	116
Branford	112	101
Manchester	109	108
Windsor	108	112
Rocky Hill	106	112
Berlin	104	107
Milford	102	103
Ansonia	99	89
Stratford	95	107
Watertown	95	106
Naugatuck	91	108
East Hartford	91	103
East Haven	84	98
West Haven	84	97
Plainville	83	100
Shelton	77	97
Derby	74	91
Seymour	74	93

Source: Connecticut Town and County Fact Book, 1960 (Storrs, Conn.: Agricultural Experimentation Station, 1964).

ence between the elite suburbs (such as New Canaan, Westport, and West Hartford) and the working-class suburbs (an East Hartford, a West Haven, or a Seymour) is large indeed. New Canaan is an upper-middle-class suburb of managers and professionals, 1,670 (in 1964) of whom commute daily to New York.

Table 10. The components of socioeconomic status for the high and low Connecticut suburbs

Suburb	Percentage earning over $10,000	Percentage in white-collar jobs	Median family income	Median years of school completed	Percentage with four or more years of college
New Canaan	61.4	64.6	$13,210	13.9	33.0
Seymour	14.0	35.2	$6,404	10.4	3.6

Source: Connecticut Town and County Fact Book, 1960.

Seymour is a working-class suburb, its residents wage workers employed in manufacturing (see Table 10). Shaker Heights,

white-collar jobs. To permit combination of these "apples and oranges" in a single index figure, each was expressed as a relationship to the statewide (Connecticut) figure for the variable. This was done by determining the percentage which each suburban population is of the total Connecticut population for the variable. For example, 22% of Connecticut families in 1959 had incomes over $10,000; and the figure is 62.8% for families in Darien. 62.8 is 285.45% of 22.0. Then, the average of these five percentage figures which compare each suburb with the state population was computed, and this mean of the five variables equally weighted is called the community's socioeconomic index. Median education, percentage of college graduates, median income, percentage earning over $10,000 a year, and percentage holding white-collar jobs together give a fairly good glimpse of a town's SES. I chose to express the community's rank on each variable as a percentage relationship to the Connecticut rather than to the national figure in order to rank each community within its immedate environment and to eliminate an exaggeration of the community's SES position due to the much higher income in Connecticut than in most of the country. In 1959, for example, median family income in the United States was $5,660; in Connecticut, $6,887.

Ohio and Grosse Point Farms, Michigan; Webster Groves, Missouri and Winnetka, Illinois and New Canaan are all suburbs—but one highly specialized variety of upper-middle-class suburb.

The terms *city* and *small town* present far fewer conceptual difficulties. Still, certain highly stylized descriptions of American small towns dominate at least popular attention. A handsome church with a towering steeple, quiet tree-shaded streets, the corner store with the cracker-barrel philosopher, a slow and easygoing life with friendships strong and true: all these are part of the folklore of the town. In fact, of course, the flat, dusty South Carolina town with the railroad track down the center of Main Street is as common as the compelling New England prototype. In 1960, there were slightly more than 11,000 towns outside urbanized areas with populations between 1,000 and 10,000. These range from isolated farming villages to small industrial centers lying just beyond the edge of enormous population concentrations.

A city is a political entity, its boundary lines defined through political decisions. American cities typically are underbounded, the political city containing something less than the entire urban area. Some cities, though, are true-bounded and even overbounded. Houston is 321 square miles, its boundaries conterminous with Houston county. Compare this to Boston's 46 square miles (see Table 11). Given differences of this magnitude, many demographic comparisons of American cities obviously are strained. The city of Boston and the city of Houston are quite different kinds of places simply because the political boundary of the former includes a much narrower slice of the metropolitan region.

American cities have been settled at different points in time, by different thrusts of population movement. The great northeastern cities took in waves of immigrants from Europe in the last decades of the nineteenth and the first decades of this century. The cities of the South, Southwest and West are newer and owe their growth to the nationalizing of American social

Table 11. Boston and Houston, city and urban fringe population, and density, 1960

	City			Urban fringe	
	Population	Percentage of metropolitan population	Population per square mile	Population	Percentage of metropolitan population
Boston	697,000	26.9	15,157	1,892,000	73.1
Houston	938,000	75.5	2,923	305,000	24.5

Source: U.S. Bureau of the Census, *County and City Data Book: 1967.*

and economic life since 1940. Typically they are far less underbounded, have larger middle-class populations, and, settled by a different type of population migration, behave differently in partisan political activity than the old eastern cities. They are not, typically, Democratic anchors. Indeed, Republicans have made their greatest gains in the South in cities.

In short, each of the three categories subsumes a range of community settings which by some standards of measurement is wide indeed. This does not mean that central cities do not share some characteristics as sociopolitical settings which set them apart from all small towns. It does suggest the necessity of quite explicitly distinguishing the generic characteristics from the more specific features of some cities, some suburbs, some small towns. I will be at pains to do this as this volume unfolds.

II. THE DEMOGRAPHIC CONTRASTS

The United States has been built on massive movements of people, from foreign countries and within our boundaries. In recent decades, towns, suburbs, and cities have been variously affected by internal migrations. We have often heard that big cities have not gained nearly as fast as their surrounding rings and many in the Northeast and North Central regions have actually lost population, that small-town and rural America has not kept pace with national growth either and wide sections have stagnated or incurred absolute decline, that the suburbs have been the big gainers. But population movement and change as they affect the places of our trichotomy need to be examined a bit more closely.

In the 1950's, when national population had its largest growth in absolute numbers and its highest rate of growth since the first decade of the century, almost half of our 3,134 counties (or county equivalents) lost people. One quarter lost 10 per cent or more. Most of these declining counties were rural.[3] In Illi-

[3] A county was classified rural if less than 50% of its population was urban, by the Census definition.

nois, for example, forty-six of fifty counties losing population between 1950 and 1960 were rural and more than two-thirds of all rural counties in the state declined. The number of people living on farms has sharply declined. Between 1960 and 1966 alone, the farm population dropped by four million, to 11.5 million or 6 per cent of the total. This, in turn, has affected those towns which served as commercial centers for a farming hinterland.

Between 1950 and 1960 the population of small towns increased slightly, well below the national rate. Towns between 1,000 and 10,000 outside urbanized areas gained 6.9 per cent, only a third of the national rate. But the collective conceals a wide variation in individual experiences; many towns declined or remained static and some increased rapidly. An important condition affecting growth appears to be proximity to metropolitan areas. In Connecticut, where distances are small and urban centers numerous and nearby, many "small towns" are in fact exurban bedrooms. They frequently resemble the metropolitan fringe of less compact regions: they are places of mixed land use, with farms and suburban tracts scattered about, and are now expanding faster than the state as a whole.[4] Between 1950 and 1960, the small towns of Connecticut grew by 38 per cent, the whole state by 26 per cent. But towns such as Putnam, which are not perched on the edge of a metropolitan region, typically have not gained population. Putnam had only fifteen more people in 1960 than it had in 1920.

The abandonment of big cities is another theme of American population change. Of the sixty-seven cities with over 150,000 inhabitants in 1950, twenty-nine actually lost population by 1960. And what is more striking, eleven of fifteen cities with more than 500,000 people declined. Those declining were with

[4] The data are from the *Connecticut Town and County Fact Book, 1960.* I have classified as small towns those places of under 10,000 outside SMSAs (Standard Metropolitan Statistical Areas), excluding all Fairfield County towns because of the clearly metropolitan character of the entire county. There were 73 places in this category.

few exceptions Northeastern and North Central cities. Cities in the other parts of the country recorded gains, especially rapid in the West South Central States. These regional differences are explained by two factors. First, the cities of the South and West are newer, at a different stage in their growth than the old giants of the Northeast and North Central sections. A few are actually centralizing (that is, the density of the center is still increasing). But the larger part of the variance in regional growth patterns is only apparent, explained by the inability of eastern cities to change their boundaries, while many newer cities in the South and West have been able to annex surrounding territory and thus are far less underbounded. Table 12 shows this clearly.

Table 12. Growth patterns of metropolitan cities and rings, by region, before and after adjustments for annexation, 1950–1960

	Before adjustment for annexations		After adjustment for annexations	
Region	Centralizing	Decentralizing	Centralizing	Decentralizing
United States	64	147	8	203
Northeast	0	46	0	46
North Central	13	46	1	58
South	41	36	5	72
West	10	19	2	27

Source: Adapted from Leo F. Schnore, "Municipal Annexations and the Growth of Metropolitan Suburbs, 1950–1960," *American Journal of Sociology*, LXVII (January, 1962), 414.

A decreasing share of our national population, then, is living in central cities and small towns. If numbers are power, and they are to a substantial extent in the electoral process, power is shifting, gravitating toward the widening bands of metropolitan territory around core cities. The inhabitants of these suburban bands are, as aggregates, more prosperous than their urban or small-town counterparts. The index first introduced in Table 9 shows the clear statistical superiority of suburbanites in those values commonly associated with socioeconomic status. Some of the contrasts indicated by Table 13 are especially strik-

Table 13. Cities, suburbs, small towns, by five socioeconomic variables, expressed as a ratio to the country as a whole; U.S. = 100

Variable	Central cities	Small towns	Suburbs
Median years of school completed	101	93	113
Percentage with 4 or more years of college	105	76	142
Median family income	105	87	126
Percentage of families earning over $10,000	110	63	161
Percentage of labor force employed as white-collar workers	110	100	122
Combined SES index	106	84	133

Source: Data adapted from *U.S. Census of Population, 1960.*

ing. Compare, for example, suburbanites and small-towners for the percentage with a college education or the proportion of families earning over $10,000 per year. Small towns, the social, economic, and political fulcrum of America a half century ago, now lag by all socioeconomic indicators.

Big city and small town residents not only have a smaller share of SES values today than suburbanites, but they also are relatively less well off than in the past. Table 14 compares, for example, the relative socioeconomic position of a group of big cities in 1950 and 1960.[5] Every one of these older cities lost ground vis-à-vis the population of the rest of the state between 1950 and 1960. The city populations had a smaller share of the available socioeconomic values in 1960 than a decade before. Is this the essence of the "decline of cities" argument so often badly confused? The inhabitants of the older cities fare less well

[5] The SES Index used in Table 14 was computed for each city, and for each state in which the cities are located, as described in note 2 in this chapter. Then, the state index was divided into the city, for 1950 and 1960. The figures in Table 14 thus compare each city to its state for the 2 years, for the composite SES Index.

Table 14. Selected American cities, by a five-variable index of socioeconomic status, 1950 and 1960

City	SES index (expressed as city/state)	
	1950	1960
New York	99	95
Boston	96	91
Providence	100	96
Philadelphia	102	96
Pittsburgh	110	102
Jersey City	83	76
Baltimore	90	80
Detroit	109	96
Cleveland	94	81
Cincinnati	103	100
Chicago	105	96
St. Louis	105	91

Source: Adapted from *U.S. Census of Population, 1950;* and *U.S. Census of Population, 1960.*

than their suburban neighbors. And what is perhaps especially important, older cities have a smaller share of the affluent and well-educated. Ten of the twelve had a smaller part of their states' upper-income families in 1960 than in 1950, and eleven of the twelve had fewer of the college-educated.

The increasing concentration of Negroes in our central cities is the most often discussed and the most easily demonstrated of the major urban demographic changes. Some suburbs do have significant numbers of Negroes, but the picture of dark cities and white rings is a generally accurate one. The flow of Negroes to our largest cities is a half century old but has dramatically increased since 1950 and is now a dominant theme in the American metropolitan experience. In 1910, Negro Americans were the most rural of all Americans; today they are the most urban. In 1910, 90 per cent of the Negro population of the

United States lived in the South; in the mid-1960's, more than half reside outside the eleven states of the old Confederacy. The general movement of Negroes into northern cities, the flight of whites, and the rapid growth of suburban population which remains mostly white is summed up in Table 15.

The rapidity of the change in the white-Negro mix in the cities is more dramatically revealed by examining some of the big cities which have not annexed territory (see Table 16). Between 1950 and 1960, Detroit lost 180,000 people, but its Negro population jumped by more than 180,000 (60 per cent). Things were much the same for other Northeast and North Central cities, such as New York, Philadelphia, Boston, and Cleveland. Every city over 250,000 showed a marked increase in its Negro population between 1950 and 1966. Only in some of the smaller cities of the South has the Negro population remained stationary or declined. Suburban rings are overwhelmingly white and are getting "whiter" with the passage of time. The white population of the suburbs is increasing faster, in terms of percentages as well as numbers, than the nonwhite.

These movements of people do not involve color alone, of course, for Negro Americans rank well below whites in income, education, and other variables associated with socioeconomic status (see Table 17). Thus, the central cities are taking in increasing numbers of people whose demands for services are high.

These demographic data suggest something of the contrasting experience of town, city, and suburb. But to adequately explore differences in the social and political life of these three community settings, we must turn to the major themes which emerge from the literature on each. What distinguishes the urban, the suburban, the small town sociopolitical "ways of life"? Here we are bound by the literature and what it has emphasized. Studies of the suburb as setting, for example, have been heavily sociological; those of the city as setting more often have been done by political scientists and public administrators. The weaknesses

Table 15. White and Negro population of the United States, by place of residence, 1950, 1960, and 1966

Residence	1950 (in thousands)		1960 (in thousands)		Percentage change 1950–1960		1966 (in thousands)		Percentage change 1960–1966	
	White	Negro	White	Negro	White	Negro	White	Negro	White	Negro
Total population	134,942	15,755	158,838	18,849	17.7	19.6	170,744	21,508	7.5	14.1
Metropolitan	80,249	8,360	99,688	12,198	24.2	45.9	108,983	14,790	9.3	21.2
In central cities	45,441	6,456	47,655	9,705	4.9	50.3	46,444	12,074	−2.5	24.4
Outside central cities	34,808	1,904	52,033	2,493	49.5	30.9	62,539	2,716	20.2	8.9
Nonmetropolitan	54,693	7,395	59,144	6,674	8.1	−9.7	61,791	6,718	4.5	0.7

Source: U.S. Census of Population, 1950; and *Current Population Reports,* Series P-20, No. 157, December 16, 1966.

Table 16. White and Negro population, five northern cities, 1950 and 1960

City	White population 1950 (in thousands)	White population 1960 (in thousands)	Percentage change 1950–1960	Negro population 1950 (in thousands)	Negro population 1960 (in thousands)	Percentage change 1950–1960
Boston	759	629	−17	40	63	58
New York	7,116	6,641	− 7	748	1,088	46
Philadelphia	1,693	1,467	−13	376	529	41
Cleveland	765	623	−19	148	251	70
Detroit	1,546	1,183	−24	301	482	60

Source: U.S. Census of Population, 1950; and *U.S. Census of Population, 1960.*

Table 17. Social and economic characteristics of white and Negro population, 1960 and 1965

	1960		1965	
Characteristic	White	Negro	White	Negro
Median family income	$5,643	$2,850 (est.)*	$7,251	$3,916
Median years of school completed	10.9	8.2	12.1	9.1
Percentage high school graduates	43.2	20.1	52.2	27.8

Source: U.S. Bureau of the Census, *Current Population Reports*, Series P-20, No. 157, December 16, 1966.

* Income data for Negro population for 1959 not available from 1960 Census; data reported for nonwhites only.

and gaps in the literature become readily apparent, and we will not hesitate to comment on these.

III. THE SUBURB AS A "WAY OF LIFE"

Postwar research on the American suburb as sociopolitical setting began with the confident affirmation of suburbia as the quintessence of America's future, a future seen variously as Levittown and Park Forest. Then, in the 1960's, these ideal types were "exposed," and a swelling chorus proclaimed that suburbia is not one unbroken string of Park Forests. Bleak as these quasi-polemical peaks appear, some good work was done on the way up and down, and we are now in a better position to comment on the suburb as a "way of life" than two decades ago when the work began in earnest.

Suburbia and Individuality

Few matters have been muddied more successfully than the whole theme of conformity in American society, and this "problem" has figured prominently in the literature on suburbia. William Whyte through his *Fortune* series on Park Forest and

The Organization Man became a principal popularizer of the "conformist suburbia" theme. The old Protestant ethic, said Whyte, has withered and has been replaced by a social ethic which emphasizes the sanctity of the group and adaptation to the group. The new organization man, carrier of this social ethic, populates the suburb, and suburbia exudes his conformist, group-oriented ethic. Park Forest, according to Whyte, is on one massive "belongingness" kick.[6]

A key to the problem, he felt, is transience. People come to Park Forest from a variety of backgrounds and places, to stay but a short time and then move on, up the executive ladder. Lacking the roots which permanence feeds, they seek substitutes and find them through "togetherness," by enthroning adaptive behavior. The result is a rampantly conformist setting which abuses privacy and punishes diversity. Woe to anyone who does not "fit." Whyte relates the sad, sad story of "Estelle" who so much wanted "in" with the gang, but who made little social fluffs. Estelle was ostracized, and "even her two-year-old daughter gets kept out of kids' parties." Estelle and her husband finally moved out to make a fresh start.[7] Demands to adapt to others must be more extensive in a big, complexly integrated society like ours than in the more isolated agrarian past. But Park Forest makes necessity a virtue and requires allegiance to an ethic which says only, "Adapt."

A. C. Spectorsky, Vance Packard, and John Keats are other prominent disseminators of this view. The suburban stereotype reveals a continuous *kaffeeklatsch* between wives in an ecologically determined common ground.

In the suburbs, in the opinion of its prominent investigators, the modern American exchanges individuality, privacy, the certain satisfactions of pride of craftsmanship and work well done, for something

[6] William H. Whyte, Jr., *The Organization Man* (New York: Simon and Shuster, 1956), pp. 284–285.

[7] *Ibid.*, p. 359.

obscurely defined as the social ethic, being a good fellow, and group cooperation.[8]

But recently, there has been something of a reaction to this picture of suburbs as places filled with rootless souls who sacrifice individuality for a niche in The Group. It is argued that Whyte and Keats were describing only the behavior of an aspiring and upwardly mobile segment of the population, not universal suburban traits. On another track, it is said that assaults on individuality are hardly new, that a half century ago they were seen principally in the independent small town, on Main Street, and that the forms of adaptive behavior which worried Whyte may be nothing more than the extension to a new environment of traditional responses.[9]

No final judgment on rootlessness and conformity in the suburb can be attempted here, but some things are clear. We adapt to the styles and values which surround us as part of the process of self-identification. In one sense, society and nonconformity are mutually exclusive. On occasion, either those pressured to adapt or outside observers become conscious of the demands for adaptive behavior. Once exposed, these easily can be ridiculed and lamented, whether in Lewis' *Main Street* or Whyte's Park Forest. There *is* a form of conformity which is unwanted (by those on whom the adaptive demands are made), but there is no indication this appears more frequently in suburbs than in other residential settings.

Present-day Americans probably are more conscious of adaptive behavior than their counterparts in other times. Ours is an egalitarian society, one which has broken down fixed status positions. Individuals can and do change their status and are asked

[8] Robert Wood, *Suburbia: Its People and Their Politics* (Boston: Houghton Mifflin, 1958), pp. 4–5.

[9] See, for example, Thomas Ktsanes and Leonard Reissman, "Suburbia: New Homes for Old Values," *Social Problems,* VII (Winter, 1959–60), 187–195; Bennett Berger, *Working-Class Suburb* (Berkeley and Los Angeles: University of California Press, 1960); Wood, *op. cit.*; and William Dobriner, *Class in Suburbia* (Englewood Cliffs, N.J.: Prentice-Hall, 1963).

to adapt consciously to changing demands. This differs sharply from the position of dwellers in ascriptive class societies, who found status static and thus slipped naturally into the slot which their ancestors had occupied, presumably accepting it as natural. Egalitarian man, who moves from one status position to another, knows that the demands placed upon him are not "natural," and with egalitarianism, conformity becomes a conscious process. In the United States it has become truly a mass undertaking.

Moreover, American society is engulfed in rapid change, and a single generation spans great variety in life styles and aspirations. Adaptive behavior is thereby increased, and we are made more aware of it. When a person is confined to one place for a lifetime, his ties and attachments are not unaffected. He comes to know landmarks, houses, and histories, and these matter to him. He is known for what his family was as well as what it is. Now a new transportation and communications technology has given us unparalleled mobility. Those whose occupations require frequent moves from one region to another form different attachments, to national rather than local institutions—for example, to the institution which is the employer rather than to a town and its history and memorabilia. And when a community is formed of people who have moved to it within a decade and who cannot know each other by what their families have been, the whole process of adaption or conforming changes, becomes still more conscious, and in a sense more hurried.

The tone of certain American suburban places has been set by a highly mobile—spatially and socially—middle class that is most responsive to the dynamic changes of the system. If such communities did not display patterns of adaptive behavior vastly different from those of a spatially stable small town in 1900 or a French peasant village in 1600, we would indeed have cause for surprise. There is need for further work on patterns of adaptive behavior in contemporary America—as affected by such variables as residence and class position–and for further work not primarily normative. The issue has been badly confused. It never should have been "more conformity" or "less conformity," but rather what types of adaptive behavior are demanded by various settings. We would expect conformity to be far more conscious and hurried in Whyte's Park Forest than in Berger's Miltpas.

Suburbia and Specialization

Suburban specialization or uniformity is widely recognized and is both praised and viewed with alarm. Robert Wood, Anthony Downs, and others have described the use of political boundaries to create manageable and relatively homogeneous communities.

> . . . all suburbs have one major advantage regarding cultural homogeneity that is not shared by larger cities: suburban residents can make use of legal machinery to maintain their homogeneity by excluding those who may change it. Of course, they cannot directly prevent any particular group from entering by passing discriminatory laws but they can set up and enforce specific standards regarding building quality, tax rates, the character of public services, and the nature of the school system. By raising these standards high enough, they can make it economically impossible for "disrupting" elements to enter the area and dilute the homogeneity which they seek to establish.[10]

Because the suburb need not reproduce all of the parts of a self-contained economic system, it can achieve a degree of homogeneity not possible before. "The central city becomes a receptacle for all the functions the suburb dweller does not care to support." [11] The old small town typically reproduced the entire class spectrum. There was a small upper class, a middle class of entrepreneurs and storekeepers, and a working class which manned the mills and factories. Today's suburb, attached to a major city in an era of rapid transportation and communication, can be far more specialized and homogeneous (though

[10] Downs, "Metropolitan Growth and Future Political Problems," *Land Economics,* XXXVII (November, 1961), 315

[11] Wood, *op. cit.,* p. 106.

the entire metropolitan region is highly variegated). Suburbs can be identified as upper-middle-class or lower-middle-class or working-class in much the same way as neighborhoods of big cities and sections of small towns. Oliver P. Williams and his associates found Philadelphia suburbs much more differentiated and specialized than the towns beyond.[12]

David Riesman does not challenge the thesis of suburban homogeneity but argues that this may be only the use of political boundary lines to achieve what a more stratified America realized without recourse to them.

> In a highly stratified society in which people at the top feel secure about their position and people at the bottom know their place and lack the autos and the spending money to get out of their place, cities can crowd together the Gold Coast and the slum, or in the typical southern city, the Negro and the white, without explosive friction and resentment on either side. . . . Today, it goes without saying that all this has quite changed. The children of the poor do not stay in place. . . . Furthermore, the children of the rich are not immune to the values thus spread from below, and the parents of the children of the rich, or at least the moderately rich, are not well defended from their children's own demands.[13]

One of the things which people are trying to escape when they flee the city is "the need either to reject people who are less well-educated than themselves, or to accept them with all that implies for their children's education and future placement in the society."

Suburbia and Betrayal

Much of the literature, too much, has been highly normative, churned up over whether suburbanization is a good thing or a betrayal. It is usually found to be the latter. Architects, city planners, and many "metropoliticians" accuse the suburbs of

[12] Williams *et al., Suburban Differences and Metropolitan Policies* (Philadelphia: University of Pennsylvania Press, 1965).

[13] Riesman, "Flight and Search in the New Suburbs," in Riesman (ed.), *Abundance for What?* (Garden City, N.Y.: Doubleday, 1964), pp. 261–262.

despoiling the countryside, Balkanizing the metropolitan region, strangling the cities, producing miles of ugly sprawl, and generally turning urban America into one vast megalopolitan waste land.[14] Urban America, Inc. has convicted suburbs as a "clear and present danger" to urban America. "In Congress, then, city dwellers may have more to fear than farmers from the one man, one vote rule and the new power it has given the spreading suburbs." [15] To still other observers, the betrayal is in a failure to approximate the hardier and healthier virtues of the old independent small town. Whyte's *Organization Man* radiates this concern.

Reacting to the betrayal theme, some have affirmed the suburb's legitimacy and worth. Herbert Gans' *The Levittowners* (New York: Pantheon, 1967) was dedicated to putting down the myth of suburban betrayal. Gans set out with a conviction that there had been no betrayal, and he found none. Levittowners do not engage in frantic socializing (p. 154). They are not stifled by homogeneity (p. 109), and even if they were, city neighborhoods are homogeneous too. Levittowners don't suffer much unwanted conformity (p. 180), and their town is not a wasteland of sameness and blandness. (Those who say it is are applying a "tourist" perspective. The tourist wants visual excitement and exotic variety, where the resident wants a comfortable, convenient, and socially satisfying place to live.) The Levittown experience disconfirms the argument that suburbs breed depression, boredom, loneliness, and ultimately mental illness (p. 220). Suburbanites are happy with their community, like the greater spaciousness, and generally find a large supply of compatible people (p. 409). Why, then, the vitality of the "suburban betrayal myth"? It is a creation of confirmed cos-

[14] See, as illustrative, Peter Blake, *God's Own Junkyard* (New York: Holt, Rinehart and Winston, 1963); Victor Gruen, *The Heart of Our Cities* (New York: Simon and Shuster, 1964); and Lewis Mumford, *The City in History* (New York: Harcourt, Brace & World, 1961), esp. ch. 16.

[15] The quotation is from the July 1967 issue of *City*, the newsletter of Urban America, Inc.

mopolitan urbanites, "disdainful of . . . values of lower-middle-class and working-class people," who dogmatically and blindly insist on the universality of the values they personally hold (p. 179).

So the argument goes on, and on. We have had a surfeit of such heavily normative discussion. Whether betrayal or shiny hope, the suburban appeal is compelling. The new middle class we are manufacturing in such quantity reject the city and choose instead the suburb.

Suburbia and Partisan Political Choice

Thus far, suburban life styles have been emphasized. Now we can look at suburbia more narrowly as a political setting. One of the earliest concerns was with the effect of suburbanization on party affiliations and partisan choice. For a time, most observers were convinced the Republican party would ride a suburban wave to victory. In one beautiful moment in 1952, Robert Taft proclaimed that "the Democratic party will never win another national election until it solves the problem of the suburbs."

Explanations of partisan conversion through suburbanization range from the simplistic to those which at least deserve attention. There was an abundance of the former. In April 1957, *Newsweek* declared that "when a city dweller packs up and moves his family to the suburbs, he usually acquires a mortgage, a power lawnmower, and backyard grill. Often, though a life-long Democrat, he starts voting Republican." [16] William Whyte somewhat mystically observed: "Whatever the cause, it is true that something does seem to happen to Democrats when they get to Suburbia. Despite the constant influx of Democrats the size of the Republican vote remains fairly constant from suburb to suburb." [17]

But others tried to identify what that "something" is. Three

[16] *Newsweek,* April 1, 1957, p. 42.

[17] Whyte, *op. cit.,* p. 300.

distinct points were made explaining the alleged conversion of Democrats, with some observers blending two or all three. One focused on social status. Children of the "tenement trail," upwardly mobile, arrive in suburbia. Having achieved a new and augmented social status, they seek the various symbols and attachments of that status. The older ethnic identifications and big-city attachments are sloughed off, the suburbanite bathes in his new white-collar status that is so fully American and becomes more receptive to the appeals of that respectable middle-class party, the Republicans. The working-class ethnic becomes middle-class American. Closely related was a "pressure of the environment" argument. Urban dwellers move into solidly Republican suburban communities where Republican organizations are entrenched and working effectively. They find themselves in a quite different situation than their old city neighborhoods where nearly everyone was a Democrat, and the only effective organization the Democratic machine. The third explanation of conversion saw suburbs breeding conservatives. By moving to the suburb, becoming home owners and thus sharing in property tax worries, and generally becoming middle-class, large numbers of Americans were thought to develop an attachment to "financial responsibility," and thus to the more "responsible" of the two parties, the Republicans. Suburbanites are more conservative, and the G.O.P. is the more conservative party.[18]

Conversion thus postulated was not implausible. Things might have worked out this way. As astute an observer as Edward Banfield, assuming a 60 per cent Republican suburban plurality, asserted that the metropolitan-wide Democratic advantage would disappear shortly after 1956, and predicted that by 1975 the imbalance between city and suburban population

[18] Louis Harris, *Is There a Republican Majority?* (New York: Harper and Brothers, 1954) is one of the more complete statements of conversion. See, also, Harry Gersh, "The New Suburbanites of the Fifties," *Commentary,* XVII (March, 1954), 217; and Frederick Lewis Allen, "The Big Change in Suburbia," Part II, *Harper's,* July, 1954, p. 50.

would be so great that the Republican metropolitan plurality would exceed two million.[19] But we now know that the conversion statement, so plausible in many regards, was wrong, and it was Samuel Lubell who first said so.[20]

That the growth of a new suburban middle class did not, *ipso facto,* assure gains for the Republican party has been pretty well demonstrated. The percentage of Democratic decline between 1948 and 1952 was smallest in the suburbs. Stevenson did better in the suburbs in 1956 than in 1952, although he did not do as well in the country at large. And the greatest congressional gains by the Democrats between 1952 and 1956 were in suburban areas.[21] Despite the massive growth of suburban population since 1952, the Democratic share of voter loyalty has remained relatively constant (see Table 18).

Table 18. Distribution of party identification, 1952–1964 (in per cent)

Party	1952	1954	1956	1958	1960	1962	1964
Democrat (strong, weak, independent)	57	56	51	54	54	53	53
Republican (strong, weak, independent)	34	33	37	33	34	34	33

Source: Releases, Survey Research Center, University of Michigan.

Those who saw the growth of a new class in a new residential setting eroding traditional Democratic support were not wrong. What was not appreciated was that the Democrats had become

[19] Edward Banfield, "The Changing Political Environment of City Planning," a paper delivered at the American Political Science Association Meeting, 1956.

[20] See his *The Future of American Politics* (Garden City, N.Y.: Doubleday, 1951).

[21] Bernard Lazerwitz, "Suburban Voting Trends: 1948 to 1956," *Social Forces,* XXXIX (October, 1960), 29–36. Robert Wood also noted that Republican gains between 1948 and 1956 in metropolitan areas are the result of defections from the Democratic party in the cities rather than Republican advances in the suburbs.

a fully respectable, middle-class party. There was no conflict between middle-class status and Democratic allegiance. And though some suburbs are overwhelmingly Republican and Republican identifications are thereby encouraged in newcomers, others have large numbers of Democrats and active local Democratic parties.

Suburbia and Service Politics

A style of political leadership is a response to the sociopolitical setting in which the leader operates. The urban political machines formed in our cities after 1870 were, for example, a highly pragmatic response to the rise of American urbanism. The machine served as patron to the waves of new immigrants, parceling out jobs, minor welfare, access to decision makers, and related types of public and private assistance. The suburban setting today usually is a polar opposite: few suburbanites require patronage or small favors, most are well enough educated to deal with government without intermediaries, are repelled by the image of freewheeling and corrupt politicians, and demand well-trained, professional administrators to competently execute their many service demands.

Education is a principal service demand, especially of new middle-class suburbanites. William Dobriner writes that the new suburbanites "appear willing to sacrifice all else to their children's education." [22] Why not, if as Riesman argues, a good education is the only capital equipment they can really count on passing on to their children? [23] No one pictures a big happy suburban consensus on education. It is a storm center. The childless resent the higher tax rates the "frills" will bring. The old middle class of the town typically are less willing to spend. Lower-middle-class and upper-middle-class suburbanites clash over the style and fabric of the education the system should produce.[24] But the battleground is often middle-class service poli-

[22] Dobriner, *Class in Suburbia,* p. 137.

[23] Riesman, *op. cit.,* p. 263.

[24] Herbert Gans describes the intense and continuing battle in his Levittown, especially between those who wanted what he calls a "lower-middle-

tics, and middle-class suburbs around the country have been willing to spend liberally for public education.

Political parties operate in suburban America, but they bear little resemblance to the old urban or county courthouse machines. The suburbanite is described as no longer requiring the help of the politician in managing his private or public affairs. Since he asks little of the party, the party lacks sanctions over him.[25] So the suburban boss bears little resemblance to a Hague, a Crump, or a Byrd. He is needed to perform such chores as maintaining contact with the state organization, recruiting candidates, and helping represent the suburb in dealings with various state agencies. But his sanctions are few and his power in suburban political affairs highly restricted.

Just as political parties in the suburb often bear little resemblance to their urban and county courthouse counterparts, so the rewards and incentives for party activity are different. In the small town and the big city, young lawyers have entered politics as a sound business practice: to become better known and thereby attract clients; to share in government business and other legal patronage controlled or influenced by the party, from probate management to municipal judgeships. But suburban lawyers in the employ of prosperous city law firms find suburban political participation of doubtful advantage. They will earn more in corporate law practice.[26]

---

class system," and those favoring a more cosmopolitan upper-middle-class system (*The Levittowners,* esp. pp. 90–100).

[25] On the basis of 57 county investigations Edward Janosik concluded that "traditional and flagrant types of political favoritism, such as interceding with law enforcement officers or conferring unofficial health and welfare benefits, have never played an important role in suburban politics and do not today" ("The New Suburbia," *Current History,* XXXI [August, 1956], 94).

[26] Not all suburban lawyers, of course, work in big city law firms. Many practice in their suburb and may benefit from political activity in much the same way as the small town lawyer. The suburban political leader often must rely upon this suburban legal talent to staff his modest and limited organization. Robert Wood makes this point in his *Suburbia,* pp. 173–174.

The commitment of many suburbanites to middle-class service politics, their feeling of competency to deal with political matters without intercession, their limited demands for services of the kind party organization can bestow, their image of the "good" government leader as the efficient manager—all encourage nonpartisanship in suburban government. Some suburbs, of course, remain highly partisan, but the trend appears away from this, and nonpartisanship is legally recognized in more than 60 per cent of the suburban governments reporting in the *Municipal Yearbook.* This listing includes only suburban communities of 10,000 and over, and the percentage of nonpartisan governments among suburbs under 10,000 almost certainly is higher.

Evidence of the attachment of middle-class suburbanites to the efficient manager as political hero is seen in the greater frequency of the council-manager form in suburbs in which the middle class predominates. Leo Schnore and Robert Alford studied the relationship between social and economic characteristics and forms of suburban government and concluded that "the popular image of the council-manager suburb [is verified]; it does tend to be the natural habitat of the upper-middle class." [27]

The suburban political style is seen quintessentially in the young, well-educated, self-confident, and reasonably affluent participant who is committed to efficient, nonpartisan management. This is, of course, overdrawn, most closely approximated in homogeneous middle-class suburbs, and valid only in hyperbolic contrast to urban and small town archetypes.

Suburbia as Setting: What Can Be Said?

Suburbs are not a recent invention, but massive suburbanization is. Riesman put it well: "It is the democratization and the extension of the phenomena I am describing, and the resulting

[27] Schnore and Alford, "Forms of Government and Socioeconomic Characteristics of Suburbs," *Administrative Science Quarterly,* VII (June, 1963), 15.

constriction of alternatives, which give them [suburbs] a new and cumulative quality." [28] The explosive growth was permitted by some of the technological advances of our age: motor cars, freeways, septic tanks and electric water pumps, and generally a whole new communication and transportation technology. Democratic suburbanization depends, too, on the extension of affluence, as millions could buy single-family houses and the motor cars to get between them and the job. The common man thus could live many miles from his place of work, and business could decentralize.

Much of the attention given suburbanization has come because we have seen the suburb as a window to the new America. We have assumed, I think correctly, that many of the important configurations of the new society appear first and develop fastest in suburbia. A new, white-collar, corporate middle class is our ascendant social and political class, and this class is suburban based because it is attached to corporations which need the array of skill resources which metropolitan regions provide; because it has been taught to appreciate and can afford the cultural resources of the region; and because it can avoid the least desirable residential areas. New work patterns, a new ruling class, new forms of consumption and leisure, the breaking down of old ethnic and class identifications, a vast affluence, a technologically developed society supplanting the old industrial state—all suggest a residential embodiment in the suburb rather than the big city or the small town. National in scope, these characteristics appear quintessentially in the suburban way of life.

The appeal of the suburb is hard to deny as Americans continue to vote with their moving vans. Those novitiates of the new middle class, college students, do not see their future in the small town. And the lure of the city is feeble.[29] The appeals

[28] Riesman, *op. cit.*, p. 244.

[29] Riesman found in interviews with several hundred college seniors at twenty American universities that the great majority planned to live in suburbs. Those who were reared in suburbs wanted to return to them, while city and small-town students looked longingly to suburban homes

of the suburb are for space, for private homes, "for the children," for social status (as the city evokes images of crime and dirt and lower-class life); for the protection of political boundary lines and their use to recreate the greater class homogeneity and insulation of earlier America, and thereby to pass on certain class norms and styles and values; for localism and local ties; for manageability in an age of bigness and concentration; for access to the "culture" of the city and freedom from its problems. These appeals are real and strong and can only intensify.

IV. THE SMALL TOWN AS SETTING

Most of the sociopolitical studies of American small towns have been principally concerned either with power or stratification.[30] Still, there is some basis for an attempt to construct a model of the small town as setting.

Change and Decline

Towns are much less independent today than in the past. Their historic autonomy has been lost to new transportation and communication systems, to a more nationalized society and economy. This is the central thrust of Vidich and Bensman's

---

(Riesman, "The Suburban Dislocation," in Riesman [ed.], *Abundance for What?* p. 237). In a survey of 300 University of Connecticut students, I found that about 95% both wanted and expected to live in the suburbs.

[30] Among the studies of power in American small towns are Robert Presthus, *Men at the Top* (New York: Oxford University Press, 1964); Aaron Wildavsky, *Leadership in a Small Town* (Totowa, N.J.: Bedminster Press, 1964); Ritchie Lowry, *Who's Running This Town?* (New York: Harper & Row, 1965); and in Robert Agger *et al.*, *The Rulers and the Ruled* (New York: John Wiley & Sons, 1964), the studies of "Farmdale" and "Oretown." Among the stratification studies are the well-known investigations of the Lynds, *Middletown* (New York: Harcourt, Brace, 1929), and *Middletown in Transition* (New York: Harcourt, Brace, 1937); W. Lloyd Warner's "Yankee City" series, and his *Democracy in Jonesville* (New York: Harper and Brothers, 1949).

Small Town and Mass Society: rural and small-town life today is dependent upon the institutions and processes of urban society.[31]

The assault on the old independence takes many forms. Small towns have been flooded with "outsiders," agents of the big national organizations and agencies—government and business—which figure prominently in community life. The general population turnover is extensive, even in towns regarded as relatively stable. Vidich and Bensman found that only 25 per cent of the population of "Springdale," (Candor, New York) was born in the town. And in almost all aspects of culture, the small town has come to reflect the contemporary mass culture.[32]

The loss of political independence is perhaps clearest. Though towns legally existed as agents of state government in the nineteenth century, real authority was with the local community. It collected taxes, established schools, cared for the poor, maintained the roads. But since World War I the political role has steadily eroded. To get the state or national subsidy, specific types of decisions must be made. Vidich and Bensman argue that this dependence leads to such an extensive habituation to outside control that the will to act is lost even when the town still has the power.[33] Political power comes to rest with those in the community who can best deal with the outside world and secure its largesse. Generally, those groups favorably linked to the outside society become ascendant socially, economically, and politically.[34]

There is a temptation to ask, "So what?" The whole society has grown more nationalized and interdependent. But it has been argued that the small town was built on a greater independence, and at least some small-towners have been reluctant to part with it. "The fact that Roxborough was an isolated and

[31] Arthur J. Vidich and Joseph Bensman, *Small Town and Mass Society* (Garden City, N.Y.: Doubleday, 1960).

[32] *Ibid.*, p. 87.

[33] *Ibid.*, p. 101.

[34] *Ibid.*, p. 99.

partly self-sufficient community only thirty years ago is not important in itself, but it becomes important because there are so many people still in the town who remember that period and are constantly looking back to it." [35] Independence, at least as seen through idealized hindsight, was a valued commodity and its loss is to be regretted. Perhaps, too, the loss of independence is made painful by its association with a more general decline in sociopolitical position.

As small towns have lost political independence, so have they lost political power. In the 1960's, reapportionment has sealed this political decline. The state legislature was a last stronghold, and reapportionment, whether or not it realizes the bold predictions made for it, has stormed that stronghold. The eighty-one small towns in Connecticut had 43 per cent of the seats in the lower house of the state legislature before the 1965 reapportionment, 14 per cent after (see Table 19).

Table 19. Representation of 81 small towns, Connecticut General Assembly, before and after the 1965 reapportionment

Representation	1963	1967
Number of seats	126	25*
Percentage of all seats	42.9	14.1
Percentage of state population	9.8	9.8

Source: Connecticut Register and Manual, 1965; and *Connecticut Town and County Fact Book, 1960.*

* Eleven of these representatives are from multi-town districts in which at least one other town is not one of our small towns. So the actual representation of the 81 towns is less than 25.

The loss of political power and political autonomy is described by some observers as contributing to a general deterioration of political life in small towns. Granville Hicks, for example, argues that the level of political discourse in "Roxborough" has declined. "Republicanism meant something in the past, or, rather, a series of things. . . . [Now] traditional Republicanism

[35] Granville Hicks, *Small Town* (New York: Macmillan, 1946), p. 93.

has prevailed, but it has been progressively shorn of any intellectual content."[36] Small town politics no longer counts for much and the actors know it.

The loss of economic autonomy by small towns is often discussed. What has occurred, of course, is the collapse, absorption, or transformation of certain types of independent small businesses seen as peculiarly linked to the former autonomy of the town. First, many of the small businesses which survive and even prosper—such as appliance stores and automobile and farm equipment dealerships—are dependent upon the external world for all goods sold and frequently for the creation of the demand for the goods. Farming has become highly specialized, and specialized farming is completely dependent upon national and even world markets. Small town factories and mills, once typically owned by local residents, now more often are simply branch operations of big national corporations.

Warner and Low described the loss of local control over the enterprises which intimately affected local economic life in "Yankee City" (Newburyport, Massachusetts). They noted that in the early days of the shoe industry, which was the principal industry, the owners and managers as well as the mill hands were residents of Yankee City. The factories were then under the control of the community, especially "the more pervasive informal controls of community traditions and attitudes." Managers and workers felt a responsibility to each other and to the town. All that is gone. The shoe factories more and more are being absorbed into big, New York–based firms. Those which remain independent face powerful competition.

Thus, to the Yankee City community, a very important result of both the horizontal and vertical extension of industry is to lessen its independence and freedom of choice in meeting problems having to do with the livelihood of its citizens. Thousands of other small industrial cities are also involved in the process of wider integration occurring throughout American industry. They, too, must come to

[36] *Ibid.*, p. 125.

accept the roles in this development that are assigned them by the larger society.[37]

Certain types of small business, such as grocery and general merchandise stores, cannot compete with the big city stores, brought closer by freeways, and with local outlets of big chains. The local merchant loses the trade of the mobile segments of the population, and he is left with the aged, the loyal, the infirm, and those who must buy on credit but cannot get it outside. The small businessman looks to the past, exhibits attitudes which developed in an economics of scarcity. He emphasizes the virtues of thrift and savings. His operation is based on non-expansion and cost-cutting principles, and he frequently uses obsolete equipment and merchandising methods. His appeal is essentially personal loyalty.[38] The economic autonomy of small towns required the autonomy and vitality of small business. Today, small business has either been liquidated or absorbed, or it operates in the interstices of an economy dominated by big corporations.

The response of small towners to change is generally described as highly ambivalent. Most of the technical innovations have been eagerly accepted. The comforts that modern technology is able to provide are much desired. The American small town is not some peasant village philosophically at odds with a secularized and industrialized society. Only certain results of change, like the domination of the town's economic and political life by outside agents, are considered harmful. But even here the response is mixed.[39] The response to change is confused because the undesirable is mixed with much that is desired and because the town lacks the ideological resources to resist what it does not like. Some of the primary agents of threatening change, such

[37] W. Lloyd Warner and J. O. Low, *The Social System of the Modern Factory—The Strike: A Social Analysis* (New Haven, Conn.: Yale University Press, 1947), pp. 108–133, *passim.*

[38] Vidich and Bensman, *op. cit.*, pp. 119–120.

[39] *Ibid.*, pp. 80, 106. See, too, Hicks, *op. cit.*, p. 113.

as national corporations and their efficient business practices, are fully legitimate in small-town ideology.

The lack of attractions for youth is one of the most widely lamented facets of the position in which small towns now find themselves. Young people leave because the jobs are inferior or there are not enough of them and because the small town is not "where the action is": to stay is to fail.[40]

The Personalization of Social and Political Life

In the small town, people really know each other and have close associations enriched by time. Or so we are told.[41] The urbanite's vistas are dominated by large and impersonal spectacles. Roxborough, Hicks writes, has almost no impersonal spectacles.[42] Politics in the small town is highly personalized. More than half a century ago, James Williams, writing of Waterbury, New York, observed that "town officials were chosen not for their ability to administer the affairs of their offices efficiently so much as for their personal impressiveness." [43] Contemporary commentators including Hicks, Lyford, and Vidich and Bensman have echoed this description. Vidich and Bensman suggest an interesting derivative of personalized politics. Local politicians in Springdale avoid issues or positions which might alienate them from other notables with whom they must get along month after month on a "friendly" basis. When an

[40] Joseph Lyford, for instance, found that "youngsters with an ambition to earn a respectable living and raise a family of their own cannot picture a future for themselves in Vandalia, no matter how much they may like it" (*The Talk in Vandalia* [New York: Harper & Row, 1965], p. 52).

[41] This is not universally accepted. Joseph Lyford argues that the only protection Vandalians have from the awful intimacy of the town's life is to retreat into a pattern of interaction in which they reveal little of themselves (*ibid.*, pp. 129–130).

[42] Hicks, *op. cit.*, p. 106.

[43] James Williams, *An American Town* (New York: James Kempster, 1906), p. 60.

issue arises on which the position of everyone is not known, an elaborate process of discussion takes place in which the participants avoid irrevocably committing themselves and in which they frequently contradict themselves. "This discussion, which appears so strange to the outsider, takes place for the purpose of finding a common ground on which all can agree and in which no opinion stands out." [44]

The intimacy of small town life is valued, but certain troublesome features are not ignored. The town is clannish, too close-knit. Gossip is rife. Too much privacy is sacrificed. There is the stifling intimacy of Lewis' *Main Street.* Lyford has described this in Vandalia:

> This kind of atmosphere is a mixed blessing. While many Vandalians appreciate the neighborly sort of mutual assistance in an emergency which is a standard fact of life in a small town, there is also some feeling that sympathy and first aid from one's fellow-citizens are often bought rather dearly—at the sacrifice of individual privacy, for instance. "Nobody could ever die in Vandalia and not be missed right away," says one complainer, "but sometimes I think I'd prefer a big city. At least you can live without being noticed, even if you may decay in your apartment for several days after you're dead." [45]

The Narrow Public Sector

The stakes in public life are simply not high in the town. Lyford notes that "politics in Vandalia is not a serious matter. . . . The last great political controversy in the memory of the dean of Vandalia's lawyers, ninety-year-old Will Welker, was over temperance." [46] Vidich and Bensman found that the American Legion was the most politcally significant organized group in "Springdale." And what are the Legion's interests in politics? "The Legion is interested in its liquor and gambling (bingo) privileges and in its monopoly over parking facilities

[44] Vidich and Bensman, *op. cit.,* p. 130.

[45] Lyford, *op. cit.,* p. 42.

[46] *Ibid.,* pp. 10–11.

for baseball and the July 4th Carnival."[47] Local notables agree to run for office because "they couldn't get anybody else." Nominations are bestowed on those least skillful in evading the designation.

There is some indication that, as the small town is reached by a spreading metropolis or otherwise receives an influx of cosmopolitans, its public sector expands under the demands made by the newcomers for services far beyond the level considered by the old small town leadership. Gladys Kammerer *et al.*, in a study of "Floriana," found outside businessmen who came to this Florida town quickly established themselves as proponents of "more government": vigorous activity to promote economic growth, more money for public education, and a generally higher level of public spending.[48] Lowry found this same challenge to "community conservatism" with the influx of young metropolites into "Micro City."[49]

The demands on the public sector of the town are limited not only by the modest scope of public problems within its jurisdiction but also by the conservative business ideology of the town's elite. Economy is emphasized and there is little inclination to use government as an instrument of program initiation.[50]

Small Towns as Setting: What Can Be Said?

Small town like *suburb* extends to an enormous variety of places. An isolated farm village in Montana, a fishing village in Maine, a town sustained by farming and marginal industry

[47] Vidich and Bensman, *op. cit.*, p. 126.

[48] Gladys Kammerer, Charles Farris, John DeGrove, and Alfred Clubok, *The Urban Political Community* (Boston: Houghton Mifflin, 1963), pp. 27–30.

[49] Lowry, *Who's Running This Town?* (New York: Harper & Row, 1965), especially pp. 138–159

[50] Lyford found this in Vandalia, as did Hicks in "Roxborough," Vidich and Bensman in "Springdale," Agger, Goldrich, and Swanson in "Farmdale," and Lowry in "Micro City," (although Micro City was a town in transition, with a large influx of outsiders).

in Illinois, a hamlet perched just beyond the edge of the New York metropolitan area, a South Carolina textile town in which 35 per cent of the population is Negro—all are covered by the definition. Where is the kernel of commonality that makes small towns a distinct sociopolitical setting?

American small towns are in a state of decline, occasionally absolute but more often only relative. Large numbers of people have left farms, and the position of those towns which existed as commercial centers for an agricultural hinterland has thereby deteriorated. Still other towns have seen their industries come under the control of national firms and move out, serving, perhaps, a more efficient national economic life but with a loss to the towns involved. Small towns often attract marginal industries seeking a cheaper labor supply than they could find in the metropolis.

The small town has lost a large measure of its historic autonomy, and it is now swept along in a nationalized society and economy which its elites cannot influence.[51] It was once the political, social, and economic fulcrum of this country, but no longer. Reapportionment but climaxes a decline rooted in the movement of people and in a new economy and technology. Wildavsky has cogently summarized this claim of the literature: "The small town citizen has apparently replaced the proletarian at the losing end of the socioeconomic system." [52]

Despite massive changes in its position, the small town still has been affected least of our trichotomy by the elements defining the new society. Thus, as suburbs are studied as a window to the new society, towns are seen as a window, though rapidly clouding, to the old: "Where have we come from and at what cost?" Little wonder, then, that the literature on towns is heavy with nostalgia.

[51] Though this usually is lamented, sometimes it is welcomed. Aaron Wildavsky, for example, cites such advantages as an end to parochialism, and greater and richer diversity (*Leadership in a Small Town,* ch. 21, "On the Advantages of Living in a Mass Society").

[52] *Ibid.,* p. 328.

Public life in the small town is limited but pervasive: pervasive in that it is unspecialized; limited, because the decisions made in the public sector have relatively modest impact upon how people live. Perhaps the most significant theme in the literature on small town politics, although often not stated explicitly as a theme, is the limited scope of the public sector.

V. THE CITY: CHANGE AND CRISIS

Any attempt to describe the city as setting is made perplexing by the same matters of scale which confront efforts to resolve urban problems: there is much more of everything. Certainly more has been said and written about the city as a sociopolitical setting. Here we will sample two principal themes.

The Troubled City

No adjective appears more often than "troubled," no nouns more than "problems" and "crisis." Crime, decay, the loss of a middle class, demands on services that outrun resources, loss of industry, staggering transportation problems, polluted air—all are endlessly chronicled. Problems of service, governmental organization, and physical development are serious, but probably less so than the social. How, for example, can racial strife be mitigated?

In response to this analysis of the troubled city, urban institutes spring up at universities across the country, a federal Department of Housing and Urban Development is created, conferences on the plight of the city aid at least downtown hotels, organizations such as Urban America dedicate themselves to a scrutiny of the ills of the city. There can be no doubt about our preoccupation with urban problems. But the precise nature and sources of our concern is less clear. Housing studies show that we have dramatically reduced the amount of substandard housing. The teeming slums of the late nineteenth century are rarely duplicated today. Many of the problems identified are hardly new. Vernon notes that New York had downtown traffic jams before the Civil War. Violence is old stuff. Wide sections of our major cities seventy-five years ago were subjected to anarchy or gang rule, and

> instead of having neighborhoods in which patrolmen plied their beats in pairs, many cities had neighborhoods which never saw the authority of law in any form. Chinese tongs were the law for many of San Francisco's impoverished inhabitants, while warring gangs were the recognized authority for many of New York's immigrant Irish and Italians.[53]

Water and sewage facilities, adequate fire-fighting equipment, urban snow removal, efforts to deal with air and water pollution, are all new to the twentieth century.

Vernon believes that the intensity of our concern with urban problems results not from the experience of low- or middle-income city residents, but rather from that of the rich, and the cultural and artistic elite, who feel victimized. The well-to-do urban dweller a half century ago led an insulated and comparatively idyllic life. But this is increasingly threatened and eroded. His point here is similar to Riesman's, that a half century ago an elite could live in a big city neighborhood confident that the poor would stay in their place and take out their violence only on each other. But if the prosperous are no longer assured of splendid insulation in the city, many cannot avoid the city. There are substantial business interests which must remain.

And only a big city can sustain a wide set of elite institutions: private clubs, symphony orchestras, museums. "The wonder of it is that the cry for the preservation of the old city or for improved access to its center is not even louder and more insistent than it is." [54] This is only part of the story, but the insight is useful. Urban violence and disorders may not be more extensive, but they are much less deferential.

[53] Raymond Vernon, *The Myth and Reality of Our Urban Problems* (Cambridge, Mass.: Harvard University Press, 1966), pp. 8–9.

[54] *Ibid.*, pp. 47–53.

Beyond this, of course, is the fact that although there have been absolute gains, there is relative decline. Cities have not kept pace with their surrounding areas in the passage to greater prosperity. And the contrast between the promise of our affluence and technology, and the reality of life for many urbanites demands attention.[55] Finally, our concern with urban problems is partially due to the demands—and the manner in which they are made—of one group, Negro Americans.

Race has become the new ethnic frontier in urban America. Conflict among various white ethnic groups declines and that between Negroes and whites becomes dominant. Negro Americans have fled the rural South in large numbers—three and one-half million between 1950 and 1960 alone. A rural population has thus had to adapt to the vastly different demands of urban life. The relatively gradual transition of the United States from a completely rural to a largely urban society over the last century and a half has produced serious strains, many of which can still be seen. But when the transition is rapid, over a generation or two, the effect is immensely disruptive of traditional social patterns. And two centuries of slavery was hardly the best preparation for a move from farm to city.[56] Recently, Daniel Moynihan has underlined the pathology of urban Negro family life—divorce, separation, desertion, female family head, children in broken homes, and illegitimacy—as the root of the "Negro problem." [57]

The violent ghetto expands, and most of the major urban problems are linked to this. Problems in urban education are discussed principally in terms of racial imbalance in city schools, or of equipping the school to meet the needs of Negro pupils.[58]

[55] This is demonstrated in a compelling fashion by Julius Horwitz, *The Inhabitants* (New York: New American Library, 1960).

[56] See E. Franklin Frazier, *The Negro Family* (Chicago: University of Chicago Press, 1932), pp. 298, 340.

[57] *The Negro Family: The Case for National Action* (Washington, D.C.: Government Printing Office, 1965).

[58] See, for example, James B. Conant, *Slums and Suburbs* (New York: McGraw-Hill, 1961).

Metropolitan consolidation is more than slightly affected by racial concerns: some whites appear newly interested in consolidation to head off black political control of the city; and Sayre and Polsby note that as Negroes increase in numbers in the large cities and whites in the surrounding suburbs, the question of metropolitan centralization can be phrased: "Will central city Negroes choose to forfeit the election of their own political leaders to high political office by supporting proposals to consolidate with white suburban populations large enough to outnumber them?" [59]

How can middle-income whites be induced to stay or return to central cities? Anthony Downs argues that such families will not move into central cities in large numbers until the cultural (not racial) homogeneity of local neighborhoods is somehow reconstituted. Cities must create devices for giving enough local autonomy to neighborhoods so that different levels of social service can be provided in different sections.[60] Unfortunately, Downs does not suggest how this might be accomplished—accepting for a moment its desirability—given the political and, indeed, the legal realities of our society.

The companion theme to how to lure whites back to the city is how to let Negroes out. Downs is only one of many to observe that until Negroes are permitted to escape urban ghettos there will be increasing social cleavage between whites and Negroes and the growing disaffection of the latter from our governmental system.[61]

Still another set of problems of the troubled city involves its relationship to the metropolitan region. By the 1920's, the relatively self-contained cities of earlier times had begun to decentralize, becoming surrounded by satellite communities. This metropolitanizing has, of course, continued. A key to many

[59] Wallace Sayre and Nelson Polsby, "American Political Science and the Study of Urbanization," in Philip Hauser and Leo Schnore (eds.), *The Study of Urbanization* (New York: John Wiley & Sons, 1965), p. 126.

[60] Downs, *op. cit.*, pp. 315–316.

[61] *Ibid.*, p. 318.

urban woes is found in the inability of the core to draw on the resources of the region it must serve. Suburbs are described as threats to cities. They allegedly strangle it, rob it of its middle class, devour services which they decline to pay for, refuse to aid the city in the crisis of black and white, and generally so carve up the region as to make effective government impossible. William Robson argues that when a metropolitan region is carved into numerous small governmental units, the social, political, and administrative needs of the region cannot be met. "A medley of scattered and disintegrated local authorities cannot provide the unity required for a coherent scheme of development." [62] Riesman believes that the growth of suburbs has robbed big cities of a "critical mass" of middle-class people. Middle-class people have lived in suburbs for a long time, but until World War II cities still had them in sufficient quantities.

Today, however, with the continual loss to the suburbs of the elite and the enterprising, the cities remain big enough for juveniles to form delinquent sub-cultures, but barely differentiated enough to support cultural and educational activities at a level appropriate for our abundant economy.[63]

Even those not inclined to see cities victimized by suburbs stress that the growth of metropolitan regions is transforming them. A national urban culture is developing, spreading over a wide territory, plastic, fluid in its boundaries, generating an urban life highly complex in its design and interdependences and resistant to frontal efforts to order it. The change began when technology and affluence overcame distance and crumbled the boundaries of the historic city. "Men come together in cities," Aristotle said, "in order to live. They remain together in order to live the good life." Today, Americans are finding the values of urbanism outside big cities.

[62] William A. Robson, *Great Cities of the World* (London: Macmillan, 1954), p. 62.

[63] Riesman, "The Suburban Dislocation," p. 238.

The Changing Urban Polity

Big-city political organizations, "the machine," have long been a source of fascination. But until the end of World War II, the fascination was usually muffled in blanket condemnation. The literature on urban politics was dominated by an emphasis on institutional reform, and it was the machine which was to be reformed away.[64] Recently, however, studies of urban political machines have been less normative and more analytical. What is the machine like? What characterizes its politics? What type of setting nourished it? Robert Merton, in an important essay, criticized the "naive moral judgments" which have dominated the literature on political machines, and suggested the basis for a functional analysis.

> . . . we should *ordinarily* (not invariably) expect persistent social patterns and social structures to perform positive functions *which are at the time not adequately fulfilled by* other *existing patterns and structures,* [thus] the thought occurs that perhaps this publicly maligned organization is, *under present conditions,* satisfying basic latent functions.[65]

[64] By 1915, the doctrinal evolution of municipal reform was almost complete and its main objectives firmly stated. They were directed squarely at the machines: (1) nonpartisan elections and nonpartisanship in appointments to the office; (2) the merit system for all city employment; (3) the separation of city government from the state and national parties; (4) minority representation on the city council; (5) the business corporation as a model for city government; (6) the council-manager form with the manager a professional executive. Such was the National Municipal League's *New Municipal Program* issued in 1915. An early alternative to the highly normative treatment of machines is Harold Gosnell's *Machine Politics: Chicago Model* (Chicago: University of Chicago Press, 1937). Theodore Lowi describes Gosnell as "one of the very first Americans to join that distinguished company [Ostrogorski, Bryce, Weber, Michels, Schumpeter] with anything approaching a systematic treatment of the subject [urban machines]" ("Machine Politics—Old and New," *Public Interest,* Fall, 1967, p. 84).

[65] Merton, *Social Theory and Social Structure* (Glencoe, Ill.: Free Press, 1957), p. 72.

He suggested these to be "*humanizing and personalizing all manner of* assistance to those in need," "providing those political privileges which entail immediate economic gain [for business]," and "providing alternative channels of some mobility for those otherwise excluded from the more conventional avenues for personal 'advancement.' "

The apoliticism of the machine has been emphasized. Its leaders wanted money and power rather than social change. Denis Brogan remarked that "the true character of the machine is its political indifferentism. . . . The machine exists for itself." [66] Moynihan noted that in the long years that Tammany dominated New York and had enormous power, it did not use that power to change any underlying social relationships.[67] In another vein, William Havard has argued that the big city machine was the political equivalent of the industrial robber baron.[68] And in still another depiction, the machine is seen as a natural response to the political culture of the ethnic-class groupings which became ascendant in our cities in the late nineteenth and early twentieth centuries.[69]

Whatever its role and merit, the urban machine of the sort that flourished between 1890 and 1940 is vanishing.[70] Some

[66] Brogan, *An Introduction to American Politics* (London: Hamish Hamilton, 1954), p. 123.

[67] Daniel Moynihan, "When the Irish Ran New York," *The Reporter,* June 8, 1961, pp. 32–34.

[68] Havard, "From Bossism to Cosmopolitanism: Changes in the Relationship of Urban Leadership to State Politics," *Annals of the American Academy,* CCCLIII (May, 1964), 85–86.

[69] Edward Banfield and James Q. Wilson distinguish between a "private-regarding, lower-class, immigrant ethos," which sustained machines, and a "public-regarding, Anglo-Saxon Protestant, middle-class ethos" (*City Politics* [New York: Vintage Books, 1966], pp. 329–333).

[70] Old-style machines have by no means completely disappeared. Lowi describes the survival of a strong machine in Chicago. "In 1967, political power in Chicago still has an extremely strong machine base; political power in New York has an entirely new and different base. As New York was being revolutionized by the New Deal and its successors, the structure

observers think this is due principally to government's taking over the quasi-welfare functions which the machine historically performed. Others talk of the transformation of urban political cultures. Banfield and Wilson argue that the "new immigrant" —the sons and grandsons of those who came here from Europe between 1890 and 1920—now demand candidates who have "the community-serving ethos and the public virtues that have long been associated with the Protestant elite." They concede that the exodus of middle-class families to the suburbs keeps the population of the larger, older cities still heavily lower class, and that the old-style politics of the machine remains congenial to the lower class.

> However, the nationally growing middle class has shown that it will use its control of state and federal government . . . to withhold the patronage, protection, and other political resources that are indispensable to the growth of political machines in the central cities. This means that the lower class will have to play politics of a kind that is tolerable to the middle class or not play it at all.[71]

The public sector in Urban America has become the arena for major national social programs, from antipoverty to redevelopment to public housing to efforts to secure racial justice. A new breed of urban political leaders has grown up more attuned to politics as an instrument for social change. William Havard is just one of a number of observers who detect a change from "bossism to cosmopolitanism," as the sheer scale and complexity of a technological society force attention to expertise and planning and link the local to the national.[72]

Urban America is pictured weighed down by a set of social, economic, and political problems that are among major national problems. The political culture of the cities will increas-

---

of Chicago politics was being reaffirmed. When New York was losing its last machine and entering into a new era of permanent Reform, Chicago's political machine was just beginning to consolidate" (Lowi, *op. cit.*, p. 84).

[71] Banfield and Wilson, *op. cit.*, p. 330.

[72] Havard, *op. cit.*, p. 89. See, too, Banfield and Wilson, *op. cit.*, pp. 329–346.

ingly demand a more "public-regarding" politics attractive to cosmopolitan-oriented individuals who become interested in politics only when it offers the prospect of social change. The great political machines, sustained by a kind of entrepreneurial politics, are dead or at least doomed. The sheer scale of urban problems ordains the ascendancy of experts. Such are the ingredients of a changing urban polity.

The City as Setting: What Can Be Said?

American cities historically have served as points of embarkation. Urbanism is about a century old in the United States, and at each of its various stages cities have had to play host to newcomers to the demands of urban life. And, typically, the new arrivals have been not only new urbanites but new Americans as well, first grasping for a hyphen, then trying to lose it: Italians, Italian-Americans, Americans.

Now, cities are home to increasing numbers of another group of new Americans—new, of course, in a quite different sense than European immigrants: in their long-enforced separation from main currents in American life. The demands on cities in the 1960's are not the same as those which have accompanied the entry of earlier groups because of several other developments concurrent with the arrival of large numbers of Negroes: (1) suburbanization or decentralization of metropolitan areas, as technology and affluence have permitted the more prosperous to leave, making the city now more than at any other point in time a lower-class residential setting; (2) the loss of insulation of city neighborhoods which has propelled those able to move out to smaller and more homogeneous communities whose political boundaries and governmental powers can serve as barriers to feared encroachments—physical as in crime and violence, psychological as in social status; (3) the depth of racial fears and discrimination, dwarfing that which confronted other ethnic groups, giving Negro Americans unparalleled ethnic awareness, keeping them locked in the city, and nourishing a profound alienation from the polity. Thus, the city as setting has become the predominantly lower-class core of an otherwise middle-class metropolitan region, and its politics is dominated by the clash of an angry black lower class and increasingly fearful and resentful white lower and lower-middle classes.

This is one dimension. The other is that cities remain, despite some movement out by stores and factories, major centers of economic and cultural life. A suburban-based upper middle class thus has an important stake in the future of the city and refuses to permit white and black city dwellers to fight it out by themselves. They press upon the city the modes, demands, and styles of upper-middle-class politics. They are the ones, primarily, who are insisting that the scale of urban problems requires the ascendancy of experts (requires, that is, *their* ascendancy.)

3. Hartford, Bloomfield, and Putnam: Three Community Profiles

There are at least as many ways to describe communities as there are reasons for wanting to study them. How we describe them depends upon why we want to describe them. As in the two preceding chapters, the concern here is with the context of community ideational life. Our focus narrows to the immediate experience of Hartford, Bloomfield, and Putnam, from which three community political profiles may be drawn. Three sets of variables provide the substance for these profiles: historical experience, socioeconomic structure, and political institutions and processes.

I. THE HISTORICAL SETTING

Hartford began modestly enough. When the Constitution was ratified, it was a small crossroads community of little more than 2,000 people. But its position on a navigable river (the Connecticut) about halfway between Boston and New York gave it a place in the flow of people and commerce, and the surrounding countryside was fertile farm land. Hartford was Connecticut's "co-capital," sharing the honor with New Haven, from colonial times until 1874, when over New Haven's strong protest the state legislature bowed to Hartford's offer of land and buildings and made it the sole capital. In 1800, banking was the backbone of local enterprise, but as the nineteenth century progressed a diversified industrial and commercial system developed, including firearms (Colt), automobile equipment, precision tools, and, of course, insurance. The first insurance company to survive, the Hartford Fire, was founded in 1810, and by 1846 a number of fire insurance companies were flourishing in the city. Hartford's first life insurance company, Connecticut Mutual, was established in 1846 followed by Aetna Life in 1850 and Phoenix Mutual in 1851.[1] In 1864, a white-bearded gentleman named James G. Batterson put together the Travelers Insurance Company, the first to insure travelers against loss of life and personal injury. Insurance has continued to prosper in Hartford. In 1968, there were twelve major insurance companies with home offices in the city employing more than 23,000 persons. Five Hartford firms are among the fifty largest life insurance companies in the United States, three of these in the top ten.[2]

Putnam's first economic stirrings were in 1730 when an Englishman named Howe built a gristmill on the Quinebaug River. But it was textiles on which the town was to be built. The first cotton mill in Connecticut and the third in the United States (The Putnam Manufacturing Company) began operations there in 1807, and within a few years a textile revolution had hit eastern Connecticut and Rhode Island. So rapid was the growth of textiles that in 1811 the Windham (Connecticut) *Herald* felt compelled to issue a warning:

In November, 1809, there were within thirty miles of Providence 26 cotton mills in operation, containing 20,000 spindles. . . . At the present time there are 74 mills within the same distance containing 51,454 spindles, making an increase of 46 mills and 31,454 spindles

[1] The Phoenix Mutual was formed by a group of temperance advocates, and for a time insured only teetotalers. It gave those pledging to stay on the wagon a discount in life insurance rates. However noble, this commitment proved unsound economically, and a decade after its founding The Phoenix opened its doors to those who imbibed strong spirits.

[2] The five and their rank order (on the the basis of total assets) are Aetna (6), Travelers (8), Connecticut General (9), Connecticut Mutual (14), and Phoenix Mutual (24) (*Fortune*, LXXIV [July, 1966], pp. 254–255).

in less than two years! Are not the people running cotton-mill mad? [3]

Putnam was finally incorporated in 1855 when, after six years of arguing, four area towns permitted it to be carved from their territory. The residents named their creation after Revolutionary War hero Israel Putnam.[4]

The continued growth of textiles in eastern Connecticut produced a demand for cheap, foreign-born labor, and that was supplied largely by French Canadians. By 1875, slightly more than three out of five Putnamites were Roman Catholic, mostly of French-Canadian birth or parentage.[5] Besides its textiles, Putnam was the modest rail center for eastern Connecticut. Though a small place, in 1910 it ranked eighth in New England in freight handling. Putnam was a relatively prosperous town in the late nineteenth and first years of this century.

But the future of textiles in New England was bleak. Some Putnam mills including the big Monohansett Manufacturing Company were liquidated after 1929. And in the 1930's others moved south. Putnam thus found its economy drastically transformed. As in so many New England textile towns, efforts to replace the jobs lost in the textile exodus yielded small companies (five to fifty employees) of a marginal nature, attracted by the promise of cheap labor. In the 1960's, Putnam was producing such items as corrugated boxes, plastic jars, molded plastic buttons, icepicks, and picnic coolers. This does not spell prosperity. Despite its decline, textiles continued to be

[3] Quoted in Leroy Harwood, *History of Eastern Connecticut* (Chicago: Pioneer Historical Publishing Company, 1932), II, 591.

[4] In addition to his prowess in fighting Putnam enjoys a high place in the history of American cigars. When leading a British force against the Spaniards in Havana, he noticed the natives rolling their own and later introduced this exotic smoke at his inn in Pomfret, Connecticut.

[5] These data are reported in Richard Bayles (ed.), *History of Windham County, Connnecticut* (New York: W. W. Preston, 1889), p. 788. Many New England textile towns took in large numbers of French-Canadians in this period.

an important part of Putnam's economy.[6] But textiles was a low-wage and low-profit industry, and the remaining firms stood in marked contrast to the booming aerospace, machine tool, and construction industries of metropolitan Connecticut.

Putnam's economic woes were intensified by a natural disaster, a major flood in 1955. Ironically, the flood produced fires, one in a magnesium processing plant which set off explosions for forty-eight hours. Two textile mills were burned. Sections of central Putnam were buried under tons of sand deposited by the flood waters, and half the business section was wiped out. Industrial losses were in the millions. For seven years after the flood, many of the wounds which it caused remained unattended, gaping reminders of loss and decline.

Bloomfield was a small town much longer than it has been a suburb. A largely agricultural small town was gradually engulfed by the spreading metropolis and thus transformed.

People first settled Bloomfield in 1675, and sixty-five years later the settlement was a bustling one of twenty-seven families. Not until 1835 was the town formally carved from three existing communities. Hartford and Bloomfield, though contiguous, were not linked by trolley until 1910, and to that time the town was wholly agricultural.[7] After 1910, Bloomfield began its slow transformation to a residential suburb. An east-west split (which has continued) arose as eastern Bloomfield, bordering on Hartford, became a bedroom for some Hartford workers, while the western part of town remained farm country.

[6] Putnam's biggest employer, and three of the four firms in town employing more than 250 in 1966, produced textiles.

[7] The extension of trolley service to Bloomfield was the culmination of a decade and a half of agitation by town residents. Its opening in 1910, providing a forty-minute ride from Hartford to Bloomfield Center, was a cause for great celebration replete with band music, fireworks, bell ringing, and cheering crowds. A local newspaper reported that "never since the old muster days and war news reports has the town had occasion for such rejoicing as now. The advent of the trolley line makes it possible for the small town to develop into a much greater suburb of Greater Hartford."

It wasn't until the late 1930's that Bloomfielders began to worry about a big influx from Hartford and what this would do to the character of their community. In 1941, the town was substantially up-zoned to keep out "foreign operators." Zoning requirements subsequently were further revised and made more restrictive to keep out low-cost housing. After 1950, Bloomfield's growth was far more rapid, and its suburban character firmly established. In the 1950's, it was the fastest growing suburb in Greater Hartford. Tobacco fields and other farms provided space for attractive residential properties.[8]

The population histories of our three communities are instructive, and they parallel the experience of many communities of each type. Hartford grew slowly up to the middle of the nineteenth century. In 1850 it was a town of only 13,000. But its population doubled in the next decade and tripled between 1890 and 1930. The 1950 census found Hartford at its high-water mark of population, from which it has since declined. Putnam was about as big in 1900 as it was going to get. While there have been little peaks and valleys, the town's population has remained essentially static over the last half century. Indeed, there were only fifteen fewer people in the town (the boundaries have not been changed) in 1920 than in 1960. When Putnam was a thriving industrial town of 7,500 in 1900, Bloomfield was a little farming village of 1,500. As late as 1950 Putnam still was nearly twice as large. But then the impact of Bloomfield's contiguity to a city and Putnam's separation from any in an age of metropolitanization was felt. In the next decade and a half, Bloomfield's population more than tripled while Putnam's declined by about 1,000 (see Table 20).

The natural history of Putnam is the history of a French-Canadian mill town which has not kept pace with the growth and prosperity of the rest of the state. Bloomfield's is that of a white-collar suburb evolving rapidly after World War II

[8] Bloomfield is located in that section of the Connecticut valley where shade-grown tobacco is cultivated for cigar wrappers.

Table 20. The population histories of Hartford, Bloomfield, and Putnam

	Hartford		Bloomfield		Putnam	
Year	Total population	Percentage change	Total population	Percentage change	Total population	Percentage change
1790	2,683					
1800	3,523	31.3				
1810	3,955	12.3				
1820	4,726	19.5				
1830	7,074	49.7				
1840	9,468	33.8	739			
1850	13,555	43.2	600	−18.8		
1860	26,917	98.6	683	13.8	2,722	
1870	37,180	38.1	1,473	115.7	4,192	54.0
1880	42,015	13.0	1,346	− 8.6	5,827	39.0
1890	53,230	26.7	1,308	− 2.8	6,512	11.8
1900	79,850	50.0	1,513	15.7	7,348	12.8
1910	98,915	23.9	1,821	20.4	7,280	− .9
1920	138,036	39.6	2,394	31.5	8,397	15.3
1930	164,072	18.9	3,247	35.6	8,099	3.5
1940	166,267	1.3	4,309	32.7	8,692	7.3
1950	177,397	6.7	5,746	33.3	9,304	7.0
1960	162,178	−8.6	13,613	136.9	8,412	−9.6
1966	155,000*	−4.4	18,000*	31.7	8,400*	–

Source: Connecticut Town and County Fact Book, 1960.
* Estimated by town officials.

from an agricultural town, intent on maintaining its position as a "nice place to live and raise children." The natural history of Hartford is of the core city of a metropolitan area of three quarters of a million, of diversified industrial and commercial structure.

II. SOCIOECONOMIC STRUCTURE

The decade 1950–60 was one of change for the populations of Hartford, Bloomfield, and Putnam in terms of their comparative socioeconomic status. In the 1950's, both city and town declined, the former markedly, in relative SES; and the suburb pulled away from them. In ten years, the SES gulf between Hartfordites and Bloomfielders widened from modest to enormous proportions, as Table 21 shows.

Hartford lost about 15,000 people between 1950 and 1960, a net decline of 8.6 per cent. But net loss fails to represent the magnitude of the city's population change. From 1950 to 1960, 56,000 people moved into Hartford and 95,000 moved out, many of them to the suburbs. This emigration has drastically altered the composition of Hartford's population, measured by such characteristics as family status, age, level of education, occupation, income, and race. About 6,500 young married couples left Hartford. The city sustained a population loss in its young adult and middle-age groups (twenty to sixty years), but showed gains for children and the aged. Although Hartford's population declined by 8.6 per cent between 1950 and 1960, the number of high school graduates dropped by 19 per cent and the number of college graduates by 12 per cent. In the same way, the employed of the city declined nearly twice as much as the population.

Hartford, Bloomfield, and Putnam visually convey many of their socioeconomic differences. Few buildings in Putnam were ever architecturally distinguished, and the overall appearance of the town is one of mild deterioration. The central business district displays a new shopping center, a source of great pride to residents, but the remainder is old and unattractive. At one end of the business district is Union Square, once a center of activity with the railroad station and the Putnam Hotel. But in the 1960's there is no rail passenger service from Putnam, and the hotel before its destruction by fire in 1966 had become in fact a boarding house. Those parts of Putnam adjacent to the river and the mills are crowded with deteriorating tenements. Some new residential property can be found on the outskirts, in such nice residential sections as Putnam Heights, where pleasant though still modest homes are spread

Table 21. Hartford, Bloomfield, and Putnam, by five socioeconomic variables, 1950 and 1960

Variable	Hartford				Bloomfield				Putnam			
	1950		1960		1950		1960		1950		1960	
	Variable total	Ratio to state total	Variable total	Ratio to state total	Variable total	Ratio to state total	Variable total	Ratio to state total	Variable total	Ratio to state total	Variable total	Ratio to state total
Median years of school completed	9.7	99	9.6	87	11.9	121	12.3	112	8.6	88	9.0	83
Percentage with four or more years of college	6.0	86	6.1	64	10.0	143	15.9	167	4.4	63	5.2	55
Percentage in white-collar jobs	46.7	117	43.0	98	48.5	122	61.7	141	31.1	78	31.0	71
Median family income	$2,953	83	$5,990	87	$3,259	92	$7,913	115	$2,526	71	$5,856	85
Percentage families earning over $10,000 ($5,000 in 1950) per year	16.9	78	13.9	64	24.7	114	30.9	141	9.8	45	9.8	44
SES index	–	93	–	80	–	118	–	135	–	69	–	68

Source: Connecticut Town and County Fact Book, 1960; and *U.S. Census of Population, 1950.*

on ample lots. An older section where Putnam's elite once lived in large Victorian homes has lost its preeminence, and many of the houses have been carved into apartments. But others still have a single occupant and most are well maintained. The Quinebaug River which runs through Putnam is not one of America's distinguished streams. Except in wet seasons, it is slow-moving and shallow, running alongside decaying textile mills. Textile towns in New England generally are not attractive, and Putnam is no exception.

Bloomfield is an attractive town. But it is also a mixed place. Its Blue Hills section in the extreme southeastern corner borders on the north end of Hartford, has small lots (four houses per acre), small houses and small shops, and a slightly run-down appearance. At the other end of the town, in northern Bloomfield, there is still open farm land and tobacco fields and the appearance of utmost rurality. In between are the homes of the residents who control Bloomfield, whose life styles and political demands now shape the suburb's response. These are the homes of white-collar professionals and managers, a mixture of ranches, raised ranches, and colonials of the $25,000 to $40,000 range, resting on half-acre and acre lots. In the southwestern corner of Bloomfield there are a small number of dwellings of very substantial size and cost, set on large tracts of land and nestled among the trees along narrow and winding lanes. Bloomfield, then, is a middle-class suburb, but its internal range is wide, and we are reminded that although it is in some ways more homogeneous than the old independent town, the extent of the homogeneity can easily be overstated. Table 22 points to the real internal variety of this suburb in another way, comparing its census tracts for four socioeconomic characteristics. The southeastern corner is, socioeconomically, sharply set off from the rest of Bloomfield, and we shall see that various facets of this divide appear in most phases of community life.

Hartford is a central city, more attractive perhaps than many others. Its central business district has been rejuvenated by

Table 22. Bloomfield census tracts, by four socioeconomic variables, 1960

Variable	Tract 1	Tract 2	Tract 3	Tract 4
Percentage with four or more years of college	9.6	10.0	23.6	20.5
Percentage of employed males, managers and professionals*	32	27	54	43
Median family income	$7,096	$7,250	$9,682	$9,054
Percentage families earning over $10,000 per year	16.2	20.8	48.2	40.1

Source: U.S. Censuses of Population and Housing, 1960; census tracts, Hartford SMSA.

* "Managers" and "professionals" are the census categories *managers, officials,* and *proprietors, including farm;* and *professional, technical,* and *kindred workers.*

several new and imaginative skyscrapers, by a justly acclaimed collection of office buildings, stores, a raised shoppers' mall called Constitution Plaza, and by substantial improvements in access and off-street parking.

Like any large city, Hartford has a number of distinct neighborhoods of great ethnic and socioeconomic variety. Some of these have maintained a fairly constant identity, but others have been completely transformed. In the late 1960's, the ethnic composition and distribution of city residents was very different from what it had been a decade and a half earlier. The big changes were precipitated by redevelopment, by economic advances permitting moves to the suburbs, and by a large immigration of nonwhites.

In the early 1950's, Hartford established a redevelopment agency, applied to the federal government, and received approval for Connecticut's first urban renewal project. The area selected was the Italian section on Front Street, adjacent to the business district. Redevelopment forced the Italians into Irish areas of the South End. One Roman Catholic church in the South End, St. Augustine, switched from 90 per cent Irish to 90 per cent Italian in a few years; and in a display of ethnic politics, an attempt was made to change the name of Franklin Avenue to Columbus. Franco-Americans are the only white ethnic group to increase in numbers in their old section, typically called "Frog Hollow," of west-central Hartford. Their numbers have been swelled by a steady stream of migrants from Maine and the province of Quebec. From a small core in the North End, the Negro (and since 1960 Puerto Rican) population has spread in concentric circles to the northwest, northeast, and southeast. The older ethnic groups of North Hartford have fled before this nonwhite immigration, the Jews, for example, moving to Bloomfield and West Hartford.

The socioeconomic variations in neighborhoods are sharp. At the bottom is the Arsenal section of North Hartford. Sixty-four hundred people lived in Arsenal in 1960. Their median family income was $3,414. Half of the housing units were substandard, and more than half lacked central heat. The streets of Arsenal are narrow and congested, open space is virtually nonexistent, and there is industrial encroachment. Two public structures dominate the southern section of Arsenal: one is the Arsenal School, a superannuated elementary facility; the other Bellevue Square, a large, high-density, low-income (and all Negro) public housing project. A city consultant described Arsenal as "an area of diminishing social utility with all the earmarks of a traditional slum: social disorganization, apathy, poverty, disrespect for personal privacy and increasing nonfamily occupancy."

At the opposite end of Hartford's social and economic spectrum is the West End, or more precisely, the northwestern central section of the city bordering on the upper-middle-class suburb of West Hartford. In this section are Hartford's finest homes: Scarborough Street in the West End is the place of residence of such notable Hartfordites as John Bailey and Abraham Ribicoff. Table 23 contrasts these highs and lows in residential settings.

Map 1 summarizes the socioeconomic characteristics of Hartford neighborhoods, through the SES index described in Chapter 2. Since 1960 data are used, this map probably understates

Table 23. Two Hartford census tracts, of highest and lowest socioeconomic status, 1960

Variable	A section of northwestern Hartford (census tract 33)	A section of northeastern Hartford (census tract 9)
Median years of school completed	14.1	8.2
Percentage with four or more years of college	37.8	1.0
Percentage in white-collar jobs	75.2	11.8
Median family income	$7,959	$3,355
Percentage families earning over $10,000 per year	42.8	1.9
SES index*	201	34

Source: U.S. Censuses of Population and Housing, 1960; census tracts, Hartford SMSA.

* The SES index compares the census tract population to the state population for the five variables equally weighted.

the size of the poverty area in Hartford's North End. Any neighborhood with an index of less than 55 is extremely disadvantaged.

Negroes came late to Connecticut. In 1900 there were 15,000 and a half century later only 53,000 in the state. But in the 1950's the immigration picked up, and the number of Negroes doubled, although still only 4.4 per cent of the population. Hartford's experience parallels that of the state. Between 1950 and 1960 the Negro population of the city doubled. Negroes have continued to come in large numbers since 1960, and a substantial immigration of Puerto Ricans has begun. In 1967, there were about 40,000 nonwhites in Hartford, one quarter of the total.

Bloomfield in 1950 had a tiny Negro population of 236; it grew to nearly a thousand in 1960 and to 2,400 in 1967. Bloomfield now has the largest Negro population of any Hartford suburb, indeed, is one of only two with significant numbers of

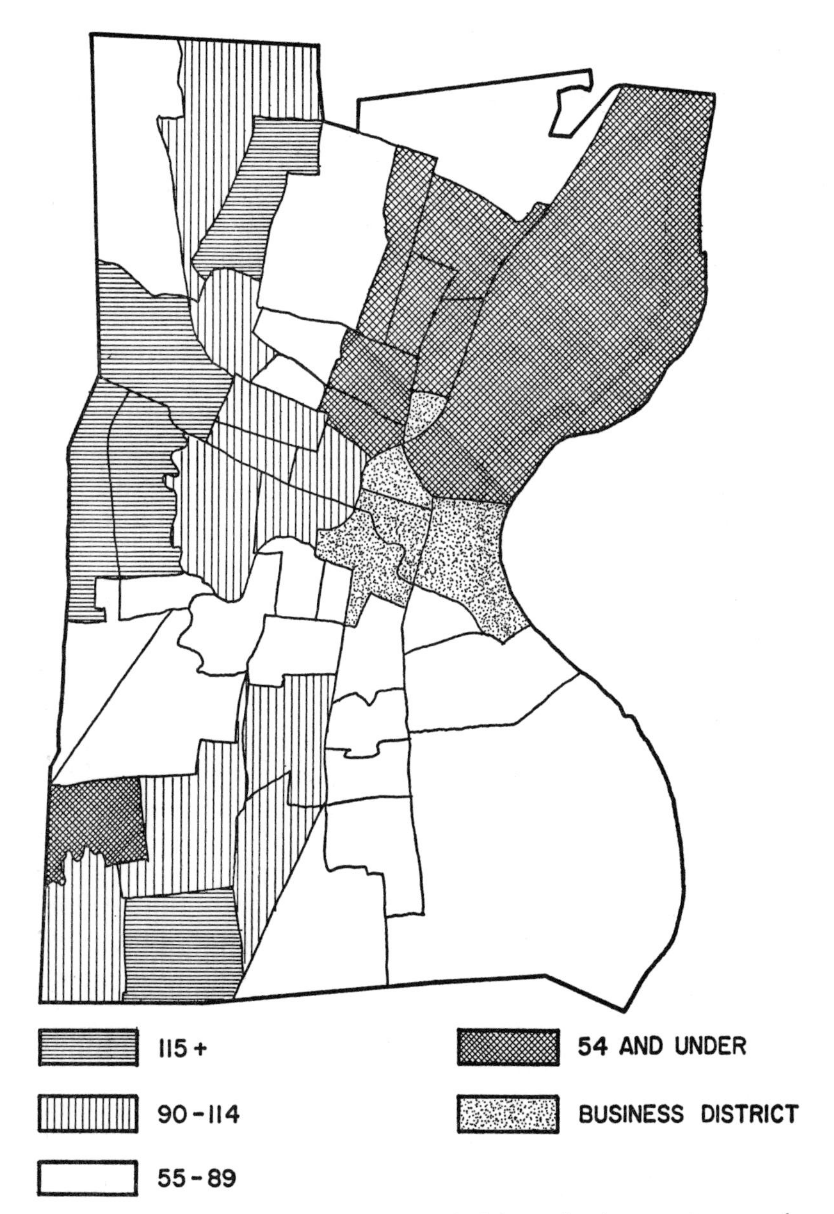

Map 1. Hartford neighborhoods, ranked by a five-item socioeconomic index, Connecticut = 100

Source: U.S. Censuses of Population and Housing, 1960; census tracts, Hartford SMSA. The construction of the index is explained in Chapter 2.

Negroes, and its Negro population is likely to increase most rapidly through the 1970's. (See Table 24).

Table 24. Nonwhite population, Hartford, Bloomfield, and Putnam, 1950, 1960, and 1967

Nonwhite population	Hartford	Bloomfield	Putnam
1950			
Number	12,790	236	9
Percentage	7.2	4.1	.3
1960			
Number	24,855	830	34
Percentage	15.5	6.1	.4
1967 (est.)			
Number	40,000	2,400	35
Percentage	25.8	12.6	.4

Source: U.S. Census of Population, 1950; Hartford census tracts, and *Connecticut Town and County Fact Book, 1960.*

Negroes are concentrated in the North End in Hartford. In 1960, there were 112 blocks (defined by the Census on Housing) which were more than 10 per cent nonwhite, or 14.6 per cent of all city blocks. Nearly 100 of these 112 were located in the North End, and there were no blocks in the South End more than 30 per cent nonwhite. Most of the small Negro population in the South End lived in public housing.

Since 1960, Negroes and Puerto Ricans have spread out in the North End: the few blocks that were mostly nonwhite have become completely so, many of the "salt-and-pepper" blocks around the old core neighborhood also have become completely nonwhite; and a whole new set of salt-and-pepper blocks on the periphery have appeared. But the Negro–Puerto Rican section has remained essentially nuclear and confined to North Hartford. In 1960, only 540 Negro families resided in the twenty-four census tracts that comprised the city's southern half, and our survey work indicates that changed very little through 1967.[9]

Bloomfield's Negro families are concentrated in the town's extreme southeastern section, bordering on North Hartford. This area's contiguity to the large concentration of Negroes in the North End together with the type of housing in the area—small, relatively low-priced homes—attracted Negroes escaping the ghetto. In addition, although the big influx of Negroes into the Blue Hills area (southeastern Bloomfield) came after 1955, Blue Hills had a small group of long-time Negro residents. So Negroes able to move out of the North End in the 1950's did not have to blaze a trail, to be among "the first Negroes to move in," if they chose Blue Hills. Between 1960 and 1967, a modest number of Negroes did find homes in other, much more expensive sections of Bloomfield. Town officials estimate that about 200 Negroes moved into predominantly white sections in this period. Map 2 shows the location of nonwhites in Bloomfield and Hartford, based on 1967 estimates rather than the already badly dated 1960 data.

Putnam, located in the northeastern corner of Connecticut, has virtually no Negroes, and racial problems are only to be read about. Putnam's historic ethnic conflict between WASPs and French Canadians has long since lost its bitterness. The town is at ethnic peace.

Several features distinguish the economy of Greater Hartford. First, the area is prospering. Its industries are principally white-collar (like banking and insurance), aerospace, and de-

[9] A team comprised of persons intimately acquainted with the neighborhoods of Hartford covered every block in the city in the summer of 1966 and attempted to make a loose but still informed assessment of changes in the location of Negro families in the six years following the 1960 Census on Housing. In addition, Hartford city officials, in the commission on the city plan, the Housing Authority, the Community Renewal Team (the Hartford antipoverty agency), and the City Manager's Office were consulted as to the movement and location of nonwhites in the city.

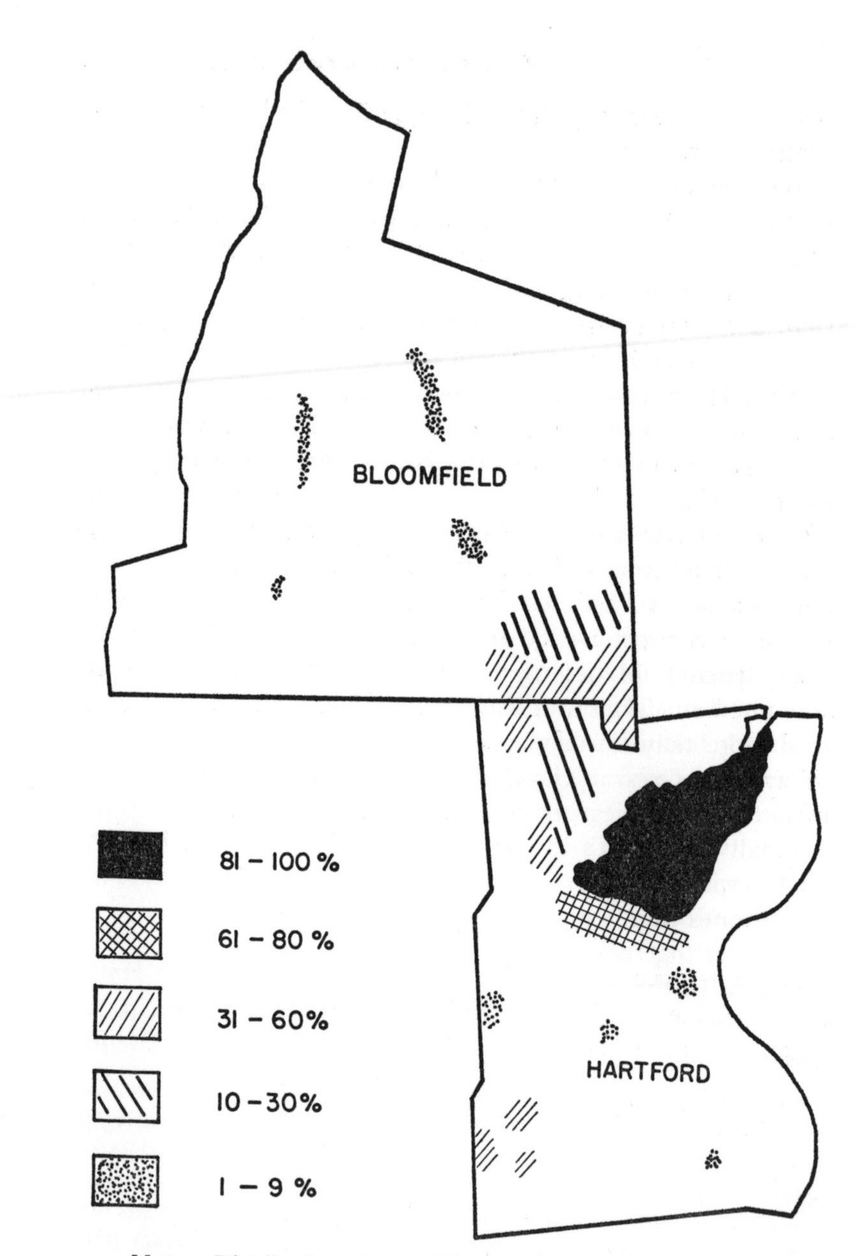

Map 2. Distribution of nonwhite population, Bloomfield and Hartford, 1967 estimates

Source: Estimates based on 1960 Census data, survey work by the principal investigator, data furnished by Hartford city officials, and data supplied by the office of the town manager in Bloomfield.

fense. They demand a relatively skilled labor force. In 1967, under pressure of the war in Vietnam, Hartford was labor-hungry. Second, Hartford is not a branch-plant city. Rather, it is the home office for a number of major national corporations. Prominent among these are the insurance companies: Travelers, Aetna, Connecticut General, Connecticut Mutual, Phoenix Mutual, The Hartford Group. That aerospace giant, United Aircraft, the area's largest employer, is based in East Hartford. The Greater Hartford Chamber of Commerce is firmly in the hands of the area's big home-office firms, has adopted a strong proprietary interest in the city, and has intervened vigorously in its public life.

A third distinctive feature of Hartford industry is its dependence on defense spending. Such major area firms as Colt Industries, Kaman Aircraft, and United Aircraft are heavily dependent on Department of Defense contracts. With the continuous high demand for defense production since the Korean War (the number of jobs in aircraft manufacturing in Greater Hartford more than doubled between 1947 and 1963, an increase of 27,500), Greater Hartford has been a major importer of labor, especially from northern New England.

Finally, the Hartford business community is a close-knit one, made especially so by the elaborate network of interlocking directorates that bring manufacturing, insurance, and banking executives together on boards of directors. In two prominent occasions in the mid-1960's, this cohesiveness brought about a marshaling of forces to resist efforts of firms outside the area to gain control of local companies.[10] But the interlocking arrange-

[10] In 1965, the Giannini Controls Corporation sought control of Veeder-Root, a Hartford firm manufacturing such counting mechanisms as gas and price gauges on gasoline pumps. Hartford's insurance companies, important holders of Veeder stock, helped the small local firm's management successfully resist the outsider's efforts. Giannini had sought to buy 35% of Veeder's stock, offering $38 a share, $7 over the market price at the time. Then, in 1966, a group of investors based in New York and Texas tried to buy 51 to 55% of the outstanding shares in the Phoenix of Hartford insurance company, a property insurance firm with assets of $350

ments of Hartford firms as well have come under criticism. In 1967, a congressional investigating team questioned the existence of competition among Hartford's commercial banks. Their report charged that both Hartford insurance companies and mutual savings banks were heavily involved in ownership and control of the city's commercial banks. "Corporate interlocks are probably as extensive as those in any comparable area in the country," the report said. Nine insurance firms held and voted 20.5 per cent of the shares in Hartford National, the area's largest commercial bank, and 21.7 per cent of the shares in the Connecticut Bank and Trust Company, the second largest. Seventeen Hartford-based insurance companies were found to have sixty-two corporate interlocks with four of the city's five largest commercial banks. "With this web of stockholder and corporate interlockings, it is hard to believe that any really effective competition among financial institutions could exist." [11] The close-knit nature of the Hartford business community is evident in all its political activity.

Putnam firms are small, typically marginal enterprises. Only one employs more than 500 workers. Wages paid manufacturing workers in the Putnam labor area have averaged 40 per cent lower than those paid in Greater Hartford.

Commuting to work (understood as crossing town lines) occurs with extravagance in Connecticut and is not peculiar to suburbanites. The state is small, and town lines are crossed by

---

million. Two days after the offer by the outside investors, Phoenix and Travelers announced that they were negotiating a "merger of interests," and subsequently the $75 a share offer of the New York–Texas group was topped by Travelers' offer of $86 a share. In the face of the Travelers' bid, the New York–Texas investors withdrew their offer. The Travelers-Phoenix merger was formally consummated May 17, 1966.

[11] "Control of Commercial Banks and Interlocks among Financial Institutions," staff report for the Subcommittee on Domestic Finance of the Committee on Banking and Currency, U.S. House of Representatives, July 31, 1967, pp. 72–79. In response to this attack, the president of one of the banks argued that "Hartford is fortunate in being the home of a number

workers from all types of places. So extensive is commuting that only 12 of 169 towns in the state fail to supply workers for the Hartford area. In 1964, 70 Hartford workers lived in Greenwich, 140 in Stamford, 120 in Norwalk, and 10 each in Darien and New Canaan—places in the southern tip of Fairfield County at the far end of the state from Hartford.[12] Still, a substantially higher segment of Bloomfield workers cross town lines each day than either Hartford or Putnam workers (See Table 25). Bloomfield is a major importer of labor, having

Table 25. Percentage of labor force employed out of town, and the ratio of in-town jobs to residents employed, Hartford, Bloomfield, and Putnam, 1964

Place	Percentage of workers employed out of town	Jobs/residents employed*
Hartford	34	1.65
Bloomfield	79	1.58
Putnam	33	.98

Source: Connecticut Department of Labor, Employment Security Division *Reports*, October, 1964.

* This index was computed by dividing the total number of jobs located in the town by the number of town residents in the labor force. It thus shows whether the town is a net importer or exporter of labor.

more jobs within its boundaries than it has persons in the labor force. Only 1,200 of the nearly 9,000 jobs within the suburb's boundaries are filled by Bloomfield residents. But the style of the community is maintained by the type of industries which it has: clean, skilled, white-collar.

III. POLITICAL INSTITUTIONS AND PROCESSES

Counties play no political role in Connecticut, and the city or town provides nearly all local government services. In this

of large national companies in both insurance and manufacturing. . . . It strikes me as only natural that a number of experienced businessmen from these companies should be directors of one or another local bank."

[12] These data are from the Connecticut Department of Labor, Employment Security Division, for October, 1964.

context, Hartford, Bloomfield, and Putnam operate with quite different local government arrangements. Bloomfield is a town with council-manager government and partisan elections. Putnam is a city not consolidated with a town; the town of Putnam is governed by a board of selectmen and the city by a mayor and board of aldermen, with partisan elections. Hartford is a consolidated town and city with council-manager government and, until November 1969, nonpartisan elections.

The town of Putnam was incorporated in 1855. Since the Connecticut constitution prohibited town governments from providing certain services made necessary by growth, such as fire protection, sidewalks, and graded streets, Putnam voters decided in 1895 to adopt a city charter establishing a council with a representative of each party from each of four wards, and one alderman-at-large holding the balance of power. But this "city of Putnam" extended only to certain built-up areas within the town. Neither the structure of Putnam city government nor ward boundaries have subsequently been changed. Putnam is one of three Connecticut cities existing as distinct units within towns. The city government provides the greater services needed by residents in the more heavily settled sections of the town. In the mid-1960's, the Town of Putnam was spending about $850,000 a year, with schools the principal claimant. And the City of Putnam was spending a little less than $400,000 for police and fire protection, city roads and recreation.

Bloomfield, incorporated in 1835, operated with a selectmen–board of finance arrangement until 1941. Then, a professional town manager was added. A manager had been urged on the town by the Bloomfield Taxpayers Association, under the leadership of a Travelers Insurance executive, Jack Hoover. Hoover and other newcomers attached to big Hartford corporations found the old selectmen–board of finance structure insufficiently professional and suited only for an essentially rural community. They argued that a manager would give government-by-expert, and that the plan was nothing more than "the application to municipalities of the method of organization found best in operating a business." A manager was hired. But the initial victory of town manager proponents was a hollow one, because the manager was only an appendage, his powers unclear. Soon, the manager, selectmen, and board of finance were at war. The conflict rapidly intensified and was replete with secret sessions of the board of finance from which the manager was excluded, outright violations of the provisions under which the manager was hired, and court injunctions. A letter to an area newspaper in the midst of the manager controversy suggests the dimensions of this conflict and its relationship to the transformation of town into suburb:

Things are occurring now in Bloomfield which have previously occurred in hundreds of small suburban towns throughout the nation. A group of comparative newcomers to Bloomfield have gradually and unsuspectingly edged themselves into various organizations, both political and nonpolitical, to the extent that many of the town's citizens have succumbed to the impression that certain newcomers are individuals of remarkable executive ability and, whether or not having had previous experience in the handling of town affairs, are capable of revolutionizing all matters of town government and procedure to the everlasting benefit of a bunch of dumb "farmers." . . . I am fully of the opinion that right will eventually prevail and the connivings of an arrogant bunch of "big shots" will be frustrated to the benefit of many humble, common, everyday, work-a-day citizens of our town.

The manager resigned, but the struggle between Bloomfield's "big shots" and the old-timers who ran the Republican party went on. The old-timers attempted in the 1943 election to eliminate the position of town manager, but, to the surprise of many and by a narrow vote, the town voted to retain it. Finally, to remove divisions and confusions of authority, a new charter was drafted and approved in 1945 which set up a town council of seven members replacing the board of finance and assuming its duties. A subsequent manifestation of the "town vs. suburb" struggle around local institutions appeared between 1956 and 1959 when a charter revision committee recommended that because of Bloomfield's increased population town meetings should be abolished. The defense of the town meeting was in ringing platitudes: "An old New England institution"; "the purest form of democracy"; "every citizen can stand up in meetin' and speak his piece and try to persuade his fellows." The proposed revision was first defeated in 1958, but finally approved in 1959. Bloomfield's town manager in 1968 had held his position since 1953 when he had become Connecticut's youngest town manager. His immense popularity and unchallenged standing among virtually all groups in Bloomfield has effectively removed the manager's position from conflict between old and newer elements of the town.

Hartford became (with Middletown, New Haven, and Norwich) one of the first places in Connecticut in which city government was established. Consolidation of city and town was achieved in Hartford in 1896. The city operated until 1947 under a weak mayoral government. Local government was a crazy quilt sewed together through the nineteenth and twentieth centuries, chiefly distinguished by an enormous diffusion of responsibility. There were twenty aldermen, fifteen representing wards and five at large. The principal administrative departments were managed by boards appointed by the mayor, but for long overlapping terms arranged to stymie a mayor seeking control. Had the mayor wanted to call a cabinet meeting, he would have needed seats for 132, and 20 more if he wanted to invite the Board of Aldermen as well. Dissatisfaction with this regime gradually accumulated, fed more by petty inefficiencies and difficulties than by major scandal or crisis.

Although Hartford was strongly Democratic, Republican William H. Mortensen won the mayoralty in 1943. Mortensen, the son of Danish immigrants, was born and raised in Hartford. In 1933 he headed the local National Recovery Administration and subsequently was appointed to the city's finance board. He won election to the Board of Aldermen, the Board of Education, and in 1942 to the Connecticut Senate, sweeping an old Democratic stronghold by 1,500 votes. Early in his term as mayor,

Mortensen felt the frustrations of Hartford's cumbersome government. The city charter, he found, "permitted responsibilty to be spread among more than 100 commissioners, all more or less subject to political pressures." [13] In July, 1945, the Board of Aldermen yielded to Mortensen's demand for authorization to appoint a committee to revise the charter. After a year of looking into various arrangements, the bipartisan committee proposed a city manager charter. This recommendation won the support of four former mayors, the Chamber of Commerce, and the League of Women Voters, but was opposed by the local Democratic party and by State Democratic Chairman John M. Bailey.

A few days after the final draft of the new charter proposals was filed in the summer of 1946, Mortensen, who had not sought reelection in 1945, was appointed honorary chairman of a newly formed Citizens Charter Committee. The CCC took the role of underdog in the hectic campaign, but won a smashing victory. The new charter was approved 21,089 to 9,748. It provided that a city manager, appointed by a city council for an indefinite term of office, would be the chief executive officer. A nine-man council would be the municipal legislature, with councilmen elected at large for two-year terms in nonpartisan elections. The first council and manager under the new charter were installed in 1948.

These arrangements survived until 1967, when, dazzled by visions of New Haven Mayor Richard Lee (visions of a strong mayor combining executive responsibilities and political power), troubled by certain clear malfunctions of the charter (like the wild free-for-all which was the "nonpartisan," at-large election for the city council), and urged on by the city Democratic party which wanted a more regular and secure control of city government, voters approved a new charter. The principal changes strengthened the mayor's position by making it full-time and providing a veto power, and returned the city to partisan council elections. The powers of the city manager, however,

[13] Interview with William H. Mortensen, April 12, 1967.

contrary to the wishes of the Democrats, remained substantially intact.[14]

American cities are in a continuing revenue crisis, as the demand for services overwhelms the local tax base and the cities become increasingly dependent upon state and federal aid. Substantial state and federal aid has been forthcoming, but the very dependence upon outside decision makers adds considerably to the anxiety of those who manage city government. Suburbs, especially white-collar, new-middle-class suburbs, are typically places with a good revenue base but are also places of high public outlays for such white-collar service priorities as schools that get children into good colleges. Small-town leaders are often committed to a low tax, low expenditure position, and the level of public expenditures per capita in the towns is

[14] Party leaders were never happy with the 1947–67 charter, for rather obvious reasons: The main thrust of the charter reform was to establish efficient, "businesslike" management, removing the parties as far as possible from the governing of the city. The charter reform grew out of an antiparty mood of which the United States has seen many. The '47–'67 charter tried to insulate management from "politics." It provided a merit system, centralized purchasing, and a city assessor and director of personnel who are in the classified service. Throughout the twenty-year life of this charter, Democratic leaders waited for an opportunity when the public would sustain a change. By 1967 the opportunity was there, especially when the leadership of the Greater Hartford Chamber of Commerce committed itself to a stronger mayor with a leading role in policy formation. New Haven was surpassing Hartford, was regularly cited as a model city, was receiving a far larger slice of federal funds for redevelopment and antipoverty exertions than the capital city. The feeling grew that a principal factor in Hartford's lag was the lack of a strong administrator and political leader. The '47–'67 charter installed the council candidate receiving the most votes as mayor, giving him no salary and no substantive powers. The city manager, it was felt, had the administrative authority but lacked the political base. The charter changes eventually agreed upon were a compromise, not all the party leadership wanted. The city manager retained his job and substantial powers although the Democratic leadership would have preferred to dispose of him. They did get a stronger mayor, salaried ($17,500 a year), and a return to partisan elections.

lower. Our three communities conform. Per capita expenditures are highest in Hartford, somewhat lower in Bloomfield, substantially lower in Putnam (see Table 26). But Bloomfield

Table 26. Per capita expenditures from current revenue, Hartford, Bloomfield, and Putnam, 1960 and 1965

Place	1960	1965	Percentage increase
Hartford	$210.49	$267.96	27
Bloomfield	176.15	250.03	42
Putnam	116.98	143.43	23

Source: Connecticut Public Expenditure Council, *Municipal Revenues and Expenditures in Hartford County and the Capitol Planning Region* (Hartford, 1966); and data supplied by the State of Connecticut Tax Department. These are the sources as well for the data in Tables 27 and 28 which follow.

spends much more per capita for education than either Hartford or Putnam, and the share of total expenditures going for schools is twice as high in the suburb as in the city (see Table 27). Public welfare is something else. The city's burden is far greater (see Table 28).

Table 27. Per capita expenditures for schools, Hartford, Bloomfield, and Putnam, 1960 and 1965

Place	1960	1965	Percentage increase	Expenditures for schools, 1965, as a percentage of total expenditures
Hartford	$60.15	$ 83.86	39	31
Bloomfield	95.75	145.43	52	58
Putnam	66.10	77.03	10	54

Hartford and Putnam are overwhelmingly Democratic. In Bloomfield, Republicans have more than held their own in local elections, although even there the Democratic majority in party registration is substantial. Not only do the Democrats

Table 28. Per capita expenditures for public welfare, Hartford, Bloomfield, and Putnam, 1960 and 1965

Place	1960	1965	Percentage change	Expenditure for welfare, 1965, as a percentage of total expenditures
Hartford	$23.39	$28.04	20	10.0
Bloomfield	1.57	.73	−54	.3
Putnam	2.11	2.45	16	2.0

have a registration majority in all three communities, but it has steadily increased in all three, a pattern followed by much of the state. Hartford first recorded a Democratic plurality in 1931, Putnam in 1935, and Bloomfield in 1959 (see Table 29).

Table 29. Democratic and Republican registration, Hartford, Bloomfield, and Putnam, selected years, 1936–1966 (as percentages)

	Hartford			Bloomfield			Putnam		
Year	Dem.	Rep.	Ind.	Dem.	Rep.	Ind.	Dem.	Rep.	Ind.
1936	42.6	30.9	26.5	na*	na	na	50.8	49.2	na
1946	44.1	24.5	31.4	na	na	na	61.5	38.5	na
1956	47.1	20.1	32.8	34.3	42.3	23.4	52.4	30.1	17.5
1960	51.8	18.6	29.6	39.4	36.2	24.4	49.7	27.9	22.4
1966	58.9	17.2	23.9	42.8	32.4	24.8	57.7	23.7	18.6

Source: Registrars of Voters, Hartford, Bloomfield, and Putnam.
* Bloomfield data is not available for 1936 and 1946. The Putnam figures for these years are for two-party registration only.

The electorate in Hartford has shrunk significantly since World War II. In November, 1944, there were more than 86,000 registered voters. Two decades later, when the city's population was about the same as in 1944, the number had dropped by 23,000, indicating that changes in population composition have brought a far higher number of those not able to vote (the transients and the young) and those not psychologically equipped to vote (the apoliticals).

Hartford, in its electoral politics, has much in common with other northeastern and north central cities. It has returned a majority for every Democratic presidential candidate since 1924 when Calvin Coolidge took 62 per cent of the city's vote against the redoubtable John Davis. It has voted Democratic in every gubernatorial election since 1926. And a majority of each Common Council between 1947 and 1967 were Democrats, although the elections were conducted formally on a nonpartisan basis.

The city of Putnam came under firm Democratic control in the 1930's, the town government in 1947. Putnam has given a majority to the Democratic presidential nominee in every election since 1924 save one, when the town "liked Ike" by almost three to two in 1956. Similarly, it has given a majority to the Democratic gubernatorial nominee in every election since 1926 except the 1936 contest. Only once between 1937 and 1967 did the Republicans elect their candidate for alderman-at-large, the position which determines control of the Board of Aldermen.[15] The G.O.P. last elected a mayor in 1946.

Bloomfield has given much more satisfaction to the Republicans. Only three Democratic presidential nominees have received a majority in the suburb since it went for Wilson in 1912: Roosevelt in 1936, Kennedy in 1960, and Johnson in 1964. Bloomfield has "gone Democratic" in gubernatorial voting only four times since 1920, although, somewhat ominously for the Republicans, three of these were the elections of '58, '62, and '66. The Democrats have managed to gain a majority on the Town Council only once in thirty years, in 1959, and were soundly defeated in 1967. Figures 1, 2, and 3 summarize Repub-

[15] Putnam elects two aldermen from each of its four wards and one alderman-at-large. Under the system of minority representation, there is one Democrat and one Republican from each ward. Thus, the only contest is for alderman-at-large, whose vote determines majority control. In fact, party affiliation is of minimal importance in the voting of the board.

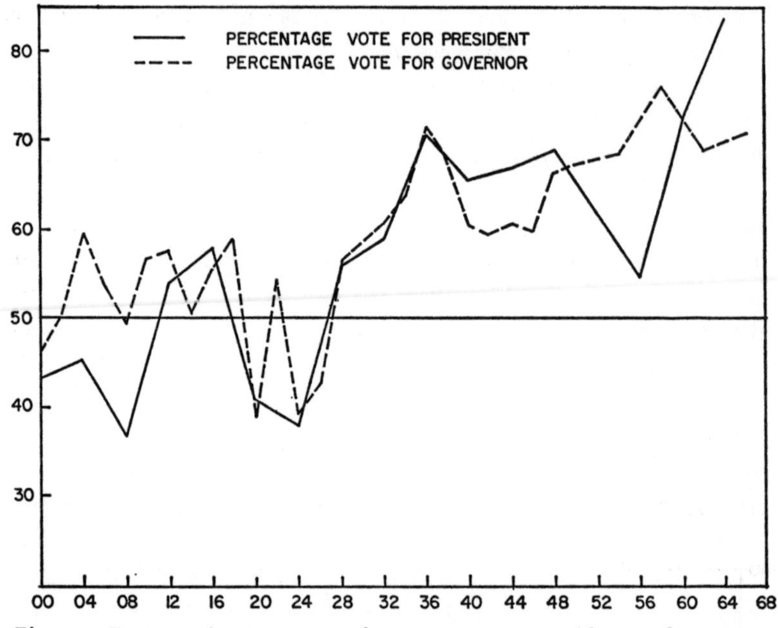

Figure 1. Democratic percentage of two-party vote, president and governor, Hartford, 1900–1967

lican and Democratic electoral experience in the three communities since 1900.

The Democratic party of Putnam has produced several notable leaders. John Dempsey, governor of Connecticut since 1961, was Putnam's mayor between 1949 and 1961. Congressman William St. Onge is another Putnam resident who served as mayor and director of the redevelopment program before his election to Congress in 1962. Before Dempsey, Perry Barber was a popular Democratic leader and mayor, and Barber went on to occupy a judgeship on the Connecticut Superior Court. In a community in which few men of talent have been active, the few with talent have stood out. They have been Democrats. The Republican party, given to frequent defeats, has found it hard to field slates of candidates.

In Bloomfield, both Republicans and Democrats are well led,

and both have combined old and new Bloomfield in their leadership. Thus, the conflict between old and new, town and suburb, has been intra-party rather than inter-party. Lewis Rome, in 1968 the chairman of the Town Council (mayor), typifies the young professionals who have gained political ascendancy in both parties. Rome, with a B.A. and LL.B. from the University of Connecticut, was in 1968 the most popular political leader in Bloomfield. Parties in Bloomfield, as in many suburbs, are organizationally weak. Bloomfielders ask little of them, and they have few sanctions. The role of party leadership is limited to assisting in the recruiting of candidates and representing the community in state party affairs.

Party activity in Hartford is a far more elaborate affair. Hartford is a Democratic city and the Democratic party of Hartford can claim the label "machine." For more than two decades,

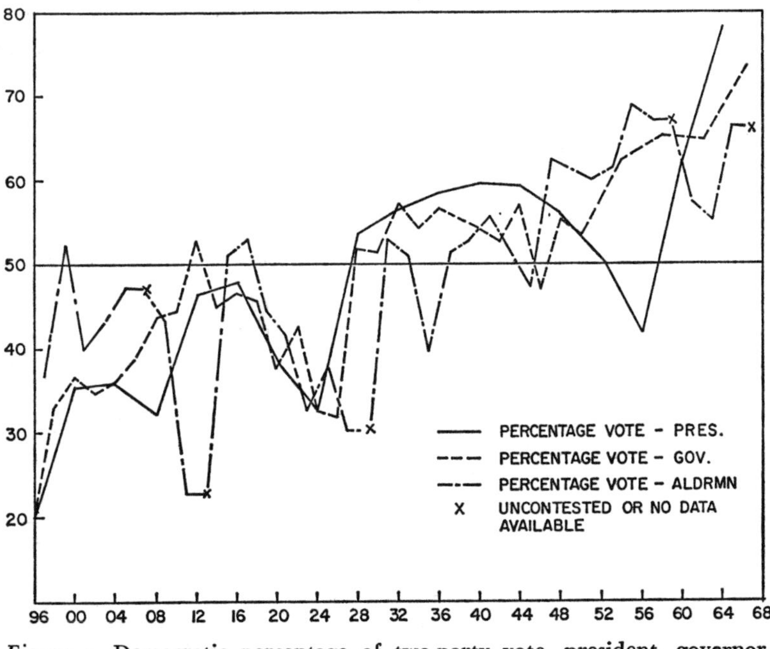

Figure 2. Democratic percentage of two-party vote, president, governor, and alderman-at-large, Putnam, 1900–1967

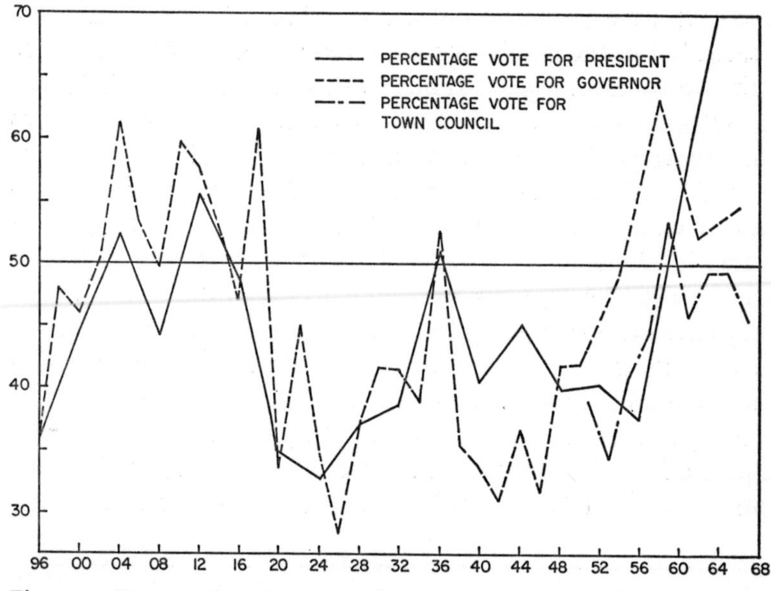

Figure 3. Democratic percentage of two-party vote, president, governor, and town council, Bloomfield, 1900–1967

Note: The Democratic percentage of the Council vote was computed from the average vote of the four Democratic and four Republican candidates.

John M. Bailey has been its seldom-questioned leader. He became Connecticut Democratic Chairman in 1946, and stayed on in that post after 1961 when he was appointed Democratic National Chairman. But despite these wider horizons, Bailey, whose home is still in Hartford, continued to take a proprietary interest in the city's political life. The Bailey machine is a traditional one in its commitment to organization maintenance more than to substantive programs, in its pragmatism, in its fear of issues, in that it does not see in politics an instrument for social change. Hartford lacks a Democratic reform movement, although it does have a collection of politicians who periodically do battle with the machine, at times in the name of reform-type goals.

Hartford, Bloomfield, and Putnam have been briefly described as community settings, based on their historical experience, social and economic structure, and their government and politics. We introduced these not as intrinsically interesting matters, but as elements essential to the construction of the contextual setting for community ideational systems. Now, we can turn to the ideational systems themselves. Chapters 4 and 5 explore the broad contours of political ideas and ideology in the town, the suburb, and the city. Chapter 4 finds in the small-town and the metropolitan ideational experience some fundamental dissimilarities. And Chapter 5 tries to describe and account for the principal lines of ideological cleavage in one metropolitan region, relating these to the sociopolitical position in which city and suburb find themselves in the America of the late 1960's.

PART II

POLITICAL IDEAS AND IDEOLOGY IN THREE AMERICAN COMMUNITIES

4. Small Town vs. Metropolitan America: The Rise of Ideology

We have been hearing so much about the end of ideology that we may have missed a beginning. Local politics in the United States has long been described as an uncongenial setting for ideology. Indeed, it has been almost commonplace to observe that conflict in American communities has dwelled on the narrow, the close-up, the specific and concrete, on personalities and immediate self-interest.[1] ("There is no ideological way to pave a road.") We see no reason to question the past validity of such analysis. But this makes all the more striking our finding a clearly ideological politics in two of the three communities studied: Hartford and Bloomfield. Putnam, the small town, appears scarcely touched by the ideologizing of local politics. Thus small town and metropolitan ideational life in one important regard are polarized; and the rise of ideology in community politics, in a metropolitanizing society, is suggested.

Historically, our local politics appears to have been given a

[1] The authors of an important recent study of community political systems in the United States acknowledge that they began expecting the abstract dimensions of ideology to be absent from local politics. They wrote: "At the outset of this study, we fully expected to find a politics of personal or, at the most, particularistic group interests in the four communities. We did not expect to find an ideological politics even to the limited extent to which it appeared to exist at the national level. When we perceived the importance of ideology as a factor 'ordering' a series of variations in the politics of the four communities . . . political ideology became a central analytic concept" (Robert Agger, Daniel Goldrich, and Bert Swanson, *The Rulers and the Ruled* [New York: John Wiley & Sons, 1964], p. 14).

distinctive flavor by the absence of ideological conflict. Most political leaders in our local communities have not seen themselves separated from other leaders by ideological divides. That astute visitor in the age of Jackson, Alexis de Tocqueville, made repeated reference to this feature of American local politics in his *Democracy*. French newspapers were regularly filled with wide-ranging political argument and discussion, he said, but in the American newspaper of the day "three quarters of the enormous sheet are filled with advertisements, and the remainder is frequently occupied by political intelligence or trivial anecdotes." When the local journalist in America writes about public figures, it is not of their "principles" but of their private lives, to "disclose all their weaknesses and vices." Americans, Tocqueville concluded, are too busy building their individual enterprises to have interest in building philosophical systems.

In brief, he found the American local community in the 1830's a place in which people were so preoccupied with the immediate demands of their employment ("I would especially remark, that they are not only employed, but that they are passionately devoted to their employments"), were such intuitive pragmatists, and, when they did turn their attention to politics, were so addicted to gossiping about politicians' personal foibles, that they simply could not indulge in ideological speculation.

> I think that it is extremely difficult to excite the enthusiasm of a democratic people for any theory which has not a palpable, direct, and immediate connection with the daily occupations of life. . . . They [the Americans] are always in action, and each of their actions absorbs their faculties: the zeal which they display in business puts out the enthusiasm they might otherwise entertain for ideas.[2]

Tocqueville was not referring only to small towns, but what he visited was an America of small towns and countryside.

A century later, Granville Hicks looked at small-town America and found the same preoccupation with the concrete and

[2] *Democracy in America* (New York: Vintage Books, 1959), II, p. 274.

the immediate, with issues of such limited and direct impact as to defy packaging. His *Small Town* is filled with accounts of arguments over the volunteer fire company and the elimination of one-room schools. Politicians vie to be road superintendent and gossip about the vices and virtues of their opponents. *And that is all.* Nowhere in *Small Town* is there indication of ideological conflict. The closest to it was a division between some "old-timers" who thought "if it was good enough for me it should be good enough for them," and the "younger folks" who were a little more inclined to change things, for example to go from one-room schools to a consolidated school. But this was hardly broad and systematic conflict over a wide set of policy preferences.

The absence of ideology was never as complete in the big city as in small and middle-size communities, but it was striking there as well. Until fairly recently, American urban politics was a politics of patronage and narrow group interests. Such a politics can be bitterly divisive, but the struggle is waged for quite different objectives than in ideological politics. Daniel Moynihan made this point writing of the Tammany machine that controlled New York City for three quarters of a century:

> But the very parochialism and bureaucracy that enable them to succeed in local politics prevented them from doing much else. In all these sixty or seventy years in which they could have done almost anything they wanted in politics, they did very little. . . . They never thought of politics as an instrument of social change—their kind of politics involved the processes of society that was not changing.[3]

And commenting on this in his introduction to *Plunkitt of Tammany Hall,* Arthur Mann echoed:

> But neither did the German, Scandinavian, or old stock American bosses whom Lincoln Steffens described some sixty years ago in *The Shame of the Cities.* What is involved here is the entire breed of

[3] Moynihan, "When the Irish Ran New York," *The Reporter,* June 8, 1961, p. 34.

organizational leader, irrespective of ethnic origins. No matter who ran them, the big city machines were designed and fueled to win elections and divide the spoils.[4]

But this nonideological view of politics was not simply the response of "an entire breed of organization leader." It was nothing less than the identifying feature of local politics for most of our history. And it was carried to its most complete statement in the homogeneous, "friends-and-neighbors," petty patronage politics of the American small town.

It remains a hallmark of the small town today. But all this appears to be changing with the metropolitanization of the United States. Put simply, elites in our suburb and city are far more inclined to an ideological view of politics than their small town counterparts. Why this is so occupies us here.

Much of the difference can be accounted for by the contrasting shape of the *public sector* in Hartford and Bloomfield on the one hand, and Putnam on the other. The public sector of a city or town comprises those political issues which concern the collectivity. Issues in the public sector often come before the formal instruments of government, but they need not always or immediately do so. To inquire about the shape of the public sector of a town is to ask what the local community as a collectivity argues about, tries to resolve.

One variable differentiating public sectors is *scope*. This refers both to "how much" happens in public life and to how important that is to the collectivity. Another is *substantive orientation*. Public sectors may deal almost exclusively in the immediate, the specific, the concrete, narrow matters of self-interest, patronage, and personal traits of the participants; or they may be oriented around matters that are broad, impersonal, and remote. A third distinguishing variable is *specialization*. When a public sector is highly specialized, most of the leaders concern themselves only with developments in a relatively small

[4] Arthur Mann, introduction to William Riordan, *Plunkitt of Tammany Hall* (New York: E. P. Dutton, 1963), p. xx.

portion of it. At the other extreme, a few leaders and organizations are involved in much of what transpires in public life. We are not talking of power here. A public sector may have a low level of specialization—most of the principals are involved in most areas—and the system still may not be of concentrated power. More likely in the American system, lack of specialization means only that the scope of the public sector is modest and very little specialization is required or desired.

The scope of public life is broadest in the central city, narrowest in the small town. The independent small town in Connecticut (that is, one which is not a satellite of a major city) is probably even less like the historic small town than its counterparts in other regions because it is less remote from big metropolitan concentrations. But at least one feature of historic small town politics survives: the limited scope of the issues of public life. There is simply not much happening in the public sector in Putnam.

It is not that Putnam lacks problems. Despite improvements in the business district, principally through the building of a new shopping center, the town exudes decline. People continue to leave Putnam, and in a state where the population doubled between 1927 and 1967, Putnam did not grow. The newer industries of the area are small and marginal, and they pay wages far below those of firms in Hartford fifty miles away. Companies in East Hartford, the home of United Aircraft, paid their workers an average weekly wage of $146 in 1965 when Putnam firms were paying $90. Putnam leaders talk constantly of attracting "one major industry that pays good wages, that will provide good jobs to keep our young people at home." But now the young do not stay, their places are not taken by young immigrants from other places, and Putnam is an "old" town. East Hartford has more than twice as many residents in the 25-34 age bracket than it has between 55 and 64, but Putnam has substantially more in the latter age group than in the former. Such problems of endemic decline, however, are not caught up in political conflict. The public sector is not shaped by argument over how to resolve them. Everyone is for new industry, like mother and country, although some work harder than others to attract it. While townsfolk lament the lack of good jobs to keep the young at home, they accept this with resignation as one accepts the visitations of the gods.

The problems sustaining conflict in Putnam are small, often petty, always limited. They cannot be packaged. School problems are limited to such questions as whether a new annex is needed. Police problems extend to whether an officer's son had been caught rifling a local sporting goods store (which, if true, had been hushed up) and to a "revolt by some policemen upset over the department's being—to their way of thinking—all chiefs and no Indians. Even urban renewal, which might suggest more, primarily involved clearing land for a shopping center.

The contrast with the public sector in Hartford could hardly be greater. There, discussions of schools include the physical rebuilding of an entire public school plant and handling a massive transformation of the social composition of the student body. In 1967, Hartford's school population was about half nonwhite, becoming more so, and was concentrated in schools in the North End. Negroes and their white allies were demanding that the board of education take immediate steps to correct racial imbalance. Many if not most of the residents of the white South End, and their political leaders, strongly opposed cross-city busing. How can Negro demands for integration be reconciled with the objective of stopping or at least slowing the exodus of whites from the city? How, in short, can Hartford induce middle-class whites to stay in the city while attempting to meet the needs and demands of nonwhites—demands which are one factor in the exodus of whites? Putnam's ethnic conflict is limited to private derogations by WASPs of Franco-Americans and vice versa, the relative lack of social exchange between the groups, and the persistence of these ethnic identifications in voting choices. Hartford, however, sits on a powder keg of potentially massive racial conflict between whites and Negroes, and there have been occasional secondary explosions, as in the limited rioting in the summer of 1967.

The public sector in Hartford is large and touches the most vital interests of the citizenry. Hartford is the declining core of a region of three quarters of a million. It has a growing population of poor nonwhites, housed mostly in physically deteriorating neighborhoods. It is preoccupied with efforts to minimize conflict between white and black. It must engage in a constant scavenging for revenues through local taxation and grants from the state and national governments to meet growing demands for public services. The contrast in the shape of the public sector in our small town and central city is not, then, limited to a simple matter of scale. What happens in the public sector in Hartford has far greater implications for the future of the city than do the issues of public life in Putnam for the town's future. Different groups push demands upon the city's public sector with the intent of achieving substantial social change. The fact that they are often thwarted does not alter the intent. When, for example, steps are proposed to achieve the integration of the city school system by busing Negroes around the city or out of the city, and by strategic locations and combinations of schools including the placement of new schools on the boundaries of white and Negro areas, the objective clearly is social change. But when, as in Putnam, the only argument involving education concerns how much to spend within narrow limits, social change is not at issue. No controversy in the public life of Putnam since World War II could have led, however resolved, to significant social change.

The scope of the public sector in Bloomfield, while more modest than that of the city, lies much closer to it than to that of the town. It is larger than Putnam's (which Bloomfield approximates in population size) for several reasons. Bloomfield is part of the metropolitan region. Its public life thus depends much more upon what happens in other communities than Putnam's. Bloomfield's sheer physical proximity to the North End of Hartford has given it a "race problem." The growth of the Negro population in Bloomfield has generated a wide-ranging argument. The issue of *de facto* segregation in the schools has been actively debated and discussed, and in 1967 it was attacked through a voluntary busing program and the decision to build a new lower middle school for the entire suburb while closing an existing K-5 (Kindergarten through grade 5) school in the area of high Negro concentration. Bloomfield citizens are more aware of the ways public power may be utilized to affect community life: zoning, for example, is not—as in Putnam—only a matter of preventing one's own ox from being gored, but becomes an instrument for shaping the social and economic composition of the community. In general, the transformation of Bloomfield from a small, still heavily agricultural town in 1950 to a bustling suburb of 19,000 in 1967 forced the development of a public sector that is wider and deals with questions of social change. Bloomfield has been transformed in the most dramatic and obvious ways, and its transformation quite clearly is not an act of God but of men, and specifically a result of the movement of men from one type of residential setting to another. Thus, it is natural rather than essentially "supernatural" as in Putnam, and as such is recognized, debated, and responded to.[5]

The stuff of conflict in Putnam defies ideologizing. The principal actors know each other intimately, and the town's politics feeds on personalities. Our interviews were peppered with tales of heavy drinking and love trysts. When we asked Putnam politicians to comment on other local leaders, they invariably treated our inquiries as an invitation to gossip about bad humor, sexual indiscretions, or petty graft. Indeed, at one time Putnam's political discourse centered on the extramarital sex life of one prominent politician. And wasn't he too often publicly drunk? Hadn't he been involved in a "brawl" in a neighboring Rhode Island town? And arrested for speeding at

[5] When I describe the transformation of Putnam as "supernatural," I mean only that it seems to town residents to be the product of rather mysterious forces quite beyond comprehension and control.

2:00 A.M., and jailed until morning? Hadn't Polly Whitman, head of the local antipornography league that was formed to clear the newsstands of obscene and suggestive literature corruptive of public morals, left her husband and "run off" with a man from a nearby town? (This was not just idle gossip. These things actually happened.)

At first, we were simply amused by these incessant revelations. But as they persisted over nearly a hundred interviews and reinterviews of the town's political leaders, we became impressed by the strength and pervasiveness of the pressures to translate political matters into "personalities." One local politician who had spent some time in the state legislature remarked that "in Hartford, you could battle with a guy on the floor [of the legislature] over some bill, then an hour later have a few beers with him and talk over some other business and legislation. You can't do that here. Everything's so personal."

Even when a broader issue intrudes through the town's narrow and immediate self-interest politics, it is stifled by the intimacy of the situation, blurred by the insistence of local leaders on seeing each other naked. Leaders were asked whether they knew of any Putnamites belonging to the Radical Right, or of any organizations of the Far Right operating in the community. Without exception, they responded that there were no "John Birch types" in Putnam. It became clear that the notables of Putnam knew each other far too well to think of each other as representatives of any abstract ideological posture. This worked both ways. It made it hard for the conservatively inclined to see other notables as "comsymps." And the "moderates" simply could not admit the possibility of the "conservatives" acting as ideologues of the Right. Bloomfield has a small Radical Right and some vociferous liberals; Putnam has neither, largely because the public sector cannot sustain them. I am suggesting that ideational inclinations can be smothered by the intimacy of a setting and thus never develop into ideological postures.

Republican leaders in Hartford, Putnam, and Bloomfield were asked to comment on the Republican Citizens Committee, a Right Wing splinter organization that figured prominently in the party's life between 1963 and 1965 and formally died in 1967. John Lupton, the Republican candidate for congressman-at-large from Connecticut in 1962, headed the Republican Citizens Committee. He was the most vocal Goldwater supporter in the state in 1964. The responses of two local Republican leaders, one from Bloomfield and the other from Putnam, typify the difference between an ideological and a nonideological view of conflict. Judging from the responses of both leaders on a wide range of issues, I could call both conservatives well to the right. The suburban Republican indeed saw himself as an ideological blood brother to Lupton:

If we are going to have Rockefeller type Republicans we might as well have Democrats. I am going to vote for Dempsey [Connecticut Democratic Governor John Dempsey] instead of Gengras [1966 Republican Gubernatorial Nominee Clayton Gengras]. Dempsey is more conservative than many of the state Republican leaders. Everywhere he goes he speaks out strongly against a state income tax. . . . I worked in New York City until a year and a half ago, and I worked some for Rockefeller his first time around—1958. Before that I supported Javits for senator in 1956. So I got burned twice, but I won't make that mistake again. Look at those guys. They are liberal Democrats! . . . I am for the Citizens Committee here, for the Conservatives in New York.

But the Putnam Republican saw the Luptonites not as ideological blood brothers—though he disagreed with them on no substantive issue at all—but as Republicans who were splintering the party:

Why, those people are willing to wreck the party. I don't go for that sort of thing. What do they think they can gain? You've got to support the party. I don't like Pinney very well [A. Searle Pinney, then Connecticut Republican State Chairman] but he has the votes [on the Republican State Committee] now. So I am a Pinney Republican.

His bewilderment before the Rightist splinter was real. He could not conceive of anyone entering party politics for another purpose than to win elections and divide the spoils. And you can divide the spoils as well with Pinney as with Lupton. That is what forty years in politics in Putnam taught him about political conflict. In this, his experience was not really different than that of the late Tammany statesman George Washington Plunkitt. Civil service reform would kill the parties, Plunkitt said, because men work in politics only to get patronage.

How are you goin' to keep up patriotism if this thing [merit service] goes on? You can't do it. Let me tell you that patriotism has been dying out fast for the last twenty years. Before then when a party won, its workers got everything in sight. That was somethin' to make a man patriotic.[6]

Not surprisingly, in this politics where everyone knows everyone else intimately and where only the most narrow and immediate interests are sources of conflict, political labels lose meaning. Putnam politicians insist that "there are no liberals or conservatives here." The only ones using such labels as liberal and conservative at all are a few "outsiders" who insist on applying categories discovered in state and national politics rather arbitrarily to the local scene. In the same way, most Putnam notables recognize that only the slightest shreds of policy difference separate the local Republican and Democratic parties. There are clear differences in the ethnicity of their constituents, and the Republicans would surely bestow the town's modest patronage on their own if they had a chance. But there is scarcely a modicum of policy difference.

The intimacy of the elites in Putnam is heightened by the lack of specialization in the public sector. Little special training is necessary to intervene in any issue area, so leaders can and do move about easily. They have little competition, partly because Putnam has not been able to attract and keep the most talented politicians, and partly because the incentives to participate in public life are modest. So Mrs. Rose Bove LaRose is the developer of Putnam's shopping center, confidant of the mayor,

[6] Riordan, *op. cit.*, p. 14.

chairman of the school board, and general woman-about-town. The public sector in Hartford, far larger and more complex, is more specialized. Some actors or organizations—principally the city manager, the Common Council, the Democratic party, and the Chamber of Commerce—are regularly at the center of discussion. But the issues of public life are of such scope and complexity as to require and receive sharply differentiated and specialized treatment: the recruitment of quite different leaders and especially subleaders; the utilization of distinct groups of experts; the involvement of different interest groups. The suburb, again, is closer to the city than to the small town. Bloomfield has a number of functionally specialized interest groups like the Bloomfield Intergroup Council (race), the Bloomfield Citizens Committee (race, an all-Negro organization), and the Bloomfield Betterment Association (tax rates, community redevelopment). The total decision audience is much larger than in Putnam, and more segmented by decision areas. The potential leadership cadre also is larger than Putnam's and possesses more personal resources.

I have dwelled at some length on the shape of the public sector in Putnam because it appears this was the ascendant form through a long sweep of American history, and because there is reason to assume that it remains common to our small towns. The view of conflict acquired through continued exposure to a politics of narrow issues, limited government activity, immediate self-interest, and personal foibles cannot readily be dropped as one moves to a situation in which the issues are more ideological. Hometown, U.S.A., has been contemptuous of ideology, and American national politics has been importantly influenced by this conditioning.

Now we are seeing in the metropolitan region the evolution of a more ideological local politics. First, metropolitan elites today simply cannot be as preoccupied with intimate personal characteristics. The metropolitan experience is far more impersonal. And ideology demands a large measure of impersonality; that is, elites cannot be so taken up with the personal frailties of their rivals that they are unable to see them as ideal types. Small-town leaders are too close to one another. The metropolitan experience provides the perspective ideology requires.

The rise of ideology owes much to the transformation of the metropolitan experience. The United States has become an interdependent society, and the metropolitan region is the microcosm of such a society. Here the pangs of interdependence are most sharply felt. The metropolitan region inflates, spreading population across existing political boundaries and creating tensions between city and suburb. The metropolitan region is the microcosm of interdependent America in race relations, the scene of persistent conflict between Negroes and whites. Here the most intense and complex racial problems are now posed: problems such as how to integrate schools while there is residential segregation, challenging the concept of neighborhood schools, forcing attention to city-wide or regional movement of pupils; problems demanding the massive and coherent commitment of resources; problems that are national rather than regional. Leaders in the metropolitan region, unlike their small-town counterparts, cannot avoid the most urgent and divisive domestic problems. And these problems admit matters often essentially remote and abstract, generate conflict that is systematic, and thus encourage ideological construction.

The massive role of the federal government adds still another dimension to the transformation of the metropolitan scene. Local leaders are brought into regular contact with national political elites. They find themselves competing with other metropolitan regions for shares in the federal pie, are called upon to mediate between purely local interests and national requirements, and come to appreciate the importance of national controversies for their local programs. Banfield and Wilson believe that

> to an increasing extent, the issues of city politics will be connected with the larger, ideological ones of national politics. Urban renewal projects, for example, are very likely to raise the national and ideological issue of race. Because of this close connection with larger

issues, local politics will be of increasing interest to those people whom Robert K. Merton has described as cosmopolitans rather than locals.[7]

A major change has occurred, then. The country is metropolitanizing, political conflict in metropolitan America is evolving in new forms, and metropolitan elites are engulfed in a sociopolitical experience quite different from what local elites have known historically. These developments appear to be closing an era of American politics, epitomized in the small town but truly national, in which most local political conflict was essentially nonideological.

Some of the new ideological postures generated in metropolitan America are positive and creative. Others are essentially reactive and reactionary: reactive, for they have been brought to coherence largely as a defense against the assaults of creative postures; reactionary, in that they are fundamentally at war with the new demands that brought the demise of the patronage politics George Washington Plunkitt knew.

There are some other developments promoting a more ideological local politics that do not so neatly relate to the contrasting experience of metropolitan areas and small towns but which deserve mention. We are equipping an increasing segment of our population with the intellectual skills to deal with abstract ideas—the stuff of ideology. An ideology is a logical or quasi-logical system of ideas that claims to deal more or less systematically with a wide range of matters of government and public policy. No one sees politics ideologically, then, unless he has a fairly high level of information and has acquired a competency or familiarity with abstract presentations. The importance of this information and training to perception of conflict was underscored by a recent study:

[7] Banfield and Wilson, *City Politics* (New York: Vintage Books, 1966), p. 333.

It is well established that differences in information held in a cross-section population are simply staggering, running from vast treasuries of well organized information . . . to fragments that could virtually be measured as a few "bits" in the technical sense. . . . The ordering of individuals on this vertical information scale is largely due to differences in education. . . . It is our primary thesis that, as one moves from elite sources of belief systems downwards on such an information scale, several important things occur. First, the contextual grasp of "standard" political belief systems [ideologies] fades out very rapidly, almost before one has passed beyond the 10% of the American population that in the 1950's had completed standard college training. . . . At the same time, moving from top to bottom of this information dimension, the character of the objects that are central in a belief system undergoes systematic change. These objects shift from the remote, generic, and abstract to the increasingly simple, concrete, or "close to home." [8]

The college experience certainly is not the only way to pick up the tools ideology demands, nor is the degree proof of acquisition. But for aggregates, exposure or the lack of exposure to standard college training seems to be extremely influential. Our rapid extension of college education thus contributes to the potential for a more ideological politics. In 1940 there were fewer than three and a half million college graduates in the United States, in 1960 more than seven and a half million, and projections call for more than fourteen million college graduates living in 1980. We have found Hartford and Bloomfield leaders somewhat better trained than their Putnam counterparts, although the long-term implications are national: an increasing share of local leaders possessing the intellectual accouterments needed for an ideological view of political life.

Beyond this, to see conflict ideologically requires time and leisure to sort things out and a degree of freedom from the

[8] Philip Converse, "The Nature of Belief Systems in Mass Publics," in David Apter (ed.), *Ideology and Discontent* (New York: Free Press of Glencoe, 1964), pp. 212–213.

most pressing economic concerns. The new middle class that has multiplied in the postwar years has this necessary leisure: psychic leisure, freedom from "survival" demands without which regular concern with abstract political matters is an over-priced luxury; and physical leisure, working days short enough, and work not so demanding physically, that one has energy to devote to thought and discussion of political questions remote from immediate experience and needs.

In sum, moving into prominence is a college-educated new middle class, with more leisure time and much more money, confident in its ability to understand politics in the way ideology demands. This new class is not exclusively metropolitan, but, as we will see in the following chapters, it is principally metropolitan. So there is a partial overlay with the more abstract and categoric (i.e., ideological) demands of the public sector in metropolitan places

It is far easier to describe the ideologizing of local politics, and to see in it marked but superficial changes in the flavor of political conflict, than to determine its impact on American political life. To talk of impact in one sense is to turn things around, because the ideologizing is itself the product of basic changes: the collapse of the independent society and the decline of the small town which was the fulcrum of that society; the staggering growth and transformation of metropolitan America as the microcosm of the interdependent society, sweeping local elites up into conflict that is broad in the range of issues, categoric in impact, and national in scope; the growth of a new political class that is trained and inclined to see politics in abstract dimensions. But it is still necessary to treat the more ideological local politics as the independent variable, and ask what we can expect from it.

In the first instance, the source and fabric of political disaffection should be substantially changed. History really doesn't furnish us with any broad-based movements of ideologues—people who themselves see politics ideologically rather than merely follow ideologues. Our protest movements, while led by ideologues, have been filled primarily by people drawn in by some very specific and pressing grievance. Thus, for most people Populism simply meant, "Let me, the farmer, reap a fair return from my labor!" "Hate the money power" is not an ideological expression any more than "hate niggers" is. By themselves, they are only testimony to bitterness and frustration.

But we appear to be building the potential for popular movements of ideologues, and contemporary right-wing conservatism can be distinguished from earlier dissents on just this basis. Less intense personal grievances are needed to sustain strong ideological protests because there is a growing body of local activists sensitized to conflict over essentially abstract policy matters and thus conscious of conflict in the absence of pressing personal stakes. This is at least characteristic of the members of organizations of the Far Right in Hartford area communities whom we have interviewed: the rank and file do not see themselves as a group of Americans singled out for particular abuse. Although other studies of right-wing conservatism have located its source in alienation and in status anxieties, our data show that the men of the Right could not have been mobilized as they have if they had not first come to see politics ideologically. When you make leaders labor in ideological gardens, you must expect they will develop a tast for the harvest, and that some will insist on cultivating different things. Men develop interests in their ideologies; and the ideologies, beyond the interests, cognitions, and orientations which nourished them, become sources of division. In this sense, a more ideological politics produces "artificial" conflict. As you come to see politics ideologically, you become aware of divisions you never knew were there.

For the political parties, the ideologizing of politics should mean that as the internal fissures produced in the past by regional, rural-urban, and ethnic differences slowly close, new ones will open in their place. Specifically, the internal conflict plaguing the Republican party, and pushing out in a number of states including New York in the form of conservative parties, should not decline but rather become a fixture of our party scene. For such conflict appears to be sustained by the involvement of a far larger segment of local leadership in an ideological view of politics. It is not coincidental that ideological splinters like the Republican Citizens Committee in Connecticut (1963–1967), and victorious right-wing Republican efforts like that behind Reagan in California, originate in the cities and suburbs—where the ideologizing of local politics is further along—and not in the small towns and rural areas which perhaps have more cause to do battle with the new society.

There are potential gains as well as problems in the developments we have sketched. Local leaders historically have not seen politics as a vehicle for changing society: patronage and personalities are not the stuff of social change. Ideologizing provides for a far more dynamic public sector at the community level, for the involvement of local elites in more rarefied reaches of public policy.

5. Metropolitan America: The Lines Form for New Ideological Conflict

Conflict of the sort which occurs in Putnam, our small town, is not ordered by the constraints of ideology. But there is ideological conflict in both the suburb and the city, and our task here is to describe its broad outlines.

Analyses of ideology in American politics, like popular commentary, generally begin with *liberal* vs. *conservative,* the Conventional Dichotomy, and this one did. It soon became apparent, however, that the conflict situation envisioned by the C.D. and the one actually present in Hartford are, in important regards, different. Our task became one of locating and describing the existing polarities and, incidentally, naming them. It is tempting to dwell on the latter exercise, but quite wrong. The demanding job is finding the patterns of ideological conflict; once located and precisely described, labeling becomes a relatively inconsequential enterprise.

Our general conclusions, which point to the "lack of fit" of the C.D. and ideological conflict in Hartford, parallel findings of a number of recent studies dealing with other community settings and with national divisions. Some of these will be discussed below. What is important, of course, is that our data and these other studies tentatively affirm the thesis that American society in the 1960's, so strikingly different from that of the 1930's, is generating at all levels conflict situations dissimilar to those of the thirties and specifically to that which the C.D. characterized.

Posit a decision sector such as local politics in Hartford, and enter in this an axis of ideological cleavage (see Diagram 1).

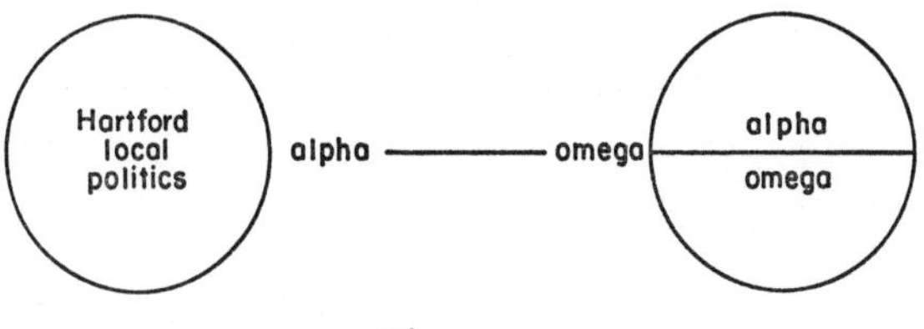

Diagram 1

Apart from definitions of the two positions, we can ask how much of the total ideational conflict is comprehended or ordered by the axis. In some systems the location and identification of a single axis accounts for a very large segment of the important conflict; in other systems no axis by itself has much explanative power. A system approaching the former model would be one in which (1) the line between alpha and omega cuts very deep; (2) the centrality of this division is clear, that is, both the alphas and the omegas see the highest values at stake; (3) both alphas and omegas are highly visible, easily identifiable, and there is little question on anyone's part where a person or group belongs; (4) no other division approaches alpha-omega in centrality, in importance to the participants, or in visibility. There is indication that some western countries at earlier points in their egalitarian and industrial revolutions approached this model.[1] Whenever the model is approached, a given axis can have tremendous explanatory power, and the analyst of this system's ideational conflict finds his job a relatively manageable one. The content of each position can be readily defined and the appearance of this division in most specific conflict situations is easily discerned. But in the United States, competing ideological positions never have had such coherence and neatness, and no single axis has had as much explanatory power. The ideological divisions which we locate will leave much conflict unaccounted for.

[1] A class-conscious industrial working class feeling itself in deep and irreconcilable conflict with capitalists suggests a situation approaching the model. The division between Fascists and Communists in Germany in 1932 would be another example of this type.

The most enduring and frequently advanced ideological axis in American politics is the Conventional Dichotomy, and at the outset we asked: How much of the ideological conflict among elites in Hartford does it subsume? [2] We expected the C.D. to have more explanative power than it proved to have. Before discussing this, however, some preliminary distinctions must be introduced.

The terms liberalism and conservatism have been used with many shades of meaning, and we need not examine these differences in any detail. But it is necessary to spell out what we understand by these categories and the type of conflict situation they appear to have ordered.

First, we agree with Hartz that American liberalism and conservatism must be understood as different strains within an overarching Liberal tradition: American political thought from the founding of the Republic has rejected the whole intellectual fabric of ascriptive class societies; it has favored republican over hereditary institutions; it has insisted that achievement rather than birth be the standard by which wealth and status are allocated; it has been profoundly secular and has spoken of progress in this world rather than looking to the next; it has been individualistic and has talked of liberating men from restraints which block them and which deny them what their talents would permit; it has posited a society in which men have natural rights, not natural duties, and one in which the right to own property looms large.[3]

If liberalism and conservatism are to be seen, then, as strains within a Liberal tradition, what distinguishes them? First, orientation to change. In a wide literature, liberals are described

[2] It was not expected that any ideological axis would account for much conflict among the rank and file of the population. Philip Converse has demonstrated that most adult Americans don't comprehend any ideological system ("The Nature of Belief Systems in Mass Publics," in David Apter [ed.], *Ideology and Discontent* [New York: Free Press of Glencoe, 1964], p. 213).

[3] Louis Hartz, *The Liberal Tradition in America* (New York: Harcourt, Brace & World, 1955).

as in some sense proponents and conservative opponents of change.[4] But unless we specify what kinds of change, the terms liberalism and conservatism become too vaguely inclusive. Moreover, common usage *has* specified the types of change: businessmen have commonly been called conservatives, yet no one denies that big business has been a prime manufacturer of certain precipitants of social change. Change, then, for what? The liberal supports change to realize a more popular or equal distribution of some important societal values. Conservatism is the ideological opposition to such change. We would expect to find in any egalitarian society an ideological posture which insists upon extending to lower socioeconomic groups more of the prerequisites of the good life: a higher standard of living; more and better public education, assurance of adequate health care. We would also expect a competing posture which opposes a more popular distribution of values. Liberals, who themselves may or may not be "little guys," concern themselves with the needs of "little guys" over the "big guys" of the society

[4] See, for example, Willmore Kendall and George Carey, "Toward a Definition of Conservatism," *Journal of Politics,* May, 1964, pp. 406–422. They maintain that resistance to change characterizes conservatism but further that since the clash between the proponents and resisters of change goes on in all kinds of groups and activities, many particular conservatisms emerge. Samuel Huntington sees conservatism as a "positional" ideology, depending upon the relations existing among groups rather than upon the continuing interest of a particular social group. It arises from distinct but recurring historical situations "in which the supporters of those [the established] institutions employ the conservative ideology in their defense" against some fundamental challenge ("Conservatism as an Ideology," *American Political Science Review,* LI [June, 1957], 454–473). Clinton Rossiter speaks of conservatism's commitment "to a discriminating defense of the social order against change and reform." The liberal is "reasonably satisfied" with his way of life but believes he can improve upon it substantially "without betraying its ideals or wrecking its institutions. . . . In short, he is optimistic rather than pessimistic about the possbilities of reform" (*Conservatism in America* [New York: Alfred A. Knopf, 1955], p. 12).

If the good society requires a proper balance of competing demands, liberals see this balance threatened by the acquisition of power and privilege by some elite, and conservatives by popular infringements on the elite. Conservatives are inclined to the rule of an elite, typically one whose fitness has been demonstrated by its economic success. Liberals look to rule "by the people" or more precisely to the leadership of spokesmen of the people. Elitist-popular splits are not new. America has always had a more elitist tradition competing with the more democratic one. One hundred and seventy-five years ago the Federalists railed against "the mob," while the Jeffersonians saw the common man as some peculiar repository of political wisdom. All of this can easily be overstated. But quite clearly persons whom we call conservatives have been more disposed to the leadership of an elite of wealth, and liberals more in sympathy with men for, if not of, the people.

The component variables in the C.D. then are: (1) orientation to change; (2) response to claims for a more equal distribution of dollars and status; and (3) preference for elite or mass rule. Despite great variations in usage, this common thread runs through much of the contemporary understanding of liberalism and conservatism. Diagram 2 locates these competing ideological positions.

		Who should lead ?	
		Minority of wealth or talent	"The people" and their spokesman
Change for what ?	Supports change toward a more popular extension of values	A	Liberals B
	Opposes change toward the more popular extension of values	Conservatives C	D

Diagram 2

We would expect to find in any egalitarian society some conflict of the liberal-conservative variety, but we would also expect that the centrality of this division would depend upon the agenda of politics. In the agenda in which Greater Hartford finds itself in the 1960's, such conflict is not the most central. Why it is not, and what is, demands our attention.

First, in this prosperous white-collar, aerospace and insurance area, "the people" are not advocating change to advance an equalitarian redistribution. Not many of the white people anyway. This is a setting in which a large portion of the common men has "arrived." A classic liberal-conservative division requires a "have" elite resisting change toward a more popular distribution of some value such as income, and a rank and file, or counter-elite speaking for the rank and file, demanding such change. Greater Hartford today does not present this type of arrangement, and such an organization as the Greater Hartford Labor Council cannot—except in a strained and limited sense—be considered a liberal force.

In fact, "the (white) people" not infrequently are the prime opponents of popular change. This is so because demands for such change in the metropolitan region ever more frequently are demands to extend benefits to nonwhites. The South End of Hartford is white and the North End black, and the residents of the former fear encroachments from the latter. These fears sustain popular neighborhood leaders who are racial reactionnaries and a number of city-wide leaders who often give expression in a more subtle way to South End racial concerns. In 1966 a South End maverick Democrat, Frank W. Russo, sought the Democratic nomination as state representative from the fourth assembly district, in South Hartford. He based his campaign on a single issue: barring Negroes from the South End. Most South End residents, Russo said, are Sicilians and accustomed to hot political battles.

They have inborn fears of Negroes coming into their neighborhoods, based primarily on the fear that their property will go down if that happens. . . . I feel a person has a constitutional right to be prejudiced, if he wants to. . . . I'm going to campaign against open housing and against busing of Negro children into our schools. . . . Homeowners should have the right to determine who will live in their neighborhood and go to their schools.

Such conflicts between lower-class and lower-middle-class whites and nonwhites in metropolitan areas across the country appears to be increasingly influential and is not comprehended by the C.D.[5] The response of the Frank Russos of Hartford would be located, in the diagram introduced above, in cell D (see Diagram 3). Genuinely popular, it is none the less reactionary.

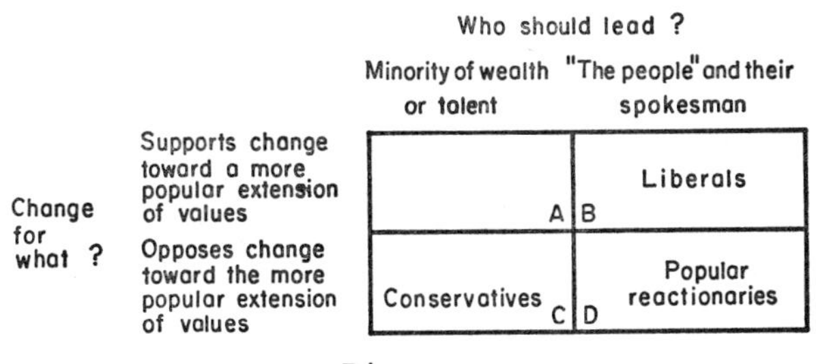

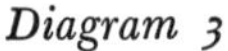
Diagram 3

Some expressions of popular reactionism in Hartford are slightly more subtle than Russo's. In 1966, for example, Hartford Mayor George B. Kinsella opposed efforts to gain voter approval of a $42 million school bond issue.[6] Aware of the tre-

[5] Enough has been written about the reaction of whites to the demands of nonwhites in metropolitan America. Discussions of urban race relations over the last decade have been dominated by the term "white backlash." Open housing ordinances, for example, have not fared well at the hands of white voters. When put to a popular vote, they have almost invariably been defeated: Seattle and Tacoma, Washington; Berkeley, California; the massive voter repudiation of the California state open housing measure ("Proposition 14") in the 1964 referendum struggle. Suburban whites have not differed here with their urban brethren. Harry and David Rosen describe the intense opposition of a prosperous North Chicago suburb, Deerfield, to a proposed integrated subdivision where twelve $30,000 houses were to be sold to Negroes (*But Not Next Door* [New York: I. Obolensky, 1959]). The rejection of the Civilian Review Board by New York City whites—to cite a different but parallel issue—was almost solely attributable to a racial reaction. We could go on, and on.

[6] In 1966 the Hartford school system's physical plant was overcrowded and in a state of physical deterioration. Lack of leadership, difficulty in finding the needed dollars, perplexing problems (largely racial in origin)

mendous hurdles that had been surmounted to bring the compromise bond issue to the vote and of the strong hostility among whites to the proposed construction ("Why take our money to build schools for Negroes?"), the Mayor told reporters shortly before the election that he opposed the bond issue as it stood. It should be replaced, he said, by one providing funds for planning and for acquisition of land in the suburbs. The next step would be building schools and housing for city Negroes in the suburbs. Unless such steps are taken, he concluded, Hartford will become a Negro ghetto financed by federal renewal funds. His proposal was greeted not as a farsighted appeal for regionalism in school planning but as "cynically [playing] on the fears of the predominantly white South End." Facing the unanimous opposition of the communications media and of business and civic leaders, along with strong criticism from within his own party, the Mayor retreated.

This points to a development of fundamental importance: popular forces are often not socially progressive forces. We tend to see an idea as progressive when its realization is recognized to be an objective toward which the system is moving. Through much of modern political history in the West, the common man was cast as supporter of socially progressive ideas. This congruence of the popular and the socially progressive never possessed a logical necessity, but it was regularly achieved and we came to see it as natural and permanent. Increasingly in Hartford, popular forces align themselves against social progress.

At the same time, nonpopular forces often are proponents of socially progressive ideas. As an example, business leaders in Hartford provided much of the muscle needed to pass the school bond issue in 1966, strongly opposing the Mayor's thinly

relating to the location and format of the new schools, had delayed decision on new school building programs to the point where a massive catch-up effort was necessary. The $42 million bond issue was only the first step in catching up. It called for funds for a new high school, three new middle schools (grades 7 and 8), and a new elementary school. The city architect estimated the total cost of planned school construction at $91 million.

veiled attempt to scuttle it. They have been among the principal backers of suburban busing. But these business leaders have hardly become political liberals. In our four-cell diagram, they probably would be better in cell A than elsewhere, but even there they are a poor fit (see Diagram 4).

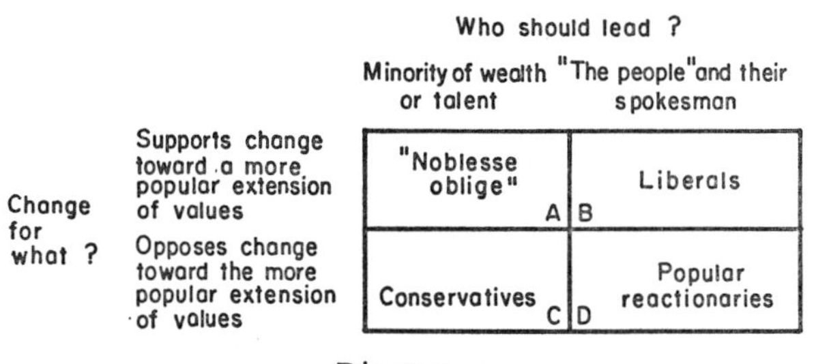

Diagram 4

Hartford's business community is clearly oriented to elite rule. In interviews with nearly all of the fifty-seven businessmen in our sample we found, when we asked for evaluations of the city's popularly elected leadership, expressions in some way disparaging: "They aren't big enough." "They don't know what is going on." "They are fairly honest, but they can't really understand the demands being made on the city today." They favored the talented manager—a man, in their view, like themselves.[7] But the position of these business leaders cannot properly be described either as support for or resistance to popular social change. The social change they are committed to is not typically perceived as redistributive—"taking from the rich

[7] This standard was regularly introduced in evaluations of national political leaders. Noteworthy was the tendency of the younger corporate manager to measure a national leader by the standard: "Is he the kind of person I would like to have cocktails with?" Is he bright, aggressive, competent in the sense of understanding the paths in which the society is moving, cosmopolitan, conversant with the norms of contemporary science? The question, "Is he probusiness, or prolabor?" loomed much larger in the thinking of the older generation of corporation leadership, but was not at all pivotal in the thinking of top management forty-five years of age and younger.

and giving to the poor"—and this is why the above diagram really has no place for them. They are committed to change primarily to realize what are conceived as broad community values. We are seeing in the metropolitan region today the rise of new progressives who do not at all resemble what we have been taught to expect in progressives. They wear button-down collars, are college-educated, and staff managerial positions in industry and in the government bureaucracy. They are certainly not disinterested or unselfish, and if they appear more attractive than their counterparts in earlier periods, that is largely because an age of affluence has permitted them to be.

Hartford corporation leaders find themselves in competition for executive talent with other national corporations and are much aware of the need to offer an attractive setting. This leads them to work for civic improvements of direct interest to their personnel. A high-ranking Travelers (insurance) executive referred to this kind of concern:

We have been discussing the building of a civic center on land cleared through the redevelopment program. The center would have a sports arena, an exhibition hall, a legitimate theater, and a cinema. All that the people on the City Council think about is how much tax revenue the city will get. The important thing is making Hartford and the Hartford area a pleasant place to live. Having a civic center is part of the equation. Business just can't attract talented young executives if the area is not pleasant. Climate is one factor, one that we can't do anything about. Motorola and General Dynamics built plants in Phoenix because of the climate. But climate isn't enough. Many wouldn't want to go to Phoenix because of the lack of cultural facilities. We're in a good starting position here, but we must move ahead. I have been a strong supporter of the RPI [Rensselaer Polytechnic Institute] Center here because industry needs this kind of thing—a place for their engineers to get their M.A.s and Doctorates. I wanted the center to be right in the downtown area and that's where it will be. . . . Things like the attractiveness of a city often involve intangibles but this is a time when intangibles have become almost tangible. We are one metropolitan area in competition with other metropolitan areas. Some of the politicians can't see this. We tell them, and they smile and nod politely and then don't act. Republicans, Democrats—party doesn't make any difference on this point.

But this relatively recent interest in the general attractiveness of the metropolitan community in which they are based commits them to change of much more fundamental importance to the health of the area, especially of the core city. A banker explained the strong Chamber of Commerce support for a new and ambitious school building program in Hartford: "There is nothing altruistic about this. We [the business community] have a big stake in what happens to the city. If the city decays or explodes, it's bad for us all around." Another, a senior vice president for Aetna (insurance) made the same point: "Why did Hartford business become involved in the issue of racial imbalance? Well, it's good business, for one thing. The businessman's investment in the core cities is jeopardized when the core cities are permitted to slide toward decay and disintegration." The important point, of course, is that activity on behalf of better housing, better education, integration, and nondiscrimination are seen as perfectly consistent with their interests as businessmen.

A politics of affluence is not a disinterested politics. Rather, the shape of compelling interests changes. What would be luxury concerns in another period became "necessities." Why should the executives of Travelers and Aetna concern themselves with what happens in the North End of Hartford? Their counterparts in other periods certainly were not notably sensitive to the needs of the urban poor. The paid manager of the corporation in Hartford today cares what his city looks like, enjoys having it cited in the *National Civic Review* and *Look* as "dynamic" and "progressive." And he has come to believe that the building of a better community will not cost him anything essential. He is not obsessed with a "rich-poor" struggle. The affluent society is beyond that. There are some basic community values that benefit all or nearly all including, perhaps incidentally, the Negroes of the North End. And in the pursuit of these community values, he not infrequently becomes a socially progressive force.

There is still substantial conflict in Hartford of the kind the C.D. orders. It can be found in problems of race and poverty. Negroes in Hartford, as in other American cities, have found themselves repeatedly victimized. Rent gouging, for example, is a continuing problem. A drab four-room apartment in a deteriorating building in Hartford's North End may cost $140 a month, while a white family rents four rooms in a much more attractive suburban setting for $120. In the spring of 1966, a detailed American Public Health Association (APHA) survey of every room and every building within proposed redevelopment areas in North Hartford found between 70 and 85 per cent of the housing units substandard. A population confined to a deteriorating neighborhood in the central city not infrequently pays high rent for its substandard housing. In March, 1966, Hartford became the first city in Connecticut to adopt a state rent receivership law as a local ordinance and to set up the machinery to implement it.[8] Very little has been done with this sweeping ordinance. Around situations such as this, there is conflict of the kind the C.D. embraces.

Hartford is in the middle of an ambitious redevelopment program, and a matter of priorities frequently arises: making land available for commercial development or expanding the amount of attractive low income housing. In 1961, the city completed a massive and long-delayed property reassessment, and charges and countercharges were exchanged over the fair-

[8] Under this ordinance, if inspectors from the city's housing authority find that the owner of a tenement house fails to correct fire hazards or other serious threats to life, health, or safety within a reasonable time, the city's corporation counsel may ask the Court of Common Pleas for a "show cause" order. This compels the property owner to appear in court within five days to show cause why the city should not be given the right to collect all rents and profits from the buildings and use this money for correction of the hazards. The rent receivership petition is to be given precedence over other business of the court. The state law puts strong emphasis on speed of action.

ness of the revaluation.[9] One fact clearly emerges from the tangle: that reassessment brought into conflict the interests of Hartford's extremely influential business community and those of the city's small property holders. Our point here is simply that conflict situations nourishing divisions of the liberal-conservative type are not hard to locate, and they almost certainly will never disappear. But in the agenda of politics in which the Hartford region now finds itself, they typically are not the most central.

Today a large portion of the working class sees its demands broadly satisfied. Economic discontents are muffled in a blanket of affluence that has opened to a very large segment of the population a range of consumption that was previously limited to a narrow elite. Not since the Civil War has the middle appeared so large and the extremes so small. The new marginal "haves" do not sustain pressure for popular change. On the contrary, they often resist it. For the frontier of popular change no longer pits a white working class against a white middle class, but typically sets white lower and lower-middle groupings against a black lower class. The new marginal "haves" find threats to property and status in the demands of a great mass of urban black "have-nots." The resistance ranges from passivity (refusal to strike alliances with Negro Americans) to what we have called popular reactionism. At the same time, a large segment of that socioeconomic group which earlier nourished conservatism finds itself in an age of affluence willing to endorse change to better harness technology on behalf of a generally more attractive society.

[9] Revaluation of all real property in the city was started by Valuation Associates Incorporated in April, 1960, under a $187,500 contract. The matter of the fairness of the reassessment was made a prominent issue in the 1961 City Council campaign, principally by Councilman George Ritter. Ritter charged repeatedly that moderate and low-priced dwellings in Hartford were being increased in valuation by very substantial margins—frequently in excess of 50%—through the method being used by the city's assessor, while downtown business valuation was being substantially reduced.

What, then, is the primary axis of ideological conflict in Greater Hartford? Broadly stated, our conclusions are that the most comprehensive axis separates *Cosmopolitanism* from *Parochialism*. The precise dimensions of these ideologies can now be sketched.

We were first struck by the inordinate complexity of the principal sociopolitical problems posed in the Hartford region. Their greater complexity testifies in part to the greater complexity of the society itself: metropolitanized, the economy far more integrated, in almost every sense more interdependent. It results, too, from the growing preoccupation of a highly developed system with "fine adjustments." But above all, the greater complexity of the major problems with which Hartford elites must deal follows from an enormous expansion of the public sector and the insistence that this society ought to be able to resolve a host of problems that previously were considered beyond reach; in short, the recognition *as problems to which the political system should respond* of things that less affluent and less technologically advanced societies looked upon simply as the woes of mankind.

The "race problem" posed in Greater Hartford is not of such elemental simplicity as was lynching.[10] Instead it asks whether Negro pupils should be bused from their neighborhoods to integrate schools despite segregated residential areas. What should be done about the growth of the Negro ghetto? How can the unemployment rate of Negro Americans, two and one half times that of whites in Hartford as nationally, be lowered? How can the income of Negro families, only 60 per cent of white family income in the Hartford SMSA, be brought up to parity? Such problems in one sense are not new: Negro Americans, for example, have always been economically disadvantaged. But

[10] To describe a problem as of "elemental simplicity" is not to minimize the difficulties confronting those who try to resolve it. But certainly the nature of the lynching problem—and this was a central concern of the civil rights movement in the 1920's and 1930's—was not hard to comprehend.

in another sense they are new, for only recently have they been seen as inequities for which the political system should supply solutions.

As problems become more complex, so the matter of their comprehension becomes more important in distinguishing responses. Victor Palmieri has described the city of the near future as "a black island spreading like a giant ink blot over the heart of a metropolis which is bankrupt financially and paralyzed politically."[11] The political leadership of Greater Hartford is divided into two groups: one comprehends this situation and its component problems and can at least envision the outline that the necessary response must assume; the other cannot comprehend either the scope of the problem or of the needed response.

We are not merely distinguishing between the bright and the not so bright. There have always been differences in ability among leaders. In the same sense, the quality and quantity of available information have always been important but are not what we are referring to here. The ideational axis we shall call *comprehension* vs. *noncomprehension* owes its centrality to the enormous expansion of the public sector in the metropolitan region, the close connection of issues of metropolitan politics to those of national politics, the awful complexity of these problems, the growth of knowledge about them, and the existence of physical resources often sufficient to their solution. At a conference held in Hartford in March, 1967, on "Racial Imbalance and Education in the City," vice presidents of Aetna Life and Casualty, officials from the Connecticut Department of Education, the United States Office of Education and the educational department of the AFL-CIO, leaders of civil rights organizations, and superintendents of municipal school systems found themselves "talking the same language." They agreed in both analysis and prescription with reference to problems at-

[11] Victor Palmieri, "The Future of Our Cities," *Center Diary*, XVI (January–February, 1967), p. 25. (The *Center Diary* is a publication of the Center for the Study of Democratic Institutions.)

tending the growing racial imbalance in city schools. The effects of ghetto education on students, the possibility of significant educational advantages through busing Negro pupils out of the ghetto, the demands for new teaching methods and restructured curricula in racially impacted schools, the possibilities through metropolitan school consolidation of reducing the exodus of whites from central cities: *knowing* here does not assure a "proper" response, but it does make for a set of responses dramatically different from those of leaders not understanding either the depth of the problem or the possibilities in solution. For a host of major urban problems such as the plight of the poor, urban redevelopment, and better job opportunities for Negroes, the key question often is not "Is the leader liberally or conservatively inclined?" but rather "Is he conversant with the body of expert knowledge dealing with these problems?"

We detected another axis closely related to the one identified in terms of comprehension. Political leadership in Greater Hartford is fractured by what could be called "two cultures": those who comprehend a new scientific culture, statement, or orthodoxy, and those who do not. The boundaries of this "scientific" culture are broad, and they include the "world view" of the contemporary physical, biological, and social sciences.[12] Increased attention has been given to the divide between the scientific statement (understood as the current state of the orthodoxy) and everything else (labeled here as pre-science). For example, David Apter has written that

> this distinction reflects itself more and more in a division between a scientific elite and the rest of the community. . . . Any political conflict quickly becomes a problem of evaluating evidence. . . . Modern society, then, is composed of a small but powerful group of intellectually participant citizens, trained, educated, and sophisti-

[12] We place quotation marks around "scientific" from time to time only to indicate that the popular equation of science and truth is not intended. The best scientific thought is culture-bound and, to some degree, "interested" thought.

cated, while all others are reduced in stature if they are scientifically illiterate. . . . The new "ideology" is increasingly rooted in a professional cadre of highly trained men.[13]

There is a scientific statement on how this system should function. A conference is held to discuss problems of the core city and the need for metropolitan cooperation; business executives, city managers, federal government officials, and college professors find they can readily accept a "scientific" statement both of the nature of the problems and how they should be met. They find, too, that differences among them as liberals and conservatives appear much less imposing than differences between them and those not sharing in this scientific view of urban problems. A conference is held to discuss the employment problems of Negro Americans; and again social scientists, bankers, antipoverty officials, and members of a state civil rights commission conceptualize the problem before them in the same way. They accept a "scientific" analysis of the causes of poverty in nonwhite America, and the "scientifically" valid solutions to it.

What are the sources of poverty? The scientific orthodoxy speaks of the cycle of poverty; of a socialization of the children of the poor so as to stifle expectations, which is to say, to crush motivation; of cultural deprivation which is not met by welfare checks. It speaks of the difficulty in ending the cycle and of the poor as victims not of the machinations of the rich but of the cycle itself. This analysis of the causes commits us to specific categories of societal response. The older orthodoxies, on the other hand, hold up quite different pictures of the causes of poverty, portraying it largely in terms of redistribution. Such descriptions typically cut two ways: either poverty is seen to result from the hoarding of the rich, and hence is resolvable through redistribution; or the poor are depicted as victims of their own sloth and lack of talent, and their continuing efforts to take from the industrious the fruits of honest toil and thereby

[13] David Apter, "Ideology and Discontent," an introductory essay in *Ideology and Discontent*, pp. 30–31.

to destroy incentive are to be stoutly resisted. These older orthodoxies are not mere straw men; they, primarily the latter, are broadly accepted by a significant segment of Hartford leadership, especially of the lower-middle-class, small business and professional men who staff the dominant Democratic party organization in Hartford.

The new scientific statement, like its earlier rivals, is essentially ideological: it specifies responses to a wide range of major political problems that collectively define the nature of the "good society." It is shared by people from whom we have been taught to expect—and who until fairly recently did in fact reflect—sharply divergent ideological positions: "conservative" corporation officials and "liberal" college professors. This scientific community is separated from those who do not comprehend the new orthodoxy by a very wide chasm, and this division intrudes with increasing frequency in a series of major national problems.

We located a third ideational axis in the division between local and cosmopolitan perspectives. Robert Merton first introduced this distinction between cosmopolitans and locals, applying it to community elites to identify different orientations to the local community.[14] Locals are far more attached to their town and draw their influence, Merton observed, from an elaborate network of personal ties and friendships. In contrast, the cosmopolitan gains his influence from the high prestige, skills, and experience that his corporate or professional position confers upon him. He went on:

> The localite largely confines his interests to this community. Rovere is essentially his world. Devoting little thought or energy to the great society, he is preoccupied with local problems, to the virtual exclusion of the national and international scene. He is, strictly speaking, parochial. Contrariwise with the cosmopolitan type. He

[14] Robert Merton, "Patterns of Influence: Local and Cosmopolitan Influentials," in *Social Theory and Social Structure* (Glencoe, Ill.: Free Press, 1957), pp. 387–420.

has some interests in Rovere and must of course maintain a minimum of relations with the community since he, too, exerts influence there. But he is also oriented significantly to the world outside Rovere, and regards himself as an integral part of that world. He resides in Rovere but lives in the great society. If the local type is parochial, the cosmopolitan is ecumenical.[15]

Ever since Merton introduced this polarity, social scientists have been turning to it, finding it a useful conceptual tool for ordering variations in the ideational responses of community leaders. Thomas Dye explained conflict over metropolitan-wide approaches to urban problems in terms of the polarity.[16] Dobriner hypothesized that cosmopolitan orientations are largely a function of metropolitan experience, (and local of the rural small town), and thus that as small towns are engulfed in expanding metropolitan regions they typically experience sharp cosmopolitan-local conflict between the new suburbanites and the old villagers.[17] Gans related cosmopolitanism and localism to policy choice in Levittown, New Jersey. For example, he found that cosmopolitans wanted a high quality school system to prepare their children for the best universities and professional careers. They thought in terms of nationwide competition for admission to prestigious universities. On the other side were those who had spent all their lives in the area, who were strongly attached to the township, and who were quite satisfied with the local colleges.[18] And Ritchie Lowry, in his study of leadership and ideology in Chico, California, took Merton's local-cosmopolitan polarity and linked it to "two cultural orientations," one which he called Conservative, the other Utopian. This yielded what was, in effect, a typology of commu-

[15] *Ibid.*, p. 393.

[16] Thomas Dye, "The Local-Cosmopolitan Dimension and The Study of Urban Politics," *Social Forces,* XLI (March, 1963), 239–246.

[17] William Dobriner, "Local and Cosmopolitan as Contemporary Suburban Character Types," in Dobriner (ed.), *The Suburban Community* (New York: G. P. Putnam's Sons, 1958), pp. 132–143.

[18] Herbert Gans, *The Levittowners* (New York: Pantheon, 1967), esp. pp. 346–349.

nity ideology which Lowry found useful to ordering conflict in this northern California community.[19] Implicit in each of these studies, we might add, was the assumption that the C.D. could not adequately account for the ideational divisions detected.

Merton's focus was on the bases of different patterns of influence. But the same factors provide for divergent ideational responses, and these ideational responses are what concern us here. We found cosmopolitan and local responses differentiated principally by three characteristics.

(1) *Types of political information.* There are well-informed locals and cosmopolitans who are poorly informed. It is not the amount of information which distinguishes these positions. But some community leaders deal primarily in "inside dope" about community affairs. They are informed about the history of the community, about the town's controversies extending back in time. They know who said what, when. They are informed about the personal traits of other notables, about their foibles —they know "where the skeletons are." Their information, then, is of the immediate and the concrete, of personalities, of the rich, intimate detail of community life. Another group, the counterparts of Merton's cosmopolitans, are knowledgeable about different things, are little interested in "inside dope" on community controversies. Their familiarity is with the broad, more abstract issues of national and international politics. Typically, they become conversant with local issues only when these "connect up" with national politics.

(2) *The evaluational context.* The Hartford cosmopolitan evaluates the adequacy of his area's response to public problems against the background of the responses of regions across the country. He measures present activity in Hartford against what is being done in Minneapolis and Miami and Seattle. The local typically compares the city's current activity to that of its historical past. This matter of the evaluational context is a sur-

[19] Ritchie Lowry, *Who's Running This Town?* (New York: Harper & Row, 1965), pp. 121–159.

prisingly important ideational component and intrudes in discussions of a wide range of public questions. The distinction can easily be overdrawn. There are few city-wide leaders in Hartford who are totally unaware of the activity of other metropolitan regions in meeting common problems. Still, the evaluational context for a broad segment of the city's leadership including, for example, most of the Hartford Common Council, is the city itself and what has been done there, not the larger world of metropolitan experience and change outside.

(3) *The town vs. the region.* The local's political vision does not penetrate the boundaries of his town. The Bloomfield local, for example, is so completely town-oriented that he does not recognize any need for steps toward more regional planning, coordination, cooperation, or consolidation. He considers the town's boundaries realistic, and emphasizes the intimacy and responsiveness of local government as it is now constituted. As one locally oriented leader put it, "the way things are I know who to call when something comes up. And I know I will get a hearing. I think it would be dangerous to set that [regional government] up. It would be too remote and impersonal." The cosmopolitan response often acknowledges this value, but goes on to insist that without adequate regional planning and cooperation some parts of the region, especially the old central city, must bear inordinate burdens. Problems such as racial imbalance in housing and schools have been created by fundamental national changes, and national and regional attack is called for.

This ideational component does not appear to involve in any way "selfishness" and "altruism." To the cosmopolitan, racial imbalance in the Hartford schools is a problem affecting all who work in the region: concentration of Negroes pushes city schools past the "tipping point" contributing to the exodus of whites from the city, and this in turn helps to create the partial vacuum that expands the ghetto. It is certainly possible to arrive at this position without much empathy or sympathy with the Negroes of Hartford's North End. The cosmopolitan response insists that desirable public values—broadly, an attractive, pleasant, and relaxed metropolitan area—cannot be realized without some commitment to regionalism.

The cosmopolitanism-localism division subsumes a surprisingly large amount of continuing ideational conflict in Hartford. For example, the professional administrators of city government and the party leadership are sharply distinguished by this ideational axis, the former of cosmopolitan orientations, the latter locals. At the same time, there are no systematic and consistent differences between these two groups of leaders of a liberal-conservative variety.

A fourth ideational axis was located in conflict arising from what is called *status politics*. Status politics, we have noted, refers to a situation in which people project worries and concerns about their social status onto political objects. Such status concerns become especially acute in an egalitarian society, which of course opens the entire population to status mobility, when most people are freed from the most pressing economic worries.

In an era of class politics, business and labor were at opposite poles, and "liberal vs. conservative" was the ideological statement of their differences. The businessman was in competition with labor for pieces of an economic pie not large enough to go around and generally resisted measures to redistribute economic values. He felt threatened by such demands. But in an era of status politics, quite different collections of individuals are threatened by demands for popular change. The most persistent pressures for popular change in Hartford today come from Negroes, and the weight of these—in housing and schools, for example—falls largely on the common man of the metropolitan region, white "haves" of marginal socioeconomic status. Who has something to lose from efforts to integrate the Hartford school system, that is, from busing Negroes into the South End? Not Chamber of Commerce executives, ensconced in

$75,000 houses in two-acre zones in the suburbs, their children attending elite private schools. This is putting it much too crudely. But it is clear that demands for change in the metropolitan region thrust status concerns to the fore and bifurcate metropolitan political elites into those of marginal and those of relatively secure status; and the C.D. tells us little about the ideational responses generated around this bifurcation.

The Chamber of Commerce of Hartford in the 1960's has urged such programs and projects as low-rent integrated housing and setting up a corporation to promote it; the busing of Negro children from declining neighborhoods in Hartford to schools outside, including suburban schools; greater employment opportunities for Negroes; and much greater expenditures for public schools in the city. The columnist Stewart Alsop came to Hartford, at the urging of his brother John who is an insurance executive there, and left to write a piece for the *Saturday Evening Post* in which he waxed lyrical about the Hartford Chamber. They "have begun to talk like a bunch of damn New Deal spenders," and in this there is great hope for urban America. If cities are to be saved, Alsop concluded, it will be only with the help of enlightened business communities like that of Hartford.

Hartford has, of course, many real problems which its business community is doing nothing about. Businessmen have not suddenly lost sight of their economic interests, and when these conflict with the needs of other segments of the community, they can be expected to pursue their interests against the other parties. We are not urging bouquets for business, but the recognition that in an age of affluence status remains in seriously short supply and many perplexing domestic problems come to hinge on status concerns; and that in this situation those of secure status—and corporation officials are but one group—can afford to be and so become the "progressives" while those of marginal status must resist this "progress." The South End Democrat insists that Negroes should "stay where they belong";

and corporation officials find themselves cast in what is for business historically an anomalous role; they become, perhaps in spite of themselves, a socially progressive force.[20]

Each of these four ideational axes alone is substantially comprehensive. But we found that we had located much greater economies of organization and description than initially anticipated since each division overlaps all the others. What we have been describing as four different axes in fact can be seen as four dimensions of a single axis. The ideational positions described in terms of *noncomprehension, pre-science, localism,* and *marginal status* are four dimensions of a single response. The same is true for the ideational antagonists of each. What is thus defined is an ideological polarity of substantial breadth, range, and integration. We have called it *Cosmopolitanism–Parochialism.* Our argument here is primarily on empirical grounds: in interviews with metropolitan elites the overlap was found to regularly occur. The positions in fact go together.

We can suggest why. There is in Hartford (and other metropolitan regions) a group of high-status leaders who hold secure positions in well-established corporate entities: professional government administrators, business executives, educators, the upper professional stratum generally. Highly educated, they tend to share a common "scientific" analysis of the inordinately complex national problems which Hartford is required to resolve; and they are committed by their understanding and command of the orthodoxies of contemporary science to certain solutions. As high-status persons, they are little threatened by the demands made by the "have-nots" of the region and to a degree commit themselves to "scientifically" valid responses to these demands. Their training and occupations bring them in touch with national experience, and give them cosmopolitan contacts and perspectives. They must reside in the metropolitan region, and

[20] To call them "socially progressive" is not to claim that the solutions which they are willing to support are adequate, or what Hartford's Negro leadership favors. We found few white leaders in Hartford who really support the demands of the more aggressive Negro leadership.

as affluent metropolitan dwellers can afford and are interested in purchasing regional attractiveness and tranquility.

Confronting these Cosmopolitans is another loose collection of Hartford leaders whose attachments are largely local. They are, typically, small businessmen and locally-oriented professionals who have spent all or most of their lives in the community and whose horizons and connections are narrow and limited to it. Their orthodoxies—partly due to less formal training and partly because of their associations and contacts—are the older "prescientific" ones. They have influence not because of expertise or controlling positions in major corporate structures, but because of personal characteristics—their friendships and associations with the common men (typically as voters) of the community. They reflect the hostility of their marginally "have" constituents to demands for change which threaten their economic position or social status. They cannot afford many of the values which matter to high-SES Cosmopolitans. In short, Cosmopolitanism and Parochialism are relatively constrained idea systems because they speak for two broad social groupings.

Cosmopolitanism and *Parochialism* as used here are ideological categories, referring to two sets of positions on a wide range of matters on public policy. Although the terminology invites confusion with prior usage, it seems admirably suited to conveying the dominant features of these ideological positions. But Cosmopolitanism and Parochialism are hard to discuss. The labels we have introduced are not in circulation. Although leaders in Greater Hartford with few exceptions insist that the C.D. does not comprehend the divisions they see and often confuses more than it clarifies, it is popularly recognized and some general sorts of meaning are widely agreed upon. There is growing ideological conflict in Hartford of the kind we have labeled Cosmopolitan and Parochial. The policy elements in each form interrelated systems because they flow from the different interests, cognitions, and orientations of two segments of community leadership. Our survey work makes it clear that community leaders do recognize the type of conflict to which our categories point, while themselves referring to it with a variety of terms and phrases. Most grope, but at least a few bring it to a high level of articulation. And a growing literature on community ideology strongly suggests that the polarity we have located in the Hartford area is of much wider relevance, and possibly national. But there are no commonly recognized terms referring to this polarity.

The extreme diffuseness of the new ideologies adds to the difficulty in describing them. The older class or economic ideologies have been generated by a fairly specific set of dollar interests. They have spoken to these interests and thus gained focus. But status groups such as Cosmopolitans and Parochials simply do not have so clearly delimited packages of objectives. They conceptualize problems differently, bringing to them different perspectives and conflicting types of information. They have different stakes in certain aspects of social, economic, and political change. But the sources are diffuse. And the new ideologies lack a definitive statement in a sacred lore. Cosmopolitanism does emerge in a literature: the literature on the organization of the metropolitan region; the literature of social science on the sources and dimensions of the "race problem" in America; the literature of the new economics on the role of government in economic life. But there is little likelihood that it will be brought to a consolidated statement.

The content of Cosmopolitanism and Parochialism is especially hard to treat because these positions are not defined around neatly dichotomized responses. The liberal can be said to favor more government aid for the disadvantaged, and the conservative less; and while this is too simple it does describe the core of one type of conflict situation. But Cosmopolitanism is not "more" and Parochialism "less" on any single dimension. One example developed in some detail will serve to clarify this point. More than half of the public school population of Hartford is nonwhite. These pupils mostly attend, because of segregated residential patterns, *de facto* segregated schools.[21] And the nonwhite enrollment has been growing at a yearly rate of four to five per cent. What should be the response to this? The question was discussed at length with each respondent in our leadership survey, and we have summarized the replies of two respondents, one a Cosmopolitan whom we will call Simpson, and the other a Parochial here called Fillmore.[22]

Simpson discussed at some length the "damage done the student" in *de facto* segregated schools. He was able to cite a report showing that pupils in the predominantly Negro schools of the city after five years in school were a year and a half behind the Hartford average in reading achievement, spelling, and word knowledge. He discussed possible remedies for what he considered an evident wrong: open enrollment, educational parks, Princeton Plans and busing. Here, he expressed strong support for the recommendations of the "Harvard Report" [prepared for the Hartford Board of Education by the Center for Field Studies of the Harvard Graduate School of Education in 1965] calling for the busing of Negro pupils out of schools in North Hartford to suburban school systems, with the number bused to reach 6,000 by 1974.

Simpson is an insurance company executive, about 40, and clearly prides himself on a tough-minded, no-nonsense approach. He went out of his way to disassociate himself from "bleeding heart liberals," who he said "never get anything done." He did not seem to empathize very strongly with North End Negroes. "My support for busing is simple enough. We know we can get better education by busing the kids out. There is nothing sacred about town lines, and the problem must be met on a region-wide basis. Busing will be good for the 'monocultural' suburban schools as well. And we must begin to attack the problem of the North End or the lid will blow off."

[21] Specifically, 55% of the 27,100 students enrolled in the city's public schools September 27, 1967, were nonwhites (44.3% Negro, 11.1% Puerto Rican). The concentration by race is marked: 18 of the K-8 schools in September, 1967, were either more than 80% nonwhite or more than 80% white (Release of The Research Department, Hartford Public Schools).

[22] These summaries were prepared from the interview protocols. The principal investigator is speaking.

Simpson discussed the great difficulties faced in getting the small pilot busing program operating [255 Negroes bused to five suburbs in 1966–67, in "Project Concern."] He had worked with other area leaders and State Department of Education officials in getting the program started.

Fillmore "frankly [doesn't] understand what they expect to gain from busing." "When I went to school the facilities weren't nearly as good as those kids [North End Negroes] have now. . . . If there are any gaps in the education given in the North End, well, let's spend some more money to take care of the problem. You won't do much by getting the kids up early to drive them out to a suburb where they will feel they don't really belong. I know I would feel that way—out of place." On three occasions in the interview, Fillmore asked the interviewer, with no apparent sarcasm, to tell him just what advantages the proponents of busing hoped to gain.

In the middle of this discussion Fillmore suddenly volunteered that he had recently taken a "tour of the North End slums sponsored for area leaders (he operates a retail business and is active in Democratic politics in Bloomfield) by the State Welfare Department. "It was a real eye opener," he said. "Things are really bad. A lot may be lazy but a lot have had bad breaks." What should be done? "Well, I just don't know. But people shouldn't have to live like that."

"People work hard to buy their own homes in the suburbs," Fillmore went on. "Of course they don't want the kids of other people who haven't done the work to be brought in with their kids. Why should the others expect to be given this on a silver platter?" Are people afraid of busing? "Well, not in the sense of the little kids hurting anyone. You know, they're [the Negro children bused in] only little ones. But people have a right to be upset about some others getting what they have worked for without doing anything."

These two leaders are similarly divided on most of the important issues before Hartford, and only confusion results when their differences are somehow squeezed into the Conventional Dichotomy. Fillmore finds busing vaguely threatening, while Simpson has no reason to. They apply different orthodoxies in evaluating racial segregation in the schools. And Fillmore looks back to his own educational experience as a boy for guidelines just as Simpson looks to the response to *de facto* segregation of Princeton and Berkeley.

Ideological divisions of the liberal-conservative variety, we have noted, do not disappear. The new polarity demands attention because it is assuming centrality, but we have paid disproportionate attention to it because it is not nearly so well understood as the C.D. In fact, as Chapters 7 and 8 will demonstrate, the most efficient and thorough ordering of conflict in Greater Hartford is achieved by combining or linking the constraints of the two polarities, producing hyphenate ideologies (see Diagram 5).

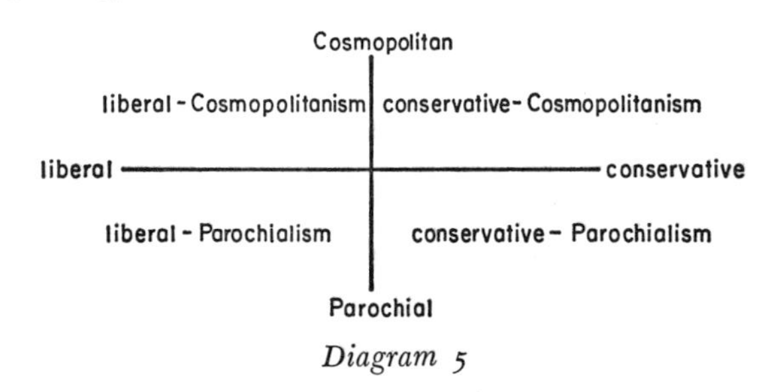

Diagram 5

Here, we have sought only to introduce the new polarity, to suggest its sources, to indicate its growing influence in ordering conflict in the Hartford region. Increasingly, the conservative-Cosmopolitan finds more in common with the liberal-Cosmopolitan than with the conservative-Parochial. A division in the Hartford business community provides a good illustration of this.

Business in the United States has always been fractured into groups defined by size, region, and production. R. Joseph Monsen and Mark Cannon in *The Makers of Public Policy* (New York: McGraw-Hill, 1965) emphasize the familiar distinction between small-business ideology and managerial ideology. But the Cosmopolitan manager of a major corporation and the Parochial owner of a small business (both typically conservatives in the older polarity) are being pushed further apart. We interviewed a top executive of a major bank, and he interrupted the interview to talk by telephone to the head of a federal agency. The federal administrator wanted to fly in with a team to observe a local, privately-sponsored conference on equal employment opportunities, to be held for the benefit of high school guidance counselors. The banker chatted amiably with the federal official and made reference to a conversation he had earlier with "Frank" Roosevelt, then head of the Equal Employment Opportunity Commission. Putting down the telephone, the banker said that he liked working with federal officials. They talk the same language. The federal officials are informed, "on top of problems." The great divide was between him and small businessmen, not between him and the officials in Washington:

> Let me give you an example. There is before Congress [this was April, 1966] a so-called "cease and desist" measure that would permit the federal agencies supervising banks to move in and issue cease and desist orders to state chartered banks that are engaging in unsafe and unsound banking practices. Now these state banks are for the most part supervised by state banking commissioners. There are a lot of small bankers who are really ignorant people, whose banks are pretty shoddy operations, and there are a lot of state banking commissioners who don't know very much either, or who play footsie with these bankers. I've just been to a conference of the American Bankers Association and have heard a lot of these people hollering about federal intrusion, about preserving states' rights, and so on. The National Association of Supervisors of State Banks are making a lot of this. This is nonsense. We support the "cease and desist" bill. There is a need for some federal intervention here because some states have not been doing their job. The calibre of federal personnel is much higher, and the quality of regulation is better. The state banks need this regulation.

The executive of the large bank sides with the federal government against the small banker. There is no place in his ideology for "states' rights," or the "evils of federal regulation," and he has even given up the rhetoric.[23] Big bankers hobnob with top federal officials, and they often find that people like "Frank" Roosevelt really aren't bad sorts. For the small banker, "Frank" Roosevelt and the federal government are mysterious and powerful forces in far-off Washington. Our big banker is a Cosmopolitan, and often finds more in common with liberal-Cosmopolitans than conservative-Parochials.

Two reservations need to be added here. First, we are discussing ideological conflict as it takes shape in the agenda of politics of Hartford in the 1960's. If the agenda of politics were markedly different in another metropolitan area—as we expect it is, for example, in Dallas—the shape of ideological cleavage would in turn differ substantially. There is indication that a portion of the Dallas business community is still fighting the battles of the early New Deal, and that the C.D. "fits" much better there than in Hartford.[24] It is likely that the Hartford agenda is more representative of metropolitan America than is Dallas', and we expect, though we cannot demonstrate, that movement is toward the Hartford pattern. But we make no firm claims for our analysis of ideological conflict, (or for the typology describing it), beyond its accuracy for Hartford in the late 1960's. And specifically we caution against applying the typology *directly* to national divisions although, again, we suspect substantial "fit." The constraints of an ideology result from the needs, interests, and cognitions of a social grouping in a particular political setting. Change the setting and the constraints may no longer be present.[25]

[23] Let the federal government propose a type of regulation he finds unpalatable, of course, and he will invoke the litany of private enterprise. We have not moved to a politics beyond self-interest!

[24] See Warren Leslie's popular but informative *Dallas Public and Private* (New York: Grossman, 1964), and R. A. Smith, "How Business Failed Dallas," *Fortune,* July, 1964, pp. 166–170.

[25] Agger, Goldrich, and Swanson, in their study of ideology in four American communities, argue that "the taxonomy constructed for these political ideologies is relevant for national as well as for American local politics. By a consistent substitution of the word 'nation' for the word

Second, we have been describing only the most prominent ideological axis. We do not mean to dismiss other sets of ideational responses: both Hartford and Bloomfield, for example, have a Radical Right and Hartford has a large Negro community, with distinctive ideational configurations. Chapters 6, 7, and 8 treat the detail of the ideational life of our three communities.

Few leaders fit neatly into the new ideological categories, but neither did they into the old. The categories represent, after all, ideal types. What is important is the emergence of the general lines of ideological conflict to which the types refer. We have so long been conditioned to see our elites divided ideologically by matters of political liberalism and conservatism that recognition of the need for substantial modifications of our conceptualization of conflict may come slowly. But in Hartford, as leaders grapple with such problems as urban renewal, poverty, *de facto* school and residential segregation, and the Balkanization of the metropolitan region, the major division with increasing frequency separates those sharing in the new scientific orthodoxy from those who do not comprehend the new and instead invoke an older orthodoxy, between those who understand the demands of a big, complexly integrated, metropolitanized society and those who necessarily cannot, between those who can afford in a period of status politics to strike a tolerant posture toward the demands of "have-nots" and those whose position makes such indulgence appear far too costly.

Other studies, we have noted, have arrived at conclusions similar to ours through different channels. Agger, Goldrich, and Swanson found the C.D. inadequate for an ordering of ideological conflict in two North Carolina and two Oregon

---

'community,' the Progressive Conservatives have their analogue in the Eisenhower administration and the Community Conservationists in Kennedy's New Frontier" (*The Rulers and The Ruled* [New York: John Wiley & Sons, 1964], pp. 31–32). We are less certain, and find the question one for empirical investigation.

communities which they studied. So did Lowry in his Chico, California, investigation. Agger and his colleagues introduced a typology strikingly similar to ours in many important regards. Their "Progressive Conservatives" and "Community Conservationists" appear to be functionally close to our conservative-Cosmopolitans, although the authors constructed their typology quite differently.[26] And Lowry's "Conservative-Local" seems to refer to a response resembling our conservative-Parochialism in some regards, as his "Utopian-Cosmopolitan" points to certain of the dimensions encompassed by liberal-Cosmopolitanism.[27] Again, the differences in construction are very great, and we are only suggesting here that investigators in quite different community settings are locating broad similarities in the structure of ideological conflict. There is growing recognition that the Conventional Dichotomy does not closely fit conflict in the new society.

[26] Agger *et al., op. cit.,* esp. pp. 14–32.
[27] Lowry, *op. cit.,* pp. 121–159.

6. Putnam: The Ideational Life of an American Small Town

What, politically, do Putnamites talk about, argue about, and concern themselves with? What are the contending policy positions? How do the political leaders of this small town see their community's problems? How do they organize conflict? What, if any, abstract conceptual dimensions are used to describe it? What are the principal sociopolitical groups in Putnam, and what distinguishes—if anything does—their ideational orientations? What, in short, is the fabric of community ideational life?

Granville Hicks in his *Small Town* gently criticized social scientists for not being enough concerned with what people *don't* talk about. He had a point. One of the principal things which Putnamites don't talk about is an ideological dimension of politics. In discussing the political problems of their town and of the country, and in their agreements and disagreements with their fellows, Putnam leaders typically do not impose the overarching dimension of ideology. Their political experience has "taught" them that there is no need to do so.

I. THE TALK IN PUTNAM

What Are the Problems?

What kinds of political problems concern the residents of Putnam? The question was pursued both by listening to what was discussed at meetings of the Board of Aldermen, Board of Education, Rotary, and other government bodies and private groups; and by asking community leaders and a community sample to locate major problem areas and to discuss the actions these demand.

Most discussions of problems in Putnam begin with the flood. The response of Democratic Alderman Thomas Bellerose is typical in the way he saw this 1955 disaster and the subsequent rebuilding. Bellerose is in his sixties and gaunt from recurring illness which has prevented him from working since about 1960; he first took his seat on the Board of Aldermen in 1959 when John Dempsey, the local boy who made good as governor of Connecticut, asked him if he wanted to fill out an unexpired term. He vividly remembers the disaster.

We were on the Gaspé when we first heard about the hurricane, so we got out of there, but it was two days before I could get back to Putnam. When my wife and I got here we could hardly believe what had happened—the main street had been flooded, in some places sand and gravel were eight to ten feet high, parts of the town were under ten or fourteen feet of water. I went down to the railroad where I worked and saw the tracks were under water and the railroad cars were scattered all over the yard. I thought to myself, "That's all for the Town of Putnam."

But it wasn't.

John Dempsey and Bill St. Onge went right to work to get renewal funds and got the ball rolling by 1957. Now we're in great shape, making great progress. Did you see those beautiful parks on either side of the river? And the new shopping center? Things were bad just after the flood, but they're good now. We just haven't any major problems now.

Most Putnamites agree that the flood and the economic dislocation which it caused, coming on the heels of loss of industry, was the real crisis in modern Putnam. And the success of the town in meeting this crisis, in attracting some new small firms and in rebuilding, make it the turning point as well.

When Putnamites ponder the question of change and their community's future, their perspectives are narrowly local: they agree that Putnam in 1967 is clearly better off than it was just after the 1955 flood. They think little of those elements of decline which would certainly strike an outside observer—for example, the relative lack of prosperity of the community and its residents individually when comparison is made to the suburban towns thirty or fifty miles to the west. Bloomfielders, in contrast, are concerned with different dimensions of change. It is true that the suburb radiates white-collar affluence, and attractive homes on well-manicured lots set the tone as much as dull flats do for Putnam. Bloomfield will soon have a redeveloped center done in handsome colonial style. And individually most Bloomfield residents have indeed never had it so good and typically have clearer channels to the new prosperity than most Putnamites. Still, there are anxieties, about riots and crime in the city, about whether these will "catch up" with Bloomfield, about Negroes and their movement around the Hartford region, and indeed about national developments such as war and inflation which loom in Bloomfield's—as in every town's—future. In sum, Putnam and Bloomfield residents concern themselves with quite different dimensions of change, and we thus have the somewhat anomalous picture of prosperous suburbanites less confident about change and their community's future than the small-towners, who are relatively less well-off. We asked the community samples in each town about their hopes for the future.

"What about [this community]? Do you think things will be better, about the same, or not as good ten years from now as they are now?" (Responses are expressed as percentages of *n*.)

	Better	*Same*	*Not as good*	*Undecided*
Putnam (*n* = 335)	78	15	1	6
Bloomfield (*n* = 488)	56	15	18	11

Putnam leaders are satisfied with their town. With the exception of a few "outsiders" who lament a "lack of culture," or monotony, or physical unattractiveness, most Putnamites are content. That "it is a good place to raise kids" is an opinion frequently offered and strongly held. Cities are not good places to raise children. Yes, wages are lower in Putnam but so, it is widely believed, are prices. The town is seen by its leaders and rank and file alike as relaxed and comfortable and tolerant. There are no demonstrations or racial problems in Putnam.

Race is "no problem" in Putnam, of course, for the simple reason that there are only twelve nonwhite families in town. The result of the relative remoteness of racial conflict has been its nearly complete absence from political discussion. The remoteness of racial problems, too, has permitted Putnamites to appear somewhat more receptive to Negro demands than their urban or suburban counterparts.[1] Integration is an "academic" question. How easily this "tolerance by default" could be upset

"Now the civil rights movement all over the country has been very active during the last few years. [This was summer, 1965.] Have Negro Americans been asking for too much, too fast?" (Responses are expressed as percentages of *n*.)

	Yes	*No*
Hartford (n = 529)	63.1	36.9
Bloomfield (n = 379)	50.4	49.6
Putnam (n = 306)	34.9	65.1

was indicated in interviews with leaders and reinterviews with a subset of the original mass sample in 1966 and 1967. The big riots in the summer of 1967 in Newark and Detroit, and smaller ones in cities of closer proximity, especially New Haven and Hartford, suddenly transformed race into a "problem," a topic of attention, though still a remote and minor one. The issue was thrust into the town's public sector in at least a marginal way and thereby lost the element of unreality which had dominated it previously. One leader put it this way: "You know, I

[1] The responses we tabulated are those of white residents only. It is hardly surprising that Negroes responded overwhelmingly in the negative. Fifty-seven Negro respondents in Bloomfield and 144 in Hartford were thus excluded from the tabulation. Also excluded in computing percentages were the *undecided, don't know*, and the *no answer* responses.

got to thinking. Providence, New Haven, Boston, Hartford—we are right in the middle. Sometime it could spread here." He was so concerned that he hurried to take his own informal census of the colored population of Putnam. (He found twelve families.) Another leader confided that were there a substantial influx of nonwhites into Putnam "the reaction would be extremely emotional." One of the original sample reinterviewed in 1967 was a local barber. He was at first reluctant to comment on the riots, but finally agreed. "I have two reactions. *Send 'em back to Africa!* That's one. *Line them up against the wall and shoot them!* That's another." One can allow for his delight in trying to shock through exaggeration and still see substantial change in his response to race relations. Two years earlier he had been talking about "how badly Negroes have been treated" and "how they have a real beef." Still, the nearest concentration of Negroes is forty miles from Putnam, and racial problems remain on the periphery of concern.

The problems which dominate both public and private discussion in Putnam can, for ease of analysis, be divided into three broad groups: "perennial pining," personal and public morality, and taxing and spending.

The problems we identify as "perennial pining" are those everyone talks about and agrees upon the need "to do something about that," but which are not in fact deemed urgent and which few actually expect to change. An example is "providing more opportunities to keep the young in Putnam." Typically, the speaker does not believe that anything much will be done to provide more opportunities for the young in Putnam, nor is he too concerned about the present situation in which most leave. His commentary on the problem is thus essentially ritualistic. He feels he should say, "We need to get better jobs." Or, he commits himself to a proposal which, however admirable, really has very little to do with why most able young people leave small towns: in Putnam, the need for a new youth center thus is often linked to a lack of opportunities for the young which causes their exodus.

Questions of personal and public morality have been a source of constant delight, consternation, and general conversation for Putnam politicians. Often, these deal with alleged sexual or financial indiscretions of individual leaders, but at other times they are somewhat more generalized. As an example of the latter, in 1964 a committee was formed calling itself the Putnam Area Committee for Decent Literature. Its membership was never large and was drawn mostly from French Catholics active in the local Democratic party. The immediate precipitating factors were the location of Henry's magazine shop and Henry's choice of literature. He reportedly was selling dirty books right on the counter, and, worse still, that counter was next door to a Catholic church. The priest thought that someone should clean "this mess" up, and he called on a local attorney who was a parishioner and an active Democratic politician. When the mayor heard of this, however, he cautioned that active association with the antipornography committee could be highly embarrassing, so the attorney turned the project over to his wife. The committee had little success generating interest. They did talk to Henry, and were told that he would take the books off the counter and put them under it, but that he had to sell them as part of a consignment arrangement he had with a Hartford dealer.

The committee brought a few speakers to town and even showed a film on lewd literature. Members talked to the operator of a local drugstore who expressed willingness to cooperate in the battle against smut because "he had only sold twenty-four copies of *Playboy* in the last year." The committee finally came to a sorry end. One of its members, a married woman, was said to be having an affair with a man from a nearby town. The affair culminated in their leaving their respective mates and going off together. One member of the committee expressed how embarrassing this was:

> Whenever I mentioned that we were interested in trying to clean up the literature sold at the stores in town, I was almost always asked whether Mrs. ——— was on the committee. And when I ad-

mitted that she was everyone would say it seemed strange that *she* was interested in getting rid of lewd magazines. And then they would laugh. So we gave the whole thing up. It's too bad though. The committee wasn't on some kind of a witch hunt. We weren't after books that are good literature but just happen to have some sexy stuff. We were after just the real trash.

Between 1964 and 1967, allegations of improper behavior by one local political leader were so common and frequent that it was hard to have a conversation on Putnam's public life without these being brought up. With no intent to exaggerate, we call it *l'affaire Bourgeois.* Recently, Putnam has produced more than its share of successful Connecticut politicians, and it seemed in December, 1963, that another political career was being launched when twenty-nine-year-old Paul Bourgeois was elected to the mayor's chair so recently warmed by Dempsey and St. Onge. Bourgeois was the youngest municipal chief executive in Connecticut and the youngest ever in Putnam. He was attractive, energetic and ambitious. More than a few agreed with the local observer who described Bourgeois as "very dynamic, perhaps the most talented mayor Putnam ever had, in many ways far more talented a man than a town of Putnam's size can normally get." This observer saw Bourgeois' interest in the mayoralty in these terms:

Paul has put in time as mayor far beyond the very modest financial return—fifteen hundred dollars a year. He has done it for the connections it has provided, for ego gratification, for the economic opportunities which it has provided. As things are now [December, 1966] he can walk into Hartford National Bank as the Mayor of Putnam, not simply as Paul Bourgeois, real estate man. This is important. It also has given him opportunities to get into various kinds of developments within the town. But still, Bourgeois has been good for Putnam. He has given good service to the town.

Not long after Bourgeois became mayor, allegations of improprieties began to circulate. They seemed almost endless: that he was using politics for profit, that he was frequently intoxicated and at least once hospitalized for alcoholism, that he had been arrested for drunken driving and had spent a night in the "cooler," and so on. These matters were never investigated and remain only allegations. But *l'affaire Bourgeois* was frequently and intensely discussed. Bourgeois managed to ride out the storm in 1965, and he was renominated by his party and reelected. In 1967, however, it appeared he could go on no longer. Some Democratic leaders professed to continue to like him, others pitied him ("He was brought along too fast." "It's a darn shame that the youngest man ever to be mayor of Putnam will now become a political nonentity.") and many gave him at least grudging credit for energy and for rescuing a languishing redevelopment program; but Bourgeois confronted in September, 1967, a Democratic town committee three to one against him, and alderman-at-large Alfred Dion was endorsed in his place. Congressman St. Onge took the unusual step of placing his prestige on the line, personally appearing and voting against Bourgeois.[2] But though the party wished to be done with him, Bourgeois was not without support. He gathered enough signatures to force a mayoralty primary, and over opposition which read like the "Who's Who" of Putnam, he won the primary 1,000 to 673. His alleged improprieties appear to have troubled middle-class voters more than the working class; he apparently won considerable sympathy from those who felt the party leaders were "ganging up on him when he's down," and the party-

[2] Bourgeois' fall from grace with his party's leaders cannot be attributed entirely to unhappiness about his personal behavior. What appears to have happened is this. Because of the rumors concerning his personal life, the party leadership felt Bourgeois had become something of a liability rather than an asset. State Democrats who at one time considered him to be a promising figure with "a future," had now given up on him. Bourgeois' own ebullience and egotism which once was at least tolerated by more senior Democrats now began to grate. Under criticism, Bourgeois became increasingly waspish. He began to pick fights with other Democratic leaders, and nominated his people for minor positions rather than the party's choices. So by September, 1967, there was little party support left. The Town Committee voted 26 to 5 against Bourgeois on a preliminary move, and the Mayor did not have his name placed in nomination at the meeting. Instead, he challenged the leadership in a primary, and won.

endorsed candidate was a colorless fellow who found it hard to say anything publicly against Bourgeois' actual work as mayor.

In his third two-year term, Bourgeois' troubles multiplied. The Travelers Insurance Company placed a $20,000 attachment on properties which he owned in January, 1968, and charged him with failing to turn in premiums which he had collected as a Travelers agent. On March 5, the Democratic Town Committee denied him a seat. On March 12, the Connecticut Insurance Commissioner suspended indefinitely all of Bourgeois' insurance licenses, as a result of the Travelers action. Then in April, the Society for Savings of Hartford filed a lawsuit against the Mayor, seeking a foreclosure on property which he owned. The bank claimed that no payments had been made for more than six months on a $145,000 mortgage which it held on Bourgeois' property. And a few days later the Democratic Town Committee formally called upon the Mayor to resign for the good of the town.

L'affaire Bourgeois is interesting and revealing, and not, of course, because there is anything unusual about allegations of personal impropriety. These abound in any political setting. But *l'affaire Bourgeois* was nothing less than the dominant political concern in Putnam for three years. The problem of public morality is construed here in its narrowest sense as the alleged improprieties of an officeholder, and it was, in terms of the amount of conversational energy devoted to it in the highest councils of local government, second to no matter before the town. The tendency to see public life largely in terms of the personal conduct or the character of officeholders is common in Putnam and appears in many cases less spectacular than *l'affaire Bourgeois.*

Matters of taxing and spending frequently arise, and while quite limited in scope, they have been intensely debated. Since 1955, the most important of these has involved redevelopment. Wide sections of the downtown area were destroyed in the 1955 flood, and although Putnam moved rapidly to establish a redevelopment agency and to apply for funds, as late as 1962 few tangible results could be seen. The devastated parts of the city's center remained a dusty wasteland filled with weeds. William St. Onge, Putnam's first redevelopment director, then its counsel, and subsequently mayor (1961–1962), became a prime target for those frustrated by the slow pace of redevelopment. St. Onge was elected mayor in 1961 by a margin of only 300 votes, the poorest performance by a Democrat in twenty years.

Criticism of the redevelopment program took several forms. Some had not wanted any program at all and seized on the subsequent lack of progress to embarrass its initiators. There were merchants who had a very direct personal interest, fearing the increased competition which the new shopping center —scheduled to be the major project—would bring. One, for example, had completed repairs on a number of business properties along the river and was quite candid in his opposition to anything threatening this relatively satisfactory source of income. A far more substantial source of opposition, however, was the unwillingness of many to support what seemed to be so large a financial commitment. The question of accepting federal funds was never raised in Putnam. The "conservatism" was not ideological, linking the specific situation to general "encroachments" by the federal government. One Putnam resident described it as "oldtime French-Canadian conservatism": "The mentality of the older French Canadians is still rooted in Quebec, stodgy, conservative, 'I've got a dollar and you won't get it.' The younger French Canadians are much more active and progressive."

But the set of economic attitudes referred to here certainly is not peculiar to one ethnic group. Rather, it is a residue of an older economic orthodoxy, widely held by an old middle class of small business owners. To prosper you save. Confronted with the economic disaster of the flood, some Putnamites answered in the way they had been "taught," retreating to public frugality. They simply could not accept the argument that by "spending" the overall economic position of Putnam could be strengthened. Opposition to establishing a renewal agency in 1956 was led by long-time Putnam Democrat Ferdinand Gagnon, who had been the first to break the Republican political monopoly in the town in the 1930's and who was a highly popular figure among old-timers. Many Putnamites believe that if the flood had not supplied an extreme need to do something, resistance to redevelopment would not have been overcome.

Once approved, redevelopment moved along slowly, but at first it did seem to move. Land acquisition and clearance were signs of action. But after an interested developer was enlisted, nothing further happened although the developer periodically promised action. The redevelopment agency was unhappy but reluctant to release the developer in view of the difficulty they had finding him initially. In the spring of 1961, the local paper editorialized about the low morale of residents and about pessimism bred of delays in the redevelopment program: six years after the flood, restoration and rehabilitation of Putnam had not reached the stage of success necessary to restore faith in the town's future. Republicans bore down hard on Democratic failures in redevelopment in the mayoralty campaign in 1961, scoring "promises but no action on the shopping center" and "too many rumors, too many promises."

> The facts still remain that the economic condition of Putnam is as follows: Increases in taxes from 25 mills to 37 mills since 1957. Loss of population in the city from 8,181 in 1950 to 6,952 in 1960. People do not generally move away from a prosperous city. Employment dropped from 1,610 in 1956 to 1,298 in March 1961. Putnam has the lowest per capita purchasing power of any city in Connecticut.

Two years later, there still were no visible results, and across a sign proclaiming "Coming Soon . . . Putnam Shopping Center" someone painted in large crude figures which appeared to speak for the town, "1955 BAH." Popular indignation over the "desert," as the cleared area came to be called, reached a breaking point; the developer was finally released, and Paul Bourgeois, alderman-at-large between 1961 and 1963 and then mayor, and a prosperous local businesswoman, Mrs. Rose Bove LaRose, took charge. Mrs. LaRose, as Putnam Shopping Center, Inc., submitted a bid for development of the center, and the plans were formally approved in January, 1964. Three months later there was groundbreaking, and to the great satisfaction and astonishment of most Putnamites the center opened in the fall of 1964. By 1965 it had become difficult to find any Putnam political figure who would admit that he ever had objections to anything other than the slowness with which redevelopment progressed. The shopping center and related work, improving an exceedingly drab downtown area and expanding local retail sales, became a source of inordinate pride to townspeople, and redevelopment disappeared as a source of political dispute. The redevelopment agency assured its reputation when in late 1966 it proclaimed the first phase of Putnam's redevelopment completed, with $371,000 unexpended. There was little opposition to the proposal that the principal be retained by the agency toward further renewal.

No issues of taxing and spending have raised broad "philosophical" questions about federal-local relations, or about "private vs. public," as Agger, Goldrich, and Swanson found in two Oregon small towns—"Farmdale" and "Oretown"—in the debate over public vs. private electrical power. There is a continuing division between those willing to tax and spend for "community progress" and others who are reluctant to spend and who minimize the urgency of Putnam's problems.

National problems are discussed in Putnam, but in an infrequent and irregular way. The great issues of national life seem curiously remote. There is a striking deference to the efforts of decision makers in Washington. "President Eisenhower knew best, President Kennedy knew best, and now President Johnson knows best" is the refrain implicit in most of our interviews with local leaders. There was, for example, great unrest over American involvement in Vietnam, but few differed from this assessment by a member of the Putnam Republican Town Committee:

I'm confused, I really don't know what to think about Vietnam. But I have to assume that President Johnson knows what is going on, and if it is an ideological battle, and not just a battlefield, then I guess I'm in favor of our being there. [What does ideological mean?] Well, if it's the Communists we're stopping, and preventing them from infiltrating the South, instead of meeting them over here, then I'm for it, but I still don't like sending our boys over there and having them come back dead or wounded. In fact, I'm confused about the whole cold war—one minute you're bitter enemies, then the next thing you're trying to work together. Maybe I just don't know enough about it. But on Vietnam, I guess I still have to go along with the President.

A small group of the citizenry, mostly Republican professional men and women, object to the activities of the Democratic administrations since 1961 (and, in a tenuous sense, since 1933) on at least quasi-ideological grounds: the government is moving into too many areas where it should not be, spending money for antipoverty and medicare programs, and doing the job badly. But such objections are exceptional. Few Putnamites, for example, saw Medicare, in 1965 when it was being enacted or in 1966 and 1967 when the program was in operation, as an extension of the role of government. Putnam is an old and relatively poor town, and Medicare was welcomed. Such reactions as this one by a Democratic politician are typical:

The next time I see Bill [Second District Congressman William St. Onge] I'm going to ask him if he would introduce a bill to lower the eligible age for Medicare to 62 for disabled persons. I'm 62 and can't work. I've got heart trouble, had it for more than ten years now, at one time the doctors gave me two years to live, but I'm still here. I just tore some ligaments in a shoulder and ripped the oil sac so they had to operate. Then the arthritis set in all my joints and I could hardly move—my hand was paralyzed so bad that when I signed my pension form they sent it back and wanted to know who had signed it. Anyhow, I'm still not eligible for Medicare and had to pay all this out of my pension money.

We must be careful on this point. Medicare was overwhelmingly endorsed by residents of all three of our communities, and indeed by Americans throughout the country.[3] Those raising ideological objections were a distinct minority in Hartford and Bloomfield. But such questions of national policy as medical aid for the aged more frequently were evaluated by the leadership of Putnam in terms of their narrowest and most immediate implications

	"Do you think there are many Communists in the United States?"			"Should anyone who is a Communist be allowed to go about the country freely?"		
	(Responses are expressed as percentages of *n*.)					
	Yes	*No*	*Undecided* and *Don't Know*	*Yes*	*No*	*Undecided* and *Don't Know*
Putnam ($n = 335$)	60	18	22	24	70	6
Hartford ($n = 732$)	52	24	24	24	67	9
Bloomfield ($n = 488$)	39	33	28	39	53	8

The problem of domestic communism has never been a vital one in this parochial, Roman Catholic community. It is not that Putnamites have unusual intellectual tolerance for Communists. Indeed, their responses to two items in the mass survey indicated a "harder" line than in Hartford or Bloomfield. Both Hartford and Bloomfield have small groups of Radical Rightists who, among other things, worry about domestic and international communism; but Putnam has been bypassed almost completely by such activity. One "outsider" was asked what would happen if a public school teacher were to assign a "left wing" magazine to her students.[4] He replied that "nothing would happen because people wouldn't be aware of anything; they

[3] In the summer of 1965, Medicare was endorsed by 74% of our Putnam sample, 75% of the Bloomfield, and 80% of the respondents in Hartford.

[4] We classed as "outsiders" business and professional men who moved to Putnam as adults, already in or launching their careers.

wouldn't recognize a 'left wing' magazine if they saw one." Another respondent, a long-time school teacher in Putnam, looked at it differently: "Why none of our teachers would ever do any such thing. And if people were told that one did, why they just wouldn't believe it." Both responses are probably overstated. It is conceivable that a "brash young fellow" could come to Putnam and to "shake the town up" assign some "far-out" political publication, and thereby generate real static. But this has not happened, partly because Putnam teachers "aren't that way" (the ideologically motivated are unlikely to choose such a town), and partly because virtually no one is thinking or talking about such things and hence searching for some taint.

In 1963, a young Putnamite who was described to us by one local leader, formerly his teacher, as "possessed of great energy but few brains," led opposition to fluoridation of the town's water supply. He made connections with a statewide ultraconservative group which furnished him literature, funds, and speakers to carry on the good fight in Putnam. He and his wife apparently adopted the ideological line of their outside sponsors, for they signed a letter published in the local weekly taking to task the newspaper's meek publisher for his endorsement of fluoridation. The newspaper's editorial was an advocacy, they argued, "of a police state." But though there was real concern in Putnam over fluorides as "poison," no one treated this effort to link fluoridation to a range of right-wing concerns as anything but a joke. Apparently no outside extremist group has attempted to intervene in Putnam since, and the local sponsor plays no role whatever in local politics.

The Use and Comprehension of Abstract Conceptual Dimensions (A.C.D.)

It is a prime characteristic of Putnam political discourse that abstract conceptual categories are either not used at all or carry no broad policy implications. As a former town official put it, "words like conservative or liberal are never used in this town. If someone is out of step with other people, politically, he is called an oddball." Approximately 20 per cent of the Putnam leaders interviewed showed no comprehension of *liberal* and *conservative*.[5] Another 35 per cent attempted a construction of the terms, but it did not make much sense or conform to any of the various constructions commonly placed on the terms. For example, an alderman who described himself as "liberal" went on to define a liberal as "a man who thinks for himself, yet who at the same time is willing to follow responsible party leadership. I follow what the leaders of the Democratic party propose, the programs which men like St. Onge and Dempsey try to get into legislation, but I am not a yes man." Another group, one-third of those interviewed, suggested constructions that were limited, even rudimentary, but which were nonetheless linked to some common usage. One Democratic leader stated that he rarely used *conservative* or *liberal* but

> I have always considered myself to be conservative, long before Senator Goldwater came on the scene. I am a conservative because I believe in reform, but believe in going slow. On the national level there are some things which we can't avoid doing. Medicare and extended social security benefits are necessary. So I am in favor of these things because the people have demanded them. We need these things, and their worth has been tested and the demand is getting greater. I don't want change for change's sake, but I don't want to hinder progress. Some things are inevitable and we must keep looking ahead.

Still another long-time Democratic politico said that if he had to choose a label for himself it would be "moderate," "because

[5] We should explain why leaders in our three communities were asked how they would construe the Conventional Dichotomy and whether they ever used it in political discussion, since in the preceding chapter it was suggested that the C.D. is of declining utility in ordering ideational conflict. The reason is simply that the C.D. remains the most familiar in our ideological lexicon and thereby offers the best opportunity to measure use and comprehension of A.C.D. But every effort was made in the loosely-structured leadership interviews to encourage the respondents to offer any other A.C.D. which they considered of greater utility. In Putnam, no one did.

though I favor progressive ideas I like to look into them before acting. I am conservative to the extent that I hold back from immediate change." This linkage of conservatism and opposition to change or insistence that change be gradual was the most common construction. Many added an additional dimension, that change meant a larger role for government.

Only 10 per cent of the Putnam leaders applied the C.D. confidently to wide-ranging sets of policy positions and to state and national political leaders. And all but one of those showing this widely integrating construction of the C.D. were "outsiders." The "outsiders," business and professional men who came to Putnam as adults and who have found reasonably comfortable economic niches, typically hold positions in local public life because of cosmopolitan skills which have made them useful. But their more cosmopolitan backgrounds at the same time serve to set them apart from the life of the town, and leave them tolerating it and being tolerated by it but not fully part of it. One of the "outsiders" who uses A.C.D. to order a broad range of political events is Dr. Robert Dinolt, a native of Czechoslovakia. Dinolt served as chairman of the town's Planning Commission and gained substantial influence although he still is not "one of us" to many Putnamites. A fellow notable called him a "radical," meaning only, it seemed, that he was highly "un-Putnamish." Dinolt's "accent" was often commented on by those who grew up in French-speaking homes and whose English still shows the effects. In something of the same position as Dinolt is Dr. Henry Johnson, a dentist of Swedish birth who arrived in the United States in 1947 and lived in Fairfield County before coming to Putnam.

We explored in each interview whether the failure of most Putnam leaders to offer broad constructions of the C.D. was merely the result of a lack of skill in verbalization. This problem was approached from several directions. Each respondent was asked whether he would use A.C.D. like liberal and conservative to locate the position of state and national political leaders. How does he categorize (and hence conceptualize) the contending forces in political conflict? Specifically how does he construe liberalism? Conservatism? What political leaders are liberals? Conservatives? What is it that they do or do not do which demands the label? Would the respondent use any A.C.D. to describe the political positions of competing elites locally or nationally? With what understanding? Would the respondent describe himself as a liberal? A conservative? If not, would he use any such conceptual category? Again with what understanding? [6]

Analysis of this interview data makes it clear that most Putnam leaders rarely if ever apply such categories, either formally articulated or informally conceived, to political life. They had, on occasion, heard the C.D. mentioned, as in newspaper descriptions of Goldwater as a conservative, and in our interviews many were willing to make an attempt at construing the terms. Some loose style categories with an ideational component like *progressive* are used in Putnam political discourse, with the progressive one willing to do things to make Putnam a little more attractive, to bring in industry, to provide better facilities for recreation. Phrases like "stuck in the mud" are applied by progressives to describe opponents unwilling to exercise themselves on behalf of such changes. But Putnam leaders are unanimous in their claim that the C.D. simply never is used in local political discourse, nor are any other comparable categories. And abstract conceptual dimensions of the kind associated with ideology are generally seen irrelevant to the ebb and flow of Putnam political life.

We can now summarize a little more precisely our findings with regard to the use and comprehension of abstract conceptual dimensions by Putnam elites:

Does not use A.C.D.; no comprehension of the C.D. or any other	(n = 11)	20%

[6] For a more complete statement, see the interview guide reprinted in the Appendix.

Does not use A.C.D.; construed the C.D. with minimal rigor and coherence	(n = 20)	36%
Limited use of A.C.D.; rudimentary but fully, coherent constructions of the C.D.	(n = 18)	33%
Frequent use of A.C.D.; a widely-integrating construction of the C.D.	(n = 6)	11%

The Political Struggle: The View from Putnam

What, for Putnamites, is political conflict all about? Exposure to the public life of Putnam hardly encourages an idealism: no Putnamite whom we interviewed saw conflict in his town between the forces of light and those of darkness. No one believed his enemies wholly perfidious, and no one seemed to expect that anything would be much better, except insofar as it is amenable to economics: that is, the economic position of the town was thought to be markedly improving. Putnam ideational life differs from that of both Bloomfield and Hartford in its closeness to the earth, in its almost absolute rejection of bold vistas. In reading over nearly nine hundred pages of interview protocols, it is striking to find that no leader ever claimed he was backing a measure to improve markedly the quality of life of a group of Putnam residents. In the city and the suburb, leaders often spoke strongly of the plight of a particular group, such as Negro Americans, and urged programs which, if implemented over rather sinister opposition, could yield great benefits. Not so in Putnam. To be sure, leaders there claimed that specific proposals would produce certain gains: consolidation of town and city, for example, would make for greater efficiency in government. But the benefits were seen to be quite immediate and limited. Also unlike Hartford and Bloomfield, no Putnam leader ever suggested that he was acting disinterestedly on behalf of others. No one saw himself the champion of a cause or of some deprived group. Interviews in Bloomfield were invariably punctuated with such remarks as "We're all working together for the good of the town." Putnam leaders obviously felt that their labors would help their community, but no one ever thought to suggest that in the process he was pursuing anything other than his own interests.

There seem to be three distinct causes for this earthy and curiously worldly approach to the question of political motivation. First and most superficial is the style of expression. Political rhetoric in Putnam is of the "no nonsense" variety. The town and the drama of its public life are modest, and so are the ways of talking about it. Discourse is as common and unpretentious as architecture and life styles. Putnam life simply does not encourage emotional appeals on behalf of the brotherhood of man or the need to eliminate poverty. But the source is deeper than style of rhetoric. The Putnam political experience itself reveals the contending elites close-up, stripped of all impersonality. People, within limits, are out to get what they can, and that's it. There is never an opportunity in Putnam politics to hide behind great impersonal causes or appeals. Finally, efforts are not made in Putnam, while they are in Hartford and Bloomfield, to enlarge the scope of government. It is, of course, precisely in efforts to expand the scope of government that the bolder and more expansive claims are made. There is argument in Putnam about the specifics of governmental activity but not about the basic scope of that activity. Putnam leaders do not perceive any need for initiatives at the local level to bring about social change. There is, in short, nothing comparable to the expectations on which an antipoverty program in a central city is predicated: that groups of people must be helped to escape an inferior status to which accidents of birth assigned them.

Political life in Putnam is almost completely devoid of conflict over the scope of government. By *scope* here we mean the basic ratio of public to private space. If a municipality substantially increases the valuation on business properties while reducing it on private residential dwellings, it does indicate that the regime is using its powers in a way at least somewhat less friendly to the interests of business than its predecessor did.

But as understood here, the scope of government is expanded only when the government unit—whether local, state, or national—starts performing a substantial function which previously had been left to the private sector. Thus, Medicare extended the scope of government because a field (health insurance for the elderly) which previously had been occupied only by private companies became a sphere of government activity.

Since World War II only urban redevelopment has involved change in the scope of local government, and redevelopment in Putnam has had very limited objectives. Few Putnam residents are much exercised about the role of the national government. Thus, a pragmatic, low-keyed conception of the political struggle emphasizing more immediate and limited interests in place of far-reaching appeals sets the tone in this small town.

Conflict between Yankee and French in Putnam, between Protestant and Catholic, has not disappeared, but it has greatly diminished. By the mid-1960's, the town's large French-Canadian population was on top politically, and the Democratic party was its vehicle. Since John Dempsey resigned in 1961, there have been four mayors, all of French-Canadian ancestry. And all the Democrats on the Board of Aldermen, along with the chairman of the town committee, have been French Canadians. The Republican party has become the receptacle for most non-French Putnamites with interests in local politics. The few Yankee Protestants active in Putnam political life work through the G.O.P. Yet, though Putnam residents continue to speak of conflict between the French and the Yankees, they do so in a matter-of-fact way. Most of the tension has gone. One Democratic politician, of French-Canadian ancestry, discussed French-Yankee conflict in terms devoid of animus:

> The division in Putnam between the Yankee Protestants and the French-Canadians goes way back, although the balance shifted because we grew so much. The division wasn't just religious. The

Yankee Protestants were the mill owners, and the French-Canadian population was mostly working families who for a long time had no interest in politics and were content to let the mill owners run the town through the Republican party. . . . Well, a lot of this [conflict between French and WASP Putnamites] has faded but it still provides an undercurrent especially in the relations between the older Yankees and the older French-Canadian residents.

Another politician, also a French Canadian, commented on his earlier difficulty in getting recognition in the Yankee-dominated Republican party.

For a long time the Republicans were a Yankee party in Putnam, and if you were like me, French, you were left out in the cold. By the early Thirties, though, they [the Yankee Republicans] could see a change coming. I remember in 1932 I told a Yankee Republican, "Grove Street isn't going to run this town any more. Give us some representation." A few days later I was invited to speak before the Republican Town Committee, and I said the same thing. And they nominated me for one of the offices. But the party no longer is a Yankee party in Putnam. Many of the old Yankees have kind of given up, though they still vote Republican. We've so few supporters that anyone who wants to work can have us.

The French now run the town, and many are among its most prosperous citizens. The sharpest resentments remaining are felt by the old Yankees who remember when Putnam was a Yankee town, and who, aspiring to positions in public life, resent the changes which have excluded them.

II. POLITICAL GROUPS AND POLITICAL IDEAS

The Principal Ideational Divide

Putnam politics, we have said, is not ideological. Conflict in the town is not ordered by any ideological dimension, and few Putnamites bind together enough policy patches to see the quilt of ideology. There are ideational divisions less constrained and wide-ranging, the most comprehensive of which we call *Progressive* vs. *Standpatter*. The terms Progressive and Standpatter are in fact sometimes used in Putnam, and the differences to which this polarity points are widely recognized.

Before examining the content of this polarity, we need to explore briefly the distinction between ideational position and *style of leadership*. In an earlier book, we defined leadership style as a combination of the goals pursued, the means selected to achieve these, and rhetoric—the language, tone and manner with which leaders describe what they are about. *Style* focuses attention on the way in which leaders perform their trade. A style is dependent upon what a leader wants to do, of course, and the values he holds, but more than this, it is the way he filters his commitments through the various demands and constraints of the sociopolitical system in which he operates. In some leadership situations, there is marked tension between different components of leadership style. A classic example is the southern Negro leader who adopted "conservative" rhetoric to survive, to cloak race objectives unacceptable to whites. We cited the case of a Greensboro, North Carolina, Negro minister whose program for race advancement (in the early 1960's) was indistinguishable from that of the most militant leaders in Greensboro.

But, in the long years which he spent in the South Carolina low country before moving to urban North Carolina, he had acquired a manner of addressing whites, a way of putting things that quite disarmed them. His speech was filled with homey anecdotes and parables, and with frequent allusions to Biblical personages and events. He spoke slowly, never raising his voice in conversation. He never used words like "demand" or "insist." He never denounced whites for discriminating against Negroes—or more precisely, his words were rarely if ever *taken* by whites as denunciations. As a result, although those who knew him well recognized that he had consistently supported direct action and had worked energetically for the most sensitive status goals, he was not universally regarded as one of the city's more militant leaders. He blended the rhetoric of a Conservative with the means and goals of a Militant.[7]

But in other leadership situations, this tension does not exist: a particular style of rhetoric is regularly found with its "appropriate" goals and means. This is the case in Putnam.

An ideational position is a conceptual dimension applied to some phase of public life, ranging from the far-reaching and highly constrained (ideology) to a fairly narrow set of policy preferences. *Progressive* vs. *Standpatter,* as used here, is a non-ideological ideational polarity. But it could also be described as a leadership style typology. For the goals defined in these ideational positions are regularly accompanied in Putnam by appropriate and complementary means and rhetoric. The Progressive is evaluated not just for the policy goals he espouses, but also for the ways he describes these and how he goes about trying to do things. And at times it appears that such a complementary component of style as rhetoric is more pivotal in evoking support and opposition than the component we focus upon —ideational position.

Progressives are committed to advancing Putnam, to making it "the industrial and commercial center of eastern Connecticut." Putnam was once an important rail center (for its size), but with the decline of railroads the town was bypassed. At the same time, its principal industry, textiles, was moving south. The physical devastation of the 1955 flood was still another blow. Now, Progressives maintain, there is need to harness available resources to permit Putnam to move ahead, to become again a dynamic and progressive town. Progressives actively court industry. They initiated the town's redevelopment program and man the Housing Authority and the Redevelopment Agency. They have endorsed long-range planning, including a master plan for Putnam. They seek improvement of the town's

[7] Everett Carll Ladd, Jr., *Negro Political Leadership in the South* (Ithaca, N.Y.: Cornell University Press, 1966), p. 170.

drab physiognomy, the extension of its commercial, industrial, and recreational facilities, and at least a modest advance in local cultural offerings. More cosmopolitan in their frame of reference, they are much more keenly aware of Putnam's shortcomings when compared to other communities in the Northeast, are impatient with delay in overcoming these, and are at least roughly conversant with the programs in use across the country to achieve community progress. Some Progressives have developed considerable expertise in dealing with the federal and state governments, especially in renewal and public housing. One, a leading Democratic politician, spoke of his expectations for Putnam:

> I want Putnam to grow, though not too fast. The growth must take place in an orderly fashion. But we must grow. Our chances are good. This town is in the middle of a tremendous east coast population belt, and soon we will have a major highway passing through. So there should be an increasing influx of population, and especially of higher income families. Given its position, the town can have a higher standard of living and increasingly capable residents. . . . So we have an opportunity but we can miss it. To prepare for it, we need to improve our appearance. Why, the way we look scares people off. We need better housing, more recreational opportunities, a youth center, and other cultural attractions.

Thus understood, "Progressivism" is a relatively constrained position. On a series of policy choices over the last decade and a half, Progressives have worked together consistently and effectively.

Still, this ideational position can easily be made to appear broader and more systematic than it is. The public sector of Putnam is modest, and the conflict between Progressives and Standpatters takes place within it. Only once have they argued over the scope of local government—the initiation of the urban renewal program—and even there the extension at issue was narrow and modest since no one expected more from renewal than help in rebuilding a shopping area. A new shopping center, a new youth center, a new fire station, an updated master plan:

these are the type of things Progressives have worked for. They are important and represent progress for Putnam. But they remain modest objectives.

The Standpatters oppose this view of progress on "philosophic" grounds. They have no ideological objections to industrial growth, commercial expansion, or nicer public facilities, nor do they believe the promotion of these is beyond the legitimate scope of government. But their Putnam is static rather than dynamic, and they typically see little need for change. They have resisted the changes urged by the Progressives, at times successfully as in town-city consolidation, sometimes unsuccessfully as with renewal. Standpatters are completely local in their orientation: Putnam is the center of their universe. They lack real understanding of the sociopolitical experience of other communities around the country and have had little contact with national institutions, whether business corporations or agencies of the federal government.

Progressives look to a Putnam growing and changing, becoming more prosperous, with more industry and better-paying jobs, physically renewed, joining the rest of Connecticut socially and economically. But the Putnam of the Standpatters is an older one, and their evaluational context is less the rest of the state than it is Putnam's past. A low tax rate and minimal expenditures by local government are their principal political objectives. Their politics is an older one than the Progressives' in another sense. They would be content to play it out exclusively for patronage and recognition with barely a whisper of issues if the Progressives would let them.

The Progressive-Standpatter polarity does have connections with Cosmopolitanism-Parochialism described in Chapter 5. Progressives are more familiar with bodies of expert knowledge, have been exposed at least superficially to the outlines of a scientific culture, and, in contrast to the Standpatters, appear to share in cosmopolitan perspectives. But the Progressive-Standpatter division is only a pale copy of certain dimensions of the ideological polarity. It orders conflict far narrower and more limited in scope. And it is generated by a vastly different political setting. Cosmopolitanism-Parochialism appears to be a principal response in a new agenda of politics that is national in its extensions and implications and in which our big metropolitan regions find themselves moving. Putnam is an older political setting, only touched by the currents sweeping the new along. Ideologies are known, indeed given shape, by their enemies. Putnam lacks Cosmopolitanism, and thus its potential for a clearly articulated Parochialism remains unrealized.

The division between Progressives and Standpatters, we have noted, is widely recognized in Putnam and frequently referred to. One politician called the perspectives of the Standpatters "the old textile mentality" that was slowly breaking down. Others described it as an old French-Canadian conservatism. A Progressive lamented that "they [the Standpatters] just don't understand the need for more commercial development, streamlining the city government, better public facilities." The Progressive-Standpatter dichotomy does order substantial ideational conflict in Putnam. Within the relatively narrow sphere of conflict which it treats, the constraints are impressive. To know a Standpatter's position on one of the issues outlined above is to be able to predict with high probability his response to the others. But it should be kept in mind that the listing of positions here which the dichotomy orders tends toward inclusiveness for a period of more than a decade.

We can get further insight into the substance of this ideational dichotomy by asking who are the Progressives, the Standpatters? Fifty-five community leaders were interviewed in Putnam between July, 1965, and November, 1967, and many were reinterviewed. On the basis of these interviews, plus close observation of political decision making in Putnam, the leaders were located in the Progressive-Standpatter dichotomy. Twenty-seven are Progressives and twenty are Standpatters, with the remaining eight not readily classifiable and hence excluded from the following analysis.[8] The Standpatters are older than

[8] Data on two of the eight was not sufficiently complete to permit clas-

the Progressives and with only four exceptions have lived in Putnam for more than three decades. Many of the Progressives themselves are lifelong Putnamites, but in their numbers are all of the "outsiders" active in the politics of the town. Occupational differences between the two groups are striking. Seventeen of the Progressives are professional men or salaried managers in contrast to only two of the Standpatters. Equally striking is the educational divide. Twenty-two of the Progressives are college graduates and thirteen took professional degrees (seven as lawyers). Only five of the Standpatters attended college and only one of those has a professional degree. A majority of both groups are of French-Canadian ancestry and Catholic in religious affiliation, but the ethnic diversity of the Progressives is much greater. These data are summarized in Table 30.

We have stressed that the Progressive-Standpatter dichotomy, although possessing substantial constraint, deals with a highly limited area of public life. This becomes evident when the positions of members of the two groups on various national issues are examined. The Progressives are *not* the liberals or the Standpatters the conservatives. The relation to national issues is minimal. A few examples should make this clear. All but two of the Standpatters warmly endorsed Medicare; in contrast, six of the Progressives voiced objections to the program. Three of the Progressives adhere to a set of national policy positions with sufficient consistency to be called "near conservatives." [9] One Progressive is a "near liberal," and another two follow liberal responses with a very high degree of constraint. Only one Standpatter is a "near conservative" and none "near liberals."

The most substantial difference in the responses of Progres-

---

sification. The other six appeared on "both sides" so frequently that to describe them as either Progressives or Standpatters would be to imply constraint not actually there.

[9] The term "near ideologue" is Converse's. The "near ideologue" uses dimensions like *conservative,* but in a peripheral way. Converse, "The Nature of Belief Systems in Mass Publics," in Apter (ed.), *Ideology and Discontent* (New York: Free Press of Glencoe, 1964), p. 216.

Table 30. Putnam Progressives and Standpatters, by a set of personal biographical data variables

Variable	Progressives (n = 27)	Standpatters (n = 20)
Age (median)	46 yrs.	53 yrs.
Residence*		
Three decades or longer in Putnam	56	80
"Outsiders"	26	0
Occupation		
Professionals and salaried executives	63	10
Lower white-collar workers	11	30
Small business operators	15	45
Blue-collar workers	11	15
Education		
Eighth grade or less	0	35
Some high school, high school graduate	19	40
Some college, college graduate	33	20
Professional degree	48	5
Ethnicity		
French	52	65
Anglo-Saxon	15	15
Irish	7	10
North European	7	5
Jewish	11	0
Other	8	5
Political party affiliation		
Democratic	63	60
Republican	30	35
Independent	7	5

Note: All figures are percentages of n unless otherwise indicated.

* These percentages do not total 100 because a third residual category into which eleven leaders fall is not included: those who have lived in Putnam less than three decades but are not "outsiders."

sives and Standpatters on national issues is in the somewhat greater awareness of the former of national politics, not in the policy positions each adopts. Within their limited comprehension of state and national affairs, the Standpatters of Putnam give general support. They are not especially critical of any national institution, whether government, business or labor. Only eight Putnam leaders expressed antilabor concerns; five of these were Progressives and three Standpatters. Only Vietnam among foreign policy matters elicited interest or attention, and again the only systematic difference was the greater familiarity of the Progressives with the specifics of American involvement. Nine leaders interviewed took unequivocal positions for or against the Administration's conduct of the war: seven were Progressives and two Standpatters. But much more typical was the response of a leading Democratic politician, a Progressive in local affairs: "The Vietnam problem is just too complex and I don't know what to think. I guess I have to go along with the Administration."

A Closer Look at Some Specific Sociopolitical Groups

John Bunzel has described profound changes in the position of small businessmen in American society.

> In many ways, as Louis Hacker has observed, the American Revolution of 1776 was the small businessman's revolution, ushering in as it did the ideal society of many small and independent units linked together in a free-market economy in which political relationships were minimal and scattered. Today, however . . . this society has been largely destroyed. The result is that the present-day pattern of living is viewed with a good deal of hostility by small businessmen, who feel that the power and authority of big business "does not fit comfortably with the American ideal." [10]

Bunzel concludes the ideological response of small business partakes of a set of attitudes circulating before the U.S. became a major industrialized system, that it has much in common with the values of an agrarian, preindustrial society. The small businessman is the contemporary spokesman for the agrarian

[10] John Bunzel, *The American Small Businessman* (New York: Alfred A. Knopf, 1962), p. 62.

spirit.[11] In the middle of the twentieth century, he finds himself increasingly out of touch with and hostile to the new society. "He would far prefer a preindustrial pattern of living that was smooth, personal, simple, concrete and homogeneous. . . ." [12]

Bunzel's description seems to be the generally accepted one. The localized, independent society of small units has collapsed and has been replaced by a society dominated by large bureaucratic structures. This is the source of a profound malaise of small businessmen. They have lost power and status, feel threatened by large controlling institutions such as big business, big government, and big labor and give vent to their frustrations through reactive movements that tend toward fascism. Writing in the 1930's, Harold Lasswell related German fascism to a long-term deterioration of the position of the lower middle class. "Psychologically speaking," he wrote, "the lower middle class was increasingly overshadowed by the workers and the upper bourgeoisie. . . ." [13] Recently, writers including Lipset and Martin Trow have found McCarthyism heavily nourished by small business frustrations. Trow argued that "the tendencies which small businessmen fear—of concentration and centralization—proceed without interruption in depression, war and prosperity, and irrespective of what party is in power; thus they are *always* disaffected." [14] Lipset described McCarthyism in the United States, Poujadism in France, Italian fascism, and German and Austrian Naziism all as middle-class movements, products of "the insolvable frustrations of those who feel cut off from the main trends of modern society." [15]

This analysis, while generally persuasive, is wide of the ide-

[11] *Ibid.*, pp. 89–92.

[12] *Ibid.*, p. 104.

[13] Harold Lasswell, "Psychology of Hitlerism," *Political Quartely,* IV (1933), 374.

[14] Martin A. Trow, "Small Businessmen, Political Tolerance, and Support for McCarthy," *American Journal of Sociology,* LXIV (1958), 279–280. See also Seymour Martin Lipset, *Political Man* (Garden City, N.Y.: Doubleday, 1960), esp. ch. 5.

[15] Lipset, *op. cit.*, p. 170.

ational orientation of Putnam small businessmen. Small businesses in Putnam can be divided into two general categories: the old merchant group, little retail establishments; and another set of firms operating in the breathing spaces within a corporation-dominated economy, where the small businessman is not in competition with the big and indeed where his services may be demanded by the activity of the big. The operator of a corner grocery store is threatened (if he has survived this long) by large food retailing corporations such as A&P and Grand Union. But Marcel Belleville, first selectman of the town of Putnam and owner of Mel's Auto Body Shop, is not threatened. The growth of the Detroit auto giants has meant for Marcel Belleville only that more Putnamites are driving more cars longer distances and smashing them more often. Nor is there any indication that such small businessmen are much troubled by their dependence on big national firms for supplies or, as in the case of new car dealers, for franchises and the basic creation of demand.

Small retail stores are in deep difficulty in Putnam. Perhaps because it is difficult for them to survive, such businessmen have not participated in Putnam's public life. They do not run for office and have not even been active in a local taxpayers association. Political activity by small businessmen has come almost exclusively from operators of "interstitial" enterprises (like auto and television repair shops). And these small business activists have not supported protest movements of any type, including those of the Right. A majority of the small business operators in our leadership sample (nine of thirteen) are Standpatters, but their orientation toward national politics is distinguished much more by disinterest than by hostility to big government or big labor. Eight of the thirteen are Democrats.

Small businessmen interviewed through their inclusion in the Putnam mass sample (rather than because of their leadership in community affairs) did show significantly greater resistance to certain federal spending programs and were more inclined to take conservative positions on a number of other national policy items. These data suggest, although they were not collected in such a manner as to permit us to say with certainty, that the economically marginal small retail merchants in Putnam are much more unhappy about political currents in contemporary America than are their counterparts who occupy comfortable "breathing spaces" in the economy, often in the service areas. But no segment of Putnam small business shows any systematic and wide-ranging concern with the scope of government activity, as the response to the question about the federal antipoverty program makes clear

	"Are you in favor of the Medicare program?" (Responses are expressed as percentages of *n*.)		"Some, like Alabama Governor George Wallace, insist that the Civil Rights Movement is Communist dominated, or at least has Communists in it in positions of influence. Do you agree or disagree?"	
	Yes	*No*	*Agree*	*Disagree*
Putnam mass sample				
Small businessmen (n = 13)	39	62	54	46
All respondents (n = 306)	81	19	34	66
Putnam leadership sample*				
Small businessmen (n = 13)	85	15	38	62

* These subjects (Medicare and Communist infiltration of the Civil Rights movement) were not explored in the leadership interviews with the same structured questions reproduced above.

"Are you in favor of the Federal Government's antipoverty program?" (Responses are expressed as percentages of *n*.)

	Yes	*No*
Putnam mass sample*		
Small businessmen (n = 11)	100	0
All respondents (n = 280)	89	11
Putnam leadership sample		
Small businessmen (n = 13)	100	0

* The number of respondents varies for the three questions described here because all *undecided* and *don't know* responses were excluded.

No systematic attempt was made here to investigate the hypothesis of the "threatened and hostile" small businessman. But our data strongly suggest that Putnam small businessmen do not feel that the twentieth century has treated them badly and are not hostile to the larger controlling institutions of the national society. In particular, the federal government is not a sinister force, although small businessmen in the mass sample showed more opposition than the sample as a whole to certain federal programs.

Brief comment must be made here about the political role of the principal employers in Putnam. As in many, probably most, smaller communities across the country, Putnam's biggest firms have long since ceased to be under local direction. The largest textile plants in town, those of Hale, Belding-Heminway, and Putnam-Herzl, are simply the local outposts of New York–based corporations with operations in many towns like Putnam. None of their top management lives in the Putnam area. We have little "hard" information on the political role of textile firms in Putnam a half century ago, although the memory of Putnam old-timers sees it as substantial. But today, the managers of the branch operations play a modest role in the town's public life. They make few demands and are rarely consulted. Most important, perhaps, they do not function collectively in Putnam politics. If the mill owners were once a power elite in Putnam, and it appears that they were, their counterparts today, our respondents agree, have little influence and rarely intervene. They are neither some shadowy elite pulling the strings on local political puppets nor a sturdy band of civic-minded leaders.

The "outsiders" are an interesting leadership group in Putnam. In a suburb like Bloomfield, a majority of the population could be classified "outsiders," and the category would lose much of its meaning. But in Putnam, business and professional men who have come to the community as adults represent a small and distinctive group. They are very much aware of themselves as a group, especially in social terms, and frequently associate. Progressives in town affairs, they represent a wide range of commitments on national policy questions. They are often impatient with Putnam for its failure to move ahead as fast as they would like and are bothered by the town's stifling drabness and general lack of "class and culture." But they are not—and perhaps this should be expected since they *chose* Putnam—especially displeased with their town. A number of times in our interviews, they acted as defenders of Putnam's honor against the expected condescensions of the interviewers. They play the role of a small, at least semi-cosmopolitan upper strata in Putnam, a role which would be denied them in a more affluent and talent-rich middle-class suburb.

The *politicians* are those who are elected to offices in Putnam, who hold the few major administrative positions in town government, and/or manage the affairs of the parties. A large majority are French Canadians and Roman Catholics. In spite of their fairly even division between Progressives and Standpatters, the politicians are strikingly alike in their orientation to public life. They are pragmatic, "close to the ground," have highly "realistic" expectations about what politics can bring,

	"Are you in favor of the Medicare program now before Congress?"			"Are you in favor of the Federal Government's antipoverty program?"		
	(Responses are expressed as percentages of *n*.)					
	Yes	*No*	*Undecided and Don't know*	*Yes*	*No*	*Undecided and Don't know*
All Republican identifiers ($n = 81$)	65	20	15	73	19	8
All Democratic identifiers ($n = 182$)	83	9	8	76	2	22
Hard-core Republicans ($n = 33$)	70	21	9	73	27	0
Hard-core Democrats ($n = 43$)	91	5	4	95	0	5

	"Some, like Alabama Governor George Wallace, insist that the Civil Rights Movement is Communist dominated, or at least has Communists in it in positions of influence. Do you agree or disagree?" (Responses are expressed as percentages of *n*.)			"Some people feel that Negro leaders pressing for full equality for Negroes at once have in fact hurt their cause by frightening responsible white leaders in the South. Do you think that this is correct?"		
	Agree	*Disagree*	*Undecided* and *Don't know*	*Yes*	*No*	*Undecided* and *Don't know*
All Republican identifiers (*n* = 81)	32	30	38	44	33	23
All Democratic identifiers (*n* = 182)	19	59	22	34	50	16
Hard-core Republicans (*n* = 33)	30	6	64	58	9	33
Hard-core Democrats (*n* = 43)	9	72	19	28	61	11

know each other well socially, and are inclined to see politics as people rather than issues. Putnam is their town and theirs is a relatively uncritical acceptance of it. None of them expects to live elsewhere.

Democratic and Republican politicians are not separated by any systematic policy differences. Neither are the rank-and-file identifiers of their parties. Democrats, especially hard-core Democrats, did show themselves to be somewhat more supportive of Great Society programs.[16] But even hard-core Republi-

[16] For purposes of analysis here, a hard-core Republican is someone who identified himself as a Republican and who remembered voting for Eisenhower in 1956, Nixon in 1960, and Goldwater in 1964. A hard-core Democrat is one who identified himself as a Democrat and remembered voting for Stevenson in 1956, Kennedy in 1960, and Johnson in 1964. The rank-and-file Republican is simply one who identifies himself as a Republican.

cans, those who had voted for Goldwater in 1964, supported Medicare by seven to three and the antipoverty program by three to one. Only civil rights, of the various policy areas explored in the mass sample, sharply polarized hard-core Republicans and Democrats in Putnam.[17] These differences are striking, but we cannot readily account for them. No other interview data suggest the basis for this polarization.

In fact, the two groups of party supporters are differentiated by little other than ethnicity and/or religion. The Republicans are not the upper-SES party of Putnam. A larger portion of Republican than of Democratic adherents were from families earning less than $5,000 a year (for 1964). By way of contrast, well over half of the Republican identifiers in Bloomfield shared in family incomes over $10,000, a plateau reached by only one quarter of the suburban Democrats. Only in religion-ethnicity did we find a variable which sharply differentiates Republicans and Democrats in our small town. Sixty-six per cent of the Democratic adherents were French Catholics compared

	Republican identifiers		Democratic identifiers	
Family income	*Putnam** (n = 77)	*Bloomfield* (n = 110)	*Putnam* (n = 161)	*Bloomfield* (n = 171)
Under $5,000	47	12	38	15
$5,000 to $10,000	39	28	50	55
Over $10,000	14	60	12	30

* All figures are percentages of *n*.

	*French-Canadian Catholics**	*Non-French Catholics*	*Non-French Protestants*
Republican identifiers (n = 81)	29	10	61
Democratic identifiers (n = 182)	66	23	11

* All figures are percentages of *n*.

[17] The full interview schedule is reproduced in the Appendix. It should be remembered that the mass sample interviews were conducted in 1965.

to only 29 per cent of the Republicans. Six in ten of the Republicans were non-French Protestants, the status of but one in ten of the Democrats.

We have described in Putnam a nonideological politics. Local government is called upon to do relatively little, and there has been little disagreement about its scope, about the ratio of public to private space. Local government is not asked to be a resolver of pressing social problems. Political leaders in Putnam are not much occupied by the great issues of national life, and although they have some opinions on such issues, are little aware of each other's opinions and do not seriously rate each other by them. Politics in this small town is highly personalized, almost smothered by the intimacy of the actors.

One fairly systematic ideational division can be detected between those, often younger, better educated, and more conversant with the world outside, who have wanted a "progressive" Putnam, and an older and more locally-oriented group who have resisted the former's instruments and programs for community progress. But *Progressive* and *Standpatter* organize only a narrow set of local controversies. The wide-ranging constraints of ideology—any ideology—are not relevant to conflict in the town. And few Putnamites make use of abstract conceptual dimensions to order and account for political life. Here in this northeastern Connecticut mill town we find, in short, an old-style local politics—narrow, immediate, personalized, and limited.

7. Bloomfield: The Ideational Life of an American Suburb

Bloomfield is a very different type of community ideational system. The public sector is larger. The metropolis continually impinges upon the suburb, thrusting problems, like race, upon it. And this regional setting, along with their occupational attachments, their educational backgrounds, and their physical mobility, gives to Bloomfield leaders more cosmopolitan perspectives and brings to the talk in Bloomfield discussions of problem areas far broader in their implications. Personalities and personal foibles are part of the talk in Bloomfield, but they do not dominate it. Issues of highly immediate and particularized self-interest intrude, but they are less central. The talk in Bloomfield deals more with the remote and impersonal.

Superficial differences in the ideational life of the small town and the suburb may exceed the actual. A white-collar, new-middle-class residential suburb that is part of the Connecticut capital region of three quarters of a million, and a French-Canadian mill town relatively self-contained and isolated and populated primarily by blue-collar workers, generate within the context of American political life in the 1960's vastly different styles of public life. But differences in the ideational life of Bloomfield and Putnam are more important than the relatively superficial matters of the style of the socioeconomic groups ascendant in each community. The nature of these more fundamental differences is one of our principal occupations here.

I. THE TALK IN BLOOMFIELD

What Are the Problems?

Much more than in Putnam, the talk in Bloomfield revolves around issues of national and international concern. Political activists in the small town rarely discuss national problems, and typically were reluctant to comment on them in our interviews. They were being asked to offer assessments of matters to which passivity often was their strongest reaction. But national and international problems are part of the talk in Bloomfield. Educational levels are substantially higher in the suburb than in the town, and many more suburbanites have been trained to see politics in terms remote and abstract, the stuff of national politics. Their metropolitan experience makes Bloomfielders less insular and exposes them to a wider range of public problems. Bloomfield leaders frequently concern themselves with policy matters which are remote and abstract, and thus "see" problems which are not there for their Putnam counterparts.

The more specific local problems and controversies which dominate the talk in Bloomfield can be divided into four categories: race, which in the period of research has generated the deepest and most wide-ranging conflict; the suburb's place in the Hartford region; taxing and spending; and change and the shape of Bloomfield's future. Questions of personal and public morality, so demanding in Putnam, really are not part of the talk in Bloomfield. We doubt that Bloomfielders are freer of vice than Putnamites. But just as the public sector in Putnam, limited in scope, invites a politics intensely personal and preoccupied with the characteristics of the actors, so public life in Bloomfield, broader and more impersonal, minimizes such concerns. There is political gossip in Bloomfield, but it is peripheral to public discourse.

Bloomfield has the largest Negro population of the Hartford suburbs, indeed is one of only two with substantial numbers of Negroes, and is the most accessible from the North End of Hartford. Not surprisingly, then, race has been the focal point for a series of relatively intense community struggles. Most Bloomfielders consider it "our greatest problem," although they differ as to the type of problem and who is at fault. Many whites fear that the growing numbers of Negroes will give Bloomfield an image injurious to its future as a growing and prosperous middle-class suburb. In its crudest form, this is a fear that Bloomfield will become a "nigger suburb." In 1963, the Hartford *Times* printed a section on area integration and listed Bloomfield as an "open community" for Negroes. Immediately thereafter a drop in real estate prices was reported. Town officials fought a continuing battle in the late 1950's and early 1960's with area real estate men. One Bloomfield administrator who has borne much of the brunt of block busting was highly critical of real estate firms:

> They have certainly made my life difficult in recent years. The high point of the trouble was between 1961 and 1963, and it has tapered off somewhat since then. They would get five or six people on the telephone and call every white home owner in the area, telling him that the Negroes were moving in, that property values would decline drastically, and that they had better sell out as fast as they could. They would get those people jumping out of their skins. . . . There is no doubt about it, a number of Hartford real estate firms engaged in block-busting tactics in the Blue Hills section of Bloomfield. We have the evidence, and a lot of it was turned over to the state insurance commissioner whose department licenses real estate people. I suppose I should try to see their side of it. The real estate business has been based historically on a commission payment system. If you don't sell, you don't get any commission. So there is a built-in interest in attempting to increase the amount of property turnover. But they certainly have made our job here that much more difficult.

Block-busting tactics might have had much greater success were it not for the vigorous response of town officials and a private biracial group, the Bloomfield Intergroup Council.

Town officials would move into a besieged neighborhood urging white residents not to sell, marshalling a battery of data to demonstrate that property values need not decline. The Intergroup Council campaigned against block busting, and their "neighborhood stabilization" program enjoyed real if not complete success:

We tried to get whites to stay, but a lot moved. Some stayed long enough to find out their Negro neighbor wasn't a bad fellow at all, and these stayed permanently. . . . One development in the southeastern corner of Bloomfield bordering on Hartford's North End, the Pershing Park development, is the one most in danger of tipping completely Negro. But block-busting tactics have largely stopped. The efforts of some real estate men to label Bloomfield "a nigger town" failed.

Up to the time of writing (1968), the response of Bloomfield's "establishment" to the entry of Negroes has been controlling and has generally succeeded in setting the tone for the community. This "establishment" is a unified group of community leaders who in the late 1950's and 1960's controlled the Council, the Board of Education, and the town administration, and whose policy choices in most areas prevailed. It is not shadowy or conspiratorial, and it has wielded influence largely through adroit appeals to the suburb's major groups. The establishment has tried to "keep the lid on" racially, to maintain an atmosphere in which Bloomfield could continue to grow, draw industry, and attract and keep prosperous families. Their position can accurately be summarized this way:

Race is an extremely delicate issue, one which has the capacity to blow the town wide open. Most whites are vaguely unhappy about Negroes moving in, and some in the threatened neighborhoods of southeastern Bloomfield extremely unhappy. Race is a powder keg, and our job is to make sure that no one sets it off. Eastern Bloomfield really does have the potential to become a largely Negro area, bordering as it does on Hartford's ghetto, with modestly priced houses and the barrier of being "the first Negro to move in" long since down. A "ghettoization" of this part of Bloomfield could only have severe social, economic and political consequences, adding a bitter and indigestible lump to our political conflict, frightening away the kind of people we need to attract, making our task of attracting and keeping industry much harder.

The establishment, then, did not approach the problem as "bleeding-heart liberals," did not see some special obligation to provide suburban housing for Hartford's Negroes. Their entry was a headache. But neither did they greet the Negro newcomers with hostility, labeling them enemies to be resisted in every possible way. Their job, instead, was management of the conflict. Bloomfield must absorb some Negroes but not be overwhelmed, and the accommodation must be peaceful. Bloomfield must continue to be an attractive place to live and "a nice place to raise children." For them, then, the principal enemies became those activists, white and Negro, who were "inflaming the race issue." One Bloomfield political leader, generally mild and soft-spoken, launched into a vehement denunciation of

> one woman [who] is nothing more than an agitator, who is always shooting off her mouth, but never offering any constructive ideas. I call her the Stokeley Carmichael of Bloomfield! I may be wrong about this, but the only reason I see for her doing this is to incite a race riot! [1]

At the same time, he expressed general satisfaction with the "character of race leadership in Bloomfield," and immediately cited Negro Councilman Alvin Wood, "our councilman and a moderate kind of guy." Given their commitment to moderating racial conflict and robbing it of its disruptive potential, it is hardly surprising that the Bloomfield establishment have reacted intensely to all efforts to heighten racial awareness and tensions.

The establishment repeatedly resisted efforts to publicize ra-

[1] The object of this attack was Mrs. Norma LeFebvre, a member of the Bloomfield Board of Education, who frequently attacked her colleagues specifically and the town generally for the continuation of segregation in the Bloomfield schools.

cial imbalance. Until mid-1966, for example, the Board of Education pretended not to see imbalance in the school system. Virtually everyone knew that most Negroes in Bloomfield lived in the Blue Hills section and that the Blue Hills school had a high proportion of Negro pupils, while two other K–6 schools, Laurel and Vincent, were very nearly all white. In April, 1966, the Board refused to participate in a classroom census jointly sponsored by the Connecticut Department of Education and the State Civil Rights Commission, claiming to adhere to a long-standing policy which prohibited keeping records which reflect race, religion, or ethnic origin of staff or students.

But pressure to conduct a racial census built up as the Intergroup Council insisted that the community could not determine what response is in order without precise information on the distribution of white and nonwhite pupils. The Board at last yielded in June, 1966, and voted four to one to conduct a racial census, but it made clear it was doing so against its better judgment. One member liked "to think of children simply as children, and counting them as white and Negro is very distasteful to me." Other Board members argued variously that they could not see what benefits the students would derive from a racial count, that Bloomfield was spending more per pupil in the allegedly imbalanced school than in any other, and that Bloomfield operated only one junior high and one senior high so that any imbalance which might occur would last only to the seventh grade. The chairman of the Board of Education, Dr. Howard Wetstone, a cancer researcher at Hartford Hospital, refused even then to agree to the special census, cast the lone dissenting vote, and warned "that the Board was embarked on a dangerous course." The school census, the establishment well understood, would provide ammunition to those insisting that there was a problem and further call the attention of whites to the entry of Negroes into the suburb.

Opposing the establishment, the Bloomfield Intergroup Council (BIC) followed a course dictated by a straightforward thesis: Bloomfield is a biracial town but really not integrated; it would be a healthier community for both Negroes and whites if genuine interaction of the two racial groups were achieved; the growing concentration of Negroes in the Blue Hills school can only hasten the exodus of whites from that area, heightening the polarization of the town into a lower-middle-class, black southeastern corner and a remainder more affluent and white. "We feel," the Intergroup Council said, "that the 'burning social question of our day' is that of human rights."

> Our children are growing up in a world populated with peoples of diverse backgrounds. If there is to be an acceptance of the concept of human rights, it is essential that all children meet and learn to live with each other. It is especially essential that this should begin at the earliest possible age, and in the schools at the elementary level since it is here that they can and will learn to relate as individuals. We can enrich the lives of all our children in the schools and help break down the provincial and preconceived attitudes of fear and intolerance. . . . Specifically, it is known that in Bloomfield the concentration of our Negro population is in the Blue Hills area and, therefore, the greatest number of Negro children attend the Blue Hills school. Already, the situation has had a negative impact in our community.

The activists of the BIC, predominantly professional, college-educated men and women, did not conceptualize the problem of race in a way very different from members of the establishment, but they give higher priority to positive steps toward integration.

The racial census revealed the expected, that the Blue Hills school was nearly half Negro and two others virtually all white. Armed with this documentation, the BIC and another interest group similarly concerned with race—the Bloomfield Citizens Committee, composed mostly of Negroes—campaigned to eliminate racial imbalance through crosstown busing.

Many Bloomfielders were less enthusiastic about busing. Nearly three hundred parents attended the May 1967 Board of Education meeting to express general disapproval. But the establishment was moving rapidly to head off further conflict. A joint committee of the Board of Education and the Human Relations Commission, an appointive body formally part of town government, had been set up a year earlier. Now, it was informally charged with providing a compromise plan. On the joint committee were Town Manager Preston King and Superintendent of Schools Edward Rogean. The manager was the moving force.

Bloomfield's assistant superintendent, Herbert Chester, was a member of the BIC and much committed to its objectives. He had been preparing a report on ways the suburb might meet racial imbalance. Three plans were included:

Plan A recommended crosstown busing and maintaining kindergarten through grade 6 in each school. This plan would have assigned pupils to the various elementary schools in a way to satisfy a statistically perfect racial balance and equal pupil-teacher ratios.

Plan B recommended developing three K–3 schools and two 4–6 schools. This plan would have established three existing K–6 schools (Laurel, Metacomet, and Wintonbury) as K–3 schools and the Vincent and Blue Hills schools as 4–6 schools. In this plan, all K–3 pupils at Blue Hills, about half Negro, would have been transferred to the three predominantly white K–3 schools.

Plan C proposed developing four K–5 schools and one grade 6 school. This plan would have taken all K–5 pupils at Blue Hills and distributed them to the other elementary schools. The Blue Hills school would then take all grade 6 pupils.

But the joint committee told Chester to add two additional options to his report:

Plan D would maintain a K–6 system with transfers from the Blue Hills school only. This plan would try to achieve racial balance by permitting Negro pupils in the Blue Hills school to enroll in the predominantly white Laurel, Vincent, and Wintonbury schools.

Plan E would maintain a K–6 system with a general volunteer enrollment plan. This plan would be based upon Negro parents volunteering to have their children transferred from the Blue Hills school and white parents enrolling their children at Blue Hills.

Plan E, it happened, was the recommendation of the joint committee. But it suggested voluntary busing as only one step toward "sound human relations . . . in the schools." Other aspects of the program included: (1) Construction of a lower middle school to house grades 5, 6, and 7. This lower middle school would be fully integrated, servicing all Bloomfield. (2) Elimination of the Blue Hills school as a teaching facility. The students in the K–4 grades living in the Blue Hills school district would be distributed among the other elementary schools and Blue Hills closed as soon as the new lower middle school is completed. (3) Establishment of an in-service human relations training program for school personnel to insure a high standard of human relations in the teaching program. Thus, the voluntary busing program would be temporary. The reason for it would disappear with the opening of the middle school for grades 5 through 7.

These establishment-engineered proposals were a tactical master stroke. And the manner of presentation was equally masterful. Parents of all Bloomfield school children were given a questionnaire listing the various plans ranging from compulsory crosstown busing to the voluntary plan. There was no mention of the status quo as a possible option. Something was going to be done. Of course, the voluntary busing plan seemed mild and acceptable in contrast to the compulsory busing. Those who had been most fearful of compulsory busing felt they had won a victory. The building of the new lower middle school was presented as desirable without regard to race. It would relieve overcrowding in the high school by permitting grade 9 to be transferred to the existing junior high, which, in turn, would give grade 7 to the new school. The latter would be part of a large and impressive campus-style educational complex—high school, junior high, and lower middle school. And (incidentally) this plan would permit the elimination of racial imbalance without busing children.

The establishment had its plan and moved quickly to push it through. The chairman of the Town Council, other leaders of the two political parties, the Superintendent of Schools, the chairman of the Board of Education and the town manager all worked actively for its adoption. The Human Relations Commission endorsed it, as did the Bloomfield Education Association.

But not everyone joined in the applause, and in a sense this was fortunate for the establishment. The insistence of some Bloomfielders that more could and should be done gave the plan an appearance of moderation and reasonableness in the eyes of probably most residents. The BIC, the Citizens Committee, and one member of the Board of Education, Norma LeFebvre, were the principal critics of the plan. The chairman of the Citizens Committee announced that the members of his group "are completely opposed to the voluntary busing plan proposed by the joint committee of the Board of Education and the Human Relations Commission, or any voluntary program. Further, we believe, this is only an excuse by the committee to escape the inevitable." His organization might be forced, he said to seek legal assistance from the NAACP and begin litigation if the voluntary plan were pursued. Leaders of the BIC argued that voluntary busing placed an unfair burden on Negro children and their parents: they must take the initiative under the voluntary plan, a responsibility which should be borne by the school administration. Further, there was no assurance that significant numbers of parents would take the initiative. Voluntary busing might not, then, do anything. Beyond this, those who would have their children bused from Blue Hills might well be the least in need, being disproportionately the more confident Negro parents whose children were already well able to compete.

At the June 1967 Board of Education meeting which adopted

the joint committee's recommendations, Mrs. LeFebvre denounced the voluntary plan as "stupid" and as a "nonplan." She made a long and impassioned plea, citing the extent of wrongs to Negro Americans. "I want to go back three centuries," she said, and described how Negroes were brought to the United States as slaves, the breaking up of Negro families, the pervasive discriminations since emancipation. Before a cool but polite audience she argued that voluntary busing sold Negroes and indeed sold the community short. Legislative bodies, like a board of education, are created to make rules, to lead, and the school board here should take decisive action implementing Plan B as educationally sound and progressive.

But Wetstone, speaking for the establishment, was in control. The proposal to build a new lower middle school was educationally sound and economically feasible, he said. Its completion would permit closing the Blue Hills school. Within three years the suburb would have a school plant satisfying its needs for at least a decade and a system effectively eliminating *de facto* school segregation without resort to compulsory busing. Pressures on whites to move from Blue Hills to escape a predominantly Negro school for their children would be removed. *De facto* school segregation is educationally bad for both Negroes and whites. Building the new school and closing the Blue Hills school will take care of this in the long run, but something must be done to reduce imbalance now. The problem is that acute. (A year earlier he had opposed even a racial census as unnecessary.) A voluntary busing program must be implemented. It will be the Board's responsibility to do whatver it can to achieve the successful implementation of the arrangements. All who sincerely believe there is a problem to which the community should respond would be urged to act through this voluntary program. If, he said to Mrs. LeFebvre, the Citizens Committee, and the Intergroup Council, compulsory busing is achieved over the objections of a majority of citizens, what would be accomplished? Integration in a hostile environment would not be educationally sound, could not help Negro and white youngsters to get along better. The voluntary program is quite as far as a majority of Bloomfielders are willing to go. We must bring Negroes and whites together and let each learn that the other doesn't wear horns. We must create a reservoir of mutual respect and understanding. Some would prefer no busing, some a more ambitious program. But let us close ranks. Wetstone appealed variously to the widespread desire to avoid "ghettoization" of the Blue Hills section, to a sense of decency, to pride in Bloomfield as a pioneering community in race relations. "We are doing something that few other places have been able to do."

The Board of Education voted to adopt the package program—voluntary busing and the eventual closing of the Blue Hills school. Bloomfield was warmly praised by the press, even, with some reservations, by the President of the Hartford NAACP. The Town Council rushed to appoint a building committee for the new lower middle school even before formally requested to do so by the Board. The Citizens Committee and the BIC, though opposed to the voluntary busing arrangements, now elected to back them, and meetings were held to urge Negro parents in the Blue Hills section to enroll their children for busing. When the Bloomfield schools opened in September, 1967, 122 Blue Hills Negro children were transported to other elementary schools, and nine white children were bused into Blue Hills. The Blue Hills school population dropped from 46 per cent Negro in 1966–67 to 31 per cent Negro in 1967–68.

The way a conflict situation becomes structured contributes mightily to the way the conflict is resolved. In Bloomfield, the structuring of conflict around the issue of race and schools is especially interesting. Our survey data suggest that in the summer of 1966 a vast majority of Bloomfield whites opposed any changes in existing school assignment policies: they favored neighborhood schools, with one of the schools thus disproportionately Negro. But one year later, Bloomfield accepted a program of voluntary busing and the prospect within two years of complete integration with discontent of quite manageable proportions. How did this happen?

The big factor is that the principal public antagonists were two groups of Cosmopolitans: the key leaders of the establishment and specifically the town manager, the chairman of the Town Council, and the chairman of the Board of Education on one side; and on the other, civil rights activists of the BIC. It could have been otherwise. Large numbers of whites, we believe, were prepared to follow Parochial or even radical rightist leadership had it been offered. But it was not, because of the astuteness of the establishment leaders, their political strength at the time the argument came to head, and general good luck. The Bloomfield establishment, such as it is, is composed of conservative-Cosmopolitans and conservative-Parochials, with the former ascendant. As we indicated in Chapter 5, this could not be a natural ideological alliance. It seems to have been achieved through a mixture of plan and chance: such conservative-Cosmopolitans as the three town government officials mentioned above deliberately cultivated the alliance for two reasons: to co-opt the conservative-Parochials would remove them as a potential threat to community progress, and besides, they needed their votes. But the alliance would not have been easily consummated if a number of leading conservative-Cosmopolitans and conservative-Parochials had not happened to get along well together, for considerations of personality rather than politics.

Once the conservative-Cosmopolitans of the establishment decided upon a course of action in the school imbalance case, their conservative-Parochial allies on the Council and the Board of Education accepted it. The former insisted that the compromise package was the only one which would prevent serious and disruptive racial strife in Bloomfield, and sponsorship by the conservative-Parochial members of the establishment served enormously to legitimize the package in the eyes of other Parochials. Those Bloomfielders of radical rightist persuasion, while bitterly resentful of the decision and hostile to the entire movement of Negroes into Bloomfield, backed off before the carefully packaged and presented decision of a unified top leadership, in which that leadership had managed to reveal itself as reasonable compromisers before more extreme demands.

Thus, the public argument over racial imbalance in the schools was dominated by those who shared a fundamentally similar conception of the problem. Parochial intervention was kept on the fringes. The contending Cosmopolitans, though each was unhappy with the position of the other, found that they could live together.

In the various areas of community race relations, a relatively small group of liberal-Cosmopolitans have worked to call attention to shortcomings, believing that "we can do better." The goal is an integrated Bloomfield, with Negroes and whites who are class equals working together in the social and political life of the town. Recognizing that there are few instances in which this has taken place, they still find it realistic and worth working for. Unless problems of *de facto* segregation are dramatized, they believe, whites will slumber on and the problems will intensify. So they dramatize the problems. They fear Bloomfield's becoming a Negro town as much as the white majority does, but believe that the majority through inaction only encourages that development.

The conservative-Cosmopolitans of the establishment depart from their more liberal counterparts on how to handle the existing black-white bifurcation. Often, they have found the primary need is to "put out fires" rather than fan them. ("Whites and Negroes are jumpy enough.") This commitment has produced inactivity before acknowledged racial problems when it was believed that activity might trigger an explosion. But their Cosmopolitan conceptualization of the dimensions of racial problems has in other situations led them to intervene actively if quietly. A conservative-Cosmopolitan leader described Bloomfield's racial situation and the responses it demands:

The big problem facing Bloomfield today is how to avoid the deterioration of the southeastern corner of the town, how to keep it a viable area and make it more attractive, thus maintaining a racial mix. The clear lesson is that if an area turning from white to black is permitted to deteriorate physically, then everything is lost. The area will go rapidly Negro. So the officials of this town are working on an ambitious program of redevelopment in the Blue Hills section, to prevent it from undergoing that deterioration. We must move fast, because already some of the small stores and dwellings along Blue Hills Avenue are beginning to decline. . . . We must spend more on various services in the Blue Hills section, to make it more attractive. But we have to be careful in doing this. People in Blue Hills are already terribly sensitive to descriptions of their neighborhood as a "second-class place." They don't want to be treated as though they are slum dwellers. I remember a few years ago a program was started to provide some additional staff, like counselors and social workers, to the Blue Hills school. We thought it was really a good idea, but I went to a meeting over there, and they really jumped on me. "Why pick on us? Why label us second-class citizens? We don't need social workers. We're as good as the rest of Bloomfield." You see, we were actually labeling the Blue Hills area the trouble spot, the junk heap of Bloomfield. . . . The key to everything now is to continue to attract industry and to expand our grand list fast enough to give us the tax dollars to work with. If we had been forced to substantially raise our tax rates while Negroes were moving into town, the lid might already have blown off, for whites would have strongly opposed seeing the added tax dollars go for remedial steps in the Blue Hills area. And even if the tax dollars didn't actually go to Blue Hills, the simple coincidence of Negroes moving in and taxes rising might well have been enough to have triggered a really nasty reaction. But the tax rate hasn't increased, and it has not because industrialization has tremendously expanded the grand list. A lot of us have worked for industrialization and broadening the tax base as part of a necessary response to the race problem, to give us the money to work with.

The Parochial persuasion has lacked effective leadership in Bloomfield and thus far has not successfully challenged the course charted by conservative-Cosmopolitans. The Radical Right of Bloomfield, small as it is, has been surprisingly quiet before the effective management of community leaders.

Necessity compels Bloomfielders to concern themselves with Greater Hartford. Their contiguity to Hartford's North End has given them a pressing racial problem. Their place in the metropolitan region brings them into competition with other suburbs for industry and residents. More than 4,500 Bloomfield residents cross town lines each day to work, and more than 8,000 workers from other area communities enter Bloomfield daily. Because of its location, Bloomfield has been transformed from a sleepy semirural village to a modern white-collar suburb in a decade and a half.

Bloomfield residents are ambivalent about their link to the region. Few leaders in the suburb are willing to see much local autonomy sacrificed to some larger regional government. Attachment to towns as units of government is strong in Connecticut, partly from habit but partly because they serve real functions for their residents. Town government provides an arena for activity, influence, and recognition. And not only Bloomfield locals fear the loss of this.

Still, when overtures to regionalism come from Bloomfield leaders, they come from Cosmopolitans. Cosmopolitans are aware of the regional dimensions of local problems; they have a wide range of regional associations, cannot romanticize Bloomfield as "our town," recognize that the price for the shield is high, and certainly do not claim that local government boundary lines are "right and natural." They are the first, then, to detect advantages for Bloomfield in specific regional approaches and to back these. It was the conservative-Cosmopolitan chairman of the Bloomfield Board of Education who proposed in September, 1967, that a regional education commission be set up to present the following proposition to boards of education in the Hartford area: "You need a new school? How would you like to have a free one, the best, the most beautiful, the most attractive and modern and efficient school that money can buy? It will be yours to own and control, it won't cost you a cent, and all you need to promise is that 25 per cent of the pupils will come from the core city and that the ratio of pupils to teachers will be kept to a certain minimum." It should not be difficult, the chairman suggested, to convince the federal and state governments and directors of foundations that schools are cheaper than riots and that they can be used to teach a generation of children of slum parents to aspire beyond the slums. School boards deciding to join the program would keep their autonomy and their control over the schools, new and old. They would be given the money to hire teachers who are psychologists and sociologists, and enough of them to provide one for every fifteen children. Education is the key to escape from the ghettos.

Similarly, it was Bloomfield's conservative-Cosmopolitan Town Council chairman who as head of the Hartford area Regional Council of Elected Officials tried to breathe life into this consultative regional assembly. Of course, the fact that in one area the shield has broken down for Bloomfield—Negroes are entering the suburb in large numbers—certainly cannot be ignored in considering this growing support for specific regional approaches.

Conflict over taxing and spending in Bloomfield has been muted by the suburb's success in attracting business. More than fifty firms opened plants and offices in Bloomfield between 1950 and 1967. The assessed valuation of all industrial property in 1950 was only $30,160, but seventeen years later the total valuation of 144 commercial buildings exceeded $20 million. Thus, Bloomfield has been able to undertake new expenditures without substantially increasing tax burdens. The sharpest divisions over taxing and spending have revolved around the varying service demands of different segments of the population. Divisions between old Bloomfielders and newcomers, east and west, the more prosperous and the least prosperous have figured prominently in these service controversies. In the early 1950's, Bloomfield was changing from a village to a suburb. Many of the newcomers were young married couples and big producers of children. Between 1950 and 1960, the school-age population jumped from 17 to 26 per cent of the total. The newcomers generally brought with them service demands greatly exceeding those of most old Bloomfielders, and the stage for conflict was thus set.

Political power had long rested with prosperous land owners and a small coterie of business executives. They ran the Council and the Board of Education. Typically, children of this ruling group attended public school only through sixth grade and then entered a fashionable private school in the Hartford area to prepare for college. Consequently, this old elite had little interest in big expenditures for public schools, in improving the quality of public education in Bloomfield. Few Bloomfield High graduates went to college, and the major emphasis in the high school seemed to be athletics. In 1951, when it was apparent that an expansion of the school plant was necessary, the old elite succeeded in blocking it. Teachers' salaries were the lowest in Hartford county, and in 1953 the teachers refused to sign their contracts. This episode culminated in the resignation of school board members when adjustments finally were made in salaries.[2] Following the resignations a new election was held, and Old Bloomfield's control of the school board was permanently ended. In 1956–57, the school board recommended construction of a new junior high school. Old Bloomfield again was opposed, and three prolonged, heated town meetings were held. The issue was finally settled in favor of the new junior high in a referendum.

Bloomfield in the 1950's was like William Dobriner's "Old Harbor," "split by the struggle of two communities to shape the prevailing character of the whole." Old Bloomfield refused support for the higher service expenditures, principally for education, which the new middle class was demanding.[3]

[2] The story still remembered by older residents is of the school board chairman commenting publicly that the tobacco crop was poor that year and thus that there could be no increase in teacher salaries.

[3] This struggle over the higher service demands of the newcomers could have been much more intense. Between 1954 and 1960, the tax rate in

Though Old Bloomfield grew steadily weaker, it made one last offensive against the increased taxing and spending. During the winter of 1960–61, the Board of Education prepared its budget for the following school year. It was a "catch up" budget designed to bring Bloomfield's school sytem into a much stronger competitive position with other suburbs. Included was a teacher salary scale to be the third highest in Hartford county. Modest reductions were imposed after consultation with the Town Council, and the budget was formally presented at a public hearing. There, a minor feud developed between the chairman of the Council, a member of the Old Bloomfield political aristocracy, and the vice-chairman of the Board of Education, a representative of New Bloomfield. "I am not alone on the Board in this opinion that the original request of the Board of Education has been cut too much," the latter remarked. "Bloomfield is not a 'Cadillac town,' " and "teachers here are very well paid," the Council chairman replied.

At this point, another representative of Old Bloomfield, an insurance company executive, declared he would devote the entire week before the annual town meeting to rally forces against the budget which he found grossly inflated even with the reductions imposed.[4] The subsequent town meeting was a heated one. "Mr. Insurance" had come well organized. Budget opponents stressed the need to hold the tax line in the interest of attracting industry. Five amendments to cut the operating budget failed, but one to reduce the Board of Education budget carried, only to have the proschool forces rally, urge that the amended budget be rejected, and get it thrown out. The town meeting thus adjourned with nothing settled.

Bloomfield increased only from 37.75 to 38 mills. The increase was kept minimal by the enormous growth of the grand list (all taxable property), which soared from $28.6 million in 1954 to $71 million in 1960. During this period the town constructed a new high school, a junior high and two elementary schools, and made sizable additions to two existing elementary schools. The number of teachers rose from 67 to 175.

[4] This resident was an official of an elite West Hartford school, and he had children attending private schools.

At this point, the budget battle added a dimension as the insurance executive, a John Birch Society member, sought to transform the controversy into a much broader rightist challenge. He organized a "Nonpartisan Citizens Committee" which refused to reveal its membership. The Committee invoked in its literature such symbols as the minutemen and Valley Forge, and charged that

in less than forty-five years we've fought two wars to destroy dictatorship on the world scene and now we're fighting, and losing, the third war to escape world enslavement. The enemy knows they're in it, but Americans are slow to admit it as they float aloft, supported by propaganda, in the "wild Blue yonder" of unrealistic hopes of appeasing a relentless dictator bent on world conquest. But you don't have to look to the Kremlin for dictators. They're right here in Bloomfield in town government, particularly in the Board and Department of Education.

But few Bloomfielders were willing to accept this new version of the conflict. The low tax, low expenditure commitments of many Old Bloomfielders had been under assault since 1953, and the budget struggle of 1961 remained primarily an expression of their opposition to the service demands of the newcomers.

On the other side, the "Citizens for the Budget" was formed. Heavily New Bloomfield, they defended the budget initially proposed and urged quality education for Bloomfield. These probudget leaders finally succeeded in rallying their forces—probably a majority throughout the controversy—and a special town meeting attended by over 1,000 persons approved the original budget.

In 1967, controversy over redevelopment pitted west Bloomfield against the east, brought a reaction from small businessmen in the community, and summoned another Radical Right intervention. Dissatisfaction with Bloomfield's business district was expressed as early as the 1930's. But by the 1960's, its somewhat shabby appearance was causing town leaders acute embarrassment, and they undertook to remedy it. A redevelopment agency was set up, with the understanding that the first target would be the town center. What was once a green of some size had been successively trimmed by road builders, and a triangle formed by the junction of major roads was virtually undeveloped except for a shopping center of blighted small shops and service stations.

The establishment and most residents of western and central Bloomfield wanted an aesthetically striking business area to improve the image of their community. The town manager was speaking for them:

> This is your center, whether it becomes beautiful or shabby, vital or stagnate, a source of community pride or meaningless crossroads, is up to you. . . . A more tangible aspect of the center's importance is image. The center of Bloomfield, like the center of any town or city, presents an image of the entire community to the observer from the outside. . . . Concern for the community's image and prestige is not mere frivolous vanity. In cold, hard, economic terms, image has a great significance to all residents. The resale value of homes is predicated upon it to no small extent, as is the price of developable land. . . . Deterioration, ugliness and blight are distressingly prevalent features of our center today. Incompatibility with the balance of the town is surely obvious to any observant person. . . . In brief, the area is blighted.[5]

The prosperous middle class wanted a center aesthetically comparable to their homes. But above all, they wanted to heighten the status of their suburb, to replace those drab little shops of old small town merchants with "smart shops" of the kind a prestigious suburb must have. With federal funds available, this pursuit of status appeared painless.

In July, 1966, the Bloomfield Redevelopment Agency announced the developer, and he unveiled plans for a center with a handsome colonial motif. Attention then turned to securing voter support for Bloomfield's dollar share of the project, and the establishment waged an extensive and impressive cam-

[5] Preston C. King, "Renewal Newsletter: Bloomfield Redevelopment Agency," September, 1966.

paign. But several sources of opposition appeared. The "Bloomfield Betterment Association" was formed to resist the project. Its members were principally small businessmen whose stores in the center would be displaced by redevelopment. One of them, the operator of a "five-and-ten," became the principal spokesman:

> I don't like urban renewal. It involves the taking away of property. I consider it un-American and against the Constitution to take property away when it isn't necessary. . . . This is no slum. . . . We [the merchants] have no guarantee our rents will remain stable after the project goes through. Once the people vote there is no recourse. . . . The elimination of free enterprise [through the project] is hardly an exercise of freedom.

These merchants drew substantial support from the less cosmopolitan segments of Old Bloomfield, from people who thought the center looked quite all right and that no changes were necessary and that the expenditure of $288,000 of their money was certainly not justified. (Bloomfield Center without renewal would have been a source of pride in Putnam, had that small town so attractive an area. Bloomfield's "blight" would have been Putnam's distinction.)

Another source of opposition was the marginal-middle-class residents of the southeastern corner. Oriented to Hartford and Hartford stores and rarely frequenting the center, they saw renewal as a device through which west Bloomfield would take their tax money to make improvements on something they rarely used. For this group, it was a straightforward east-west struggle, with the west trying to raid the town treasury.

In the ensuing campaign, the establishment left few stones unturned. Endorsements of renewal were secured from a wide range of community organizations. Meetings were held for civic leaders. The "Citizens for Redevelopment" was organized and appropriately headed by an Old Bloomfield small businessman. The leaders of both political parties backed redevelopment. A pamphlet describing the program was prepared and distributed to all citizens by the Redevelopment Agency. Even a promotional film was made by the developer.

Up to the closing days of the campaign, the tone of the opposition was set by the aggrieved small businessmen of Bloomfield Center, fighting the establishment, with only occasional hints of links to radical rightist demonology. But three days before the February 1967 referendum, a group positively identified as John Birch Society members and including a Birch section leader were discovered distributing literature against redevelopment in Bloomfield.[6] Town officials had somehow learned of the group's impending presence a week in advance, and as the Birchers began handing out literature policemen arrived and demanded identification. Supporters of redevelopment did not hesitate to remind citizens that outsiders, and specifically that Birch Society members, were intervening in the town's election. No Bloomfield residents were in this Birch group. The president of the Betterment Association charged that redevelopment supporters had "planted the Birchers" to "defame me." Town officials speculated that he had turned to the Birchers in desperation. Certainly he was not a right-wing ideologue, but just a "little guy" angry at the establishment which he believed was pushing him around.

But it's still not a slum, of course, and that's not what they're really going by; they want to "beautify" this part of town according to the colonial plans, and they don't care who they hurt about doing it. If you want to find out about that go see the Board of Directors of the Chamber of Commerce, all the industrialists from Granby Street, and bankers and insurance people. They don't give a damn about the small businessman, they just take his fifty dollars and stick him off in a corner somewhere!

In the voting, 65 per cent supported redevelopment. Sectional differences were evident, as residents of the affluent

[6] Radical rightist organizations including the Birch Society had been notably successful in organizing resistance to community redevelopment in other towns and suburbs around Connecticut.

West End endorsed it by more than 70–30, in contrast to a 50–50 division in the lower income southeastern corner.

Here, then, is a standard and recurring conflict structure in the suburb. The middle-middle-class and upper-middle-class residents of western and central Bloomfield are acutely concerned about their town's image. Redevelopment would build status. They saw Bloomfield's business district competing with more attractive shops of the Greater Hartford area, a competition which Bloomfield could only lose without redevelopment. Well-educated and affluent, they could afford to concern themselves with the aesthetics of redevelopment. Expecting that the heads of industry which might locate in Bloomfield and the new middle class generally would share their aesthetic concerns, they linked redevelopment of the center to future success in attracting the right industries and more prosperous area dwellers. Questions of public vs. private or the use of federal funds did not trouble them at all.

On the other hand, opponents were drawn from marginal or declining status groups in the suburb: from less affluent elements in the southeastern corner, on the periphery of community life; from the less prosperous survivors of Old Bloomfield, who saw no need for the change and remained committed to a low tax, low spend philosophy; from the small businessmen of the suburb who believed, quite correctly, that the establishment was committed to a commercial center in which there was no place for them. Out of this grew an opposition to redevelopment that became a fairly well articulated Parochial resistance to Cosmopolitan values and perspectives. The area's Radical Right struck a tentative alliance with the suburb's Parochials, a marriage of convenience which when exposed damaged the local Parochials.

Bloomfielders are much aware of the way communities change. A suburb where nearly 9,000 are employed in "clean" industries emerged from a small town of tobacco and dairy farms in two decades. In this same period, Bloomfield gave up the governmental form of the old New England small town—

selectmen and town meeting—in favor of a council-manager arrangement. Touching Hartford's North End, it has felt the politically sensitive entry of Negroes. It has seen power shift away from an old agricultural and business elite and toward younger professionals, most of whom are newcomers to the community. The public sector has expanded from modest "plow the roads" functions in response to far-reaching demands to make Bloomfield a high-status community, to provide a school system that will get "our children" into good colleges, to protect residents from the encroachments of the region—the service demands, in short, of a middle-class suburb. The desirability of such changes occupies a prominent place in local political discourse.

Between 1940 and 1960, argument over the form Bloomfield political institutions should assume was continuous. In the first part of this period, old-timers and newcomers clashed over the adequacy of the selectmen–town meeting arrangements, the latter urging their replacement by a council and town manager. After the newcomers' big victory in 1945 when a modified council-manager regime was approved, there were a series of minor skirmishes in which New Bloomfield succeeded in completing the transition to an efficient, highly professional local administration, over efforts by Old Bloomfield to preserve pieces of the former "friends-and-neighbors," entrepreneurial type of local government.[7] But by 1960 the new middle-class, professionalized regime was firmly entrenched. Bloomfield now has a strong town manager who hires and fires without council scrutiny a well-trained cadre of professional local government officials. It is not coincidental, of course, that as Bloomfield became a white-collar suburb it also moved toward an increasingly "pure" council-manager form. Other studies have described the general and widespread support of the suburban new middle class for professionalized, council-manager government. This class spends its careers in the bureaucratic ranks of big, effi-

[7] These struggles over the form local institutions should take are described in Chapter 3, pp. 120–122, above.

ciently managed corporations and, not surprisingly, looks for the same style of leadership in its local government.[8]

Thus far, we have been talking about our fast-growing suburb as though it were two-layered, a bottom layer of old small town residents now crushed under a big and undifferentiated layer of newcomers. In fact, New Bloomfield itself shows two quite distinct strata. "Is Bloomfield growing too rapidly?" some of the 1946–1960 arrivals ask. Is politics destined to become much more impersonal than it is now? Will the "spirit of Party"—an urban partisanship—descend on the suburb? Above all, they are concerned that many of the post-1960 entries into positions of influence are behaving like "radicals"; that is, they are unwilling to play politics by the older and more gentlemanly rules, they allow national political commitments to structure their behavior in local politics, they wish to draw party lines more sharply, and they frequently commit themselves to positions which make compromise difficult. Said one Republican leader, himself a young man who became active in local politics in the 1950's:

A lot of new people have come into Bloomfield from Hartford in the last few years. Most are Democrats but some are Republicans. With their entry the style of Bloomfield politics has changed. In the last election [1965] the Democrats waged a much tougher campaign than I feel was suitable for a town like Bloomfield. We call some of these newcomers the Jewish Mafia. They're so intense, radical. It hasn't made much difference whether you were a Democrat or a Re-

[8] Leo Schnore and Robert Alford found the council-manager structure appearing more frequently in affluent, white-collar suburbs ("Forms of Government and Socioeconomic Characteristics of Suburbs," *Administrative Science Quarterly,* VIII [June, 1963], pp. 16–17). Herbert Gans discusses the preference of the new middle class of his suburb, (Levittown, New Jersey), for the "efficient and professional" manager form. "A city manager is a good thing; we need a college man, a specialist in there to do the job. We have to get someone from the outside." He also noted that working-class Levittowners "were doubtful about a city manager—as they were about all experts and outsiders." (Gans, *The Levittowners* [New York: Pantheon, 1967], pp. 109–110).

publican on the Council in the past. With these newcomers, I think it will make much more of a difference, and I don't think I like this.

The different layers have different styles, and while the conflict among them is often blurred, it does at times break through in controversy over change and the shape of Bloomfield's future. Increasingly, the 1946–1960 layer, which engaged in running battles with the prewar strata up to about 1960, finds itself fending off assaults from the post-1960 layer, and more and more strikes alliances with the accommodating survivors of Old Bloomfield.

Putnam has changed slowly, and the effects of change, even where resented, are not sources of argument. But community change in Bloomfield is rapid and substantial and the potential for future change still greater, and local political debate is studded with the hopes and resentments of contending groups over its directions.

The Use and Comprehension of Abstract Conceptual Dimensions (A.C.D.)

Abstract conceptual dimensions, largely absent from the talk in Putnam, figure prominently in political discourse in Bloomfield. Two factors appear to converge to determine the frequency of use of A.C.D.: the intellectual training necessary to conceptualize politics abstractly and a political setting that sustains conflict of the kind which permits packaging. Both these conditions are much more common in Bloomfield than in Putnam, and in metropolitan America generally, we expect, than in the small towns. Differences in the educational backgrounds of the two sets of community elites are substantial, especially since we are dealing here with a very narrow slice of the population.

But more important at the elite level, we think, is the community experience. Elites in Bloomfield find wide-ranging conceptual dimensions relevant to conflict in the suburb, while Putnam leaders do not in their community setting.

	Bloomfield (*n* = 90)*	*Putnam* (*n* = 55)
Eighth grade or less	3	22
Some high school, high school graduate	24	29
Some college, college graduate	38	24
Professional degree	34	25

* Data are expressed as percentages of *n*.

Fully one third of our leadership sample in Bloomfield could use the Conventional Dichotomy to order a wide range of policy items. And fewer than one in seven never made use of A.C.D. in locating conflict and were unable to construe the C.D. with anything other than the most minimal coherence, the position in which we found well over half of our Putnam leadership sample

	Bloomfield (*n* = 90)*	*Putnam* (*n* = 55)
Does not use A.C.D.; no comprehension of the C.D. or any other	7	20
Does not use A.C.D.; construed the C.D. with minimal rigor and coherence	7	36
Limited use of A.C.D.; rudimentary but fully coherent constructions of the C.D.	53	33
Frequent use of A.C.D.; a widely-integrating construction of the C.D.	33	11

* Data are expressed as percentages of *n*.

As one moves below the small stratum of community activists, use and comprehension of such conceptual yardsticks as liberal and conservative is much less frequently encountered. The authors of *The American Voter* have convincingly demonstrated that only a small portion of the population applies such yardsticks. In a subsequent publication, Philip Converse concluded that "constraint" (perception of interdependence in a set of policy positions so that the use of a conceptual dimension like conservative efficiently conveys a tremendous amount of information about a specific policy or activity) is largely a function of the level of political information—having learned "what goes with what." This is acquired principally through higher education.

To recapitulate, then, we have argued that the unfamiliarity of broader and more abstract ideological frames of reference among the less sophisticated is more than a problem in mere articulation. Parallel to ignorance and confusion over these ideological dimensions among the less informed is a general decline in constraint among specific belief elements such dimensions help to organize. It cannot therefore be claimed that the mass public shares ideological patterns of belief with relevant elites at a specific level any more than it shares the abstract conceptual frames of reference.[9]

Even by a tolerant construction, Converse found, only about 11 per cent of the American population could be said to apply any "relatively abstract and far-reaching conceptual dimension" to order political events.[10]

Our data for Putnam and Bloomfield confirm this, but appear to provide a revealing supplement. The differences in the educational backgrounds of Putnam and Bloomfield residents, as shown by the 1960 Census and our 1965 sample survey data, are sharp.

	Sample 1965				Census 1960			
	0–8 yrs. school	*9–11 yrs. school*	*H.S. grad.*	*At least some coll.*	*0–8 yrs. school*	*9–11 yrs. school*	*H.S. grad.*	*At least some coll.*
Putnam (*n* = 335)*	45	21	25	10	58	18	16	9
Bloomfield (*n* = 490)	15	15	35	36	26	16	30	28

* Data are expressed as percentages of *n*.

And, as we expected, a much larger portion of the Bloomfield respondents were "at home" with abstract conceptual dimensions. Specifically, more Bloomfielders were able to use the C.D.

[9] Converse, "The Nature of Belief Systems in Mass Publics," in Apter (ed.), *Ideology and Discontent* (New York: Free Press of Glencoe, 1964), p. 231.

[10] *Ibid.*, pp. 215–216.

as a yardstick with which to measure and describe the positions of various national leaders and organizations. In one approach, respondents were presented with the names of eleven political leaders and eight nationally-known organizations. The respondents were then asked whether they considered these to be conservative(s). Five of these which appeared the least ambiguous, given common constructions of *conservative,* and which were frequently described in the media in terms of the C.D., have been selected.[11] We determined what percentage of the respondents in each community correctly located the leader/organization's position in the C.D. in each of the six possible frequencies.

	Correctly located, 5 of 5	*Correctly located, 4 of 5*	*Correctly located, 3 of 5*	*Correctly located, 2 of 5*	*Correctly located, 1 of 5*	*Correctly located, none*
Bloomfield (n = 488)*	6	11	20	34	25	4
Putnam (n = 335)	1	2	10	12	61	14

* Data are expressed as percentages of n.

[11] The five items are:

31. Former Senator Barry Goldwater?
35. Mr. John Lupton?
40. The National Association of Manufacturers?
41. The Americans for Democratic Action?
43. The American Medical Association?

The respondent was considered to have correctly located the leader/organization in the C.D. if he answered *Yes* to 31, 35, 40 and 43 (their interview schedule numbers) and *No* to 41. John Lupton, while perhaps not known to the reader, was a well-known figure in Connecticut. In 1964, he was the principal spokesman for Goldwater in Connecticut, and was executive director of the Republican Citizens Committee, a right-wing G.O.P. splinter movement. We were aware of the weaknesses in this type of measurement. A respondent could have a fully coherent understanding of the C.D. and reply, "No, Goldwater is not a conservative. He is a radical." In fact, substitution of another broad construction of the C.D. for the one which would dictate describing the 1964 Republican nominee as a conservative appears to have occurred infrequently. The low level of

Use and comprehension of the C.D. was explored through other interview schedule items. Instead of presenting leaders and organizations and asking whether they could be called conservative, we asked respondents to suggest national and community leaders whom they would classify as liberals or conservatives, and then to indicate why they would so describe these leaders. They were also asked to distinguish the "basic difference between a liberal and a conservative . . . in terms of their political beliefs." Working with seven items, we classified all respondents by their use and comprehension of *liberal* and *conservative* in much the same way as Converse did.[12] All

---

familiarity of a majority of the respondents with this conceptual yardstick in both Bloomfield and Putnam, but the significantly higher comprehension in the suburb appears well demonstrated.

[12] See Converse, *op. cit.,* especially p. 224. The seven items which we used in this classification are:

21. Are there any leaders in [this community] whom you would call conservatives? (If necessary, who are they? Can you give me their names?).
22. (If Yes) what is it they do or don't do that leads you to call them conservatives?
23. Are there any leaders in [this community] whom you would call liberals? (Again, who are they? Names?).
24. (If Yes) what is it they do or don't do that leads you to call them liberals?
25. Are there any national leaders whom you would call conservatives? (If necessary, who are they? Can you give me their names?).
26. Are there any national leaders whom you would call liberals? (If necessary, who are they? Can you give me their names?).
20. What is the basic difference between a liberal and a conservative, anyway, in terms of their political beliefs?

We were at first fearful that measurement of the use and comprehension of A.C.D. through items tailored to the C.D. might miss significant numbers who rejected consciously or unconsciously the utility of the C.D. but who at the same time did apply A.C.D. to order the issues and flow of public life. But several checks offer convincing evidence that this did not happen. Respondents were asked: "People often use labels like liberal and conservative to identify the political leanings of others. Using terms such as these, how would you describe your own political views?" Less than

respondents were placed in one of five strata, ranging from proper matching of leader and type and a broad understanding of the C.D. to an inability to locate any leader in the C.D. or to give it any coherent construction. Here again, Bloomfield respondents demonstrated markedly greater comprehension of the Conventional Dichotomy than did their Putnam counterparts (see Table 31).

Table 31. Use and comprehension of the C.D., Bloomfield and Putnam samples (expressed as percentages of *n*)

Stratum*	Bloomfield (*n* = 488)	Putnam (*n* = 335)
I	8	1
II	14	2
III	52	9
IV	21	50
V	5	39

* The precise definitions of each stratum are:

I. Correct matching of categories and leaders, the application of the categories to at least five local or national leaders, and a broad and coherent construction of the C.D.

II. Correct matching of categories and leaders, application of the categories to at least five local or national leaders, but a narrow construction of the C.D.

III. Generally correct matching of categories and leaders, but with some errors, only the most minimal construction of the C.D.

IV. Some correct matching of categories and leaders but frequent error, no construction of the C.D. at all.

V. No matching of categories and leaders whatsoever, no construction of the C.D., no apparent understanding of the terms.

1% of those respondents who did not match liberal and conservative correctly to at least some leaders and who could not manage a coherent construction of the C.D. suggested any ideational categories other than liberal and conservative in response here. Extensive probing in our mass sample subset added even more convincing indication that respondents unable to recognize and apply the C.D. are unable to apply any such ideological dimension.

All this, as we noted earlier, simply confirms the Converse conclusions. But we add a new dimension when Bloomfield and Putnam respondents are compared with education controlled (see Table 32). Every educational group in Bloomfield shows a substantially higher comprehension of the Conventional Dichotomy than its Putnam counterpart. This suggests, we believe, the importance of community setting as a conditioning instrument. College education unquestionably is an important factor introducing large numbers of Americans to abstract political constructions. But our data indicate that the type of political setting in which the individual operates is influential, too. Long exposure to a community political system in which abstract conceptual dimensions are irrelevant "teaches" us to take such dimensions lightly and provides no "training" in their use.

"Education" has still another dimension: the Bloomfield lawyer attached to a big Hartford firm and the Putnam lawyer in a small local practice show up the same in any representation of formal educational background, but the type of materials with which they work in their respective careers typically are vastly different. The latter is preoccupied with matters narrowly local, often the petty torts, assorted malfeasances, and marital habits of his fellow Putnamites.

Only 3 per cent of the Putnam population applied "any relatively abstract and far-reaching conceptual dimension" to order the flow of public life, in sharp contrast to 22 per cent in Bloomfield. This difference is even greater than it might at first appear. The ideologues of Putnam are a tiny fringe, unimportant to the ideational life of their town. But their counterparts in Bloomfield are numerous enough to dominate—that is, set the tone for—the suburb's ideational life.

II. POLITICAL GROUPS AND POLITICAL IDEAS

Politics in any setting is ideological when the policy positions taken by the participants are sufficiently constrained and wide-

Table 32. Use and comprehension of the C.D., Bloomfield and Putnam samples, by educational background (expressed as percentages of n)

	Bloomfield				Putnam			
Stratum	0–8 yrs. school (n = 72)	9–11 yrs. school (n = 73)	H.S. grad. (n = 170)	At least some coll. (n = 175)	0–8 yrs. school (n = 150)	9–11 yrs. school (n = 70)	H.S. grad. (n = 82)	At least some coll. (n = 33)
I	3	4	4	17	0	0	1	9
II	6	8	6	28	0	0	2	12
III	32	49	71	43	1	3	13	48
IV	43	30	16	12	46	61	57	21
V	17	8	3	0	53	36	27	10

ranging that the economies of ideological models speak to them. More precisely, two interdependent conditions must be met if the application of such models is to prove valid: a substantial portion (in numbers or influence) must use overarching conceptual dimensions to order conflict, and the conflict itself must be of sufficient scope to sustain packaging. It would be quite inaccurate to speak of Cosmopolitans and Parochials in Putnam, although we found individual responses which we could locate in the Cosmopolitan-Parochial polarity. The interaction of the two conditions is apparent. A principal reason why most Putnam leaders do not see politics ideologically is that they have learned that the constraints of ideology are irrelevant to the divisions they are required to deal with.

Only a portion of conflict in any system can be accounted for in terms of ideology. There will be arguments around personalities and narrow interests in the most ideological politics. Thus, an observer wishing to describe conflict in Bloomfield as efficiently and parsimoniously as possible, must apply the economies of ideological categories, but a great deal of conflict is not in any way accounted for by these categories. Few Bloomfield leaders fit neatly into one of the four ideological types: liberal-Cosmopolitan, conservative-Cosmopolitan, liberal-Parochial, conservative-Parochial. Still, this typology orders conflict in the suburb more efficiently and precisely than otherwise possible.

The Principal Ideological Divide

Conservative-Parochialism is sustained by two principal sociopolitical groups: Old Bloomfield, the old middle class of the small town; and a new lower-middle class of marginal SES position in eastern Bloomfield. Both groups appear to find current developments threatening to their status. Old Bloomfield has been inundated by post–1950 population growth. It has seen Bloomfield transformed from a farming village to a white-collar suburb, and has witnessed changes, at least in part unsatisfactory, in the distribution of influence, the structure of local government, and the level of services. This is not to say that the political role of the conservative-Parochial leadership of Old Bloomfield is uniform. A portion of the old middle class, defeated in a series of engagements, has largely withdrawn from public life. They may occasionally strike out, as in the attack on redevelopment by the Betterment Association, but for the most part are inactive. Others have bowed to the transformation of the small town into a suburb, with all that implies, and have thus far maintained an active position in local government, in alliance with conservative-Cosmopolitans. The conservative-Parochial group, including two members of the town Council and one of the Board of Education, has often deferred to the conservative-Cosmopolitans, giving the latter both votes and a broader base in contests with liberal-Cosmopolitans. In return, these conservative-Parochials have received recognition and limited influence in local political affairs, and have avoided complete displacement.

The new marginal middle class of east Bloomfield has repeatedly clashed with Old Bloomfield as east vs. west, newcomers vs. old-timers, newer ethnic groups vs. WASPs. A natural alliance of conservative-Parochials has not been realized, then, because of difference in ethnicity, religion, occupation, and orientation to the community within the ranks. The adroitness of the conservative-Cosmopolitans in preventing a more complete alienation of Old Bloomfield probably has also helped block a working alliance of conservative-Parochials. It remains possible, however, that an issue will arise—and race is the most likely—to realize the ideological potential.

Twenty-one of ninety leaders interviewed are conservative-Parochials. They have resisted the integration of Negroes into Bloomfield life by fighting the compulsory crosstown busing of school children and opposing at earlier stages the activity which culminated in the voluntary busing program and the construction of a new lower middle school. They are strong opponents of regionalism and consistently adhere to a "low tax, low expenditure" position. Conservative-Parochials have not been sources of change and innovation in community life but have confined themselves to a general resistance to the innovative activity of others. Though typically less involved with national issues and argument, they strongly criticized the domestic programs of the Great Society, especially such components of it as antipoverty and Medicare. Without exception, the conservative-Parochials in our sample defended the current American position in Vietnam on grounds of patriotism, support of the President, and resistance to communism on behalf of freedom.

We have located below each of the twenty-one conservative-Parochials on a 360° graph (see Diagram 6). No attempt was made, we should stress, to assign each leader a mathematically expressed point on the graph. But on the basis of interview materials, all leaders were located on the two axes, and our representation does describe these positions accurately in relation to all those classified in the community. The graph will have the special utility as we use it in this and the following chapter of suggesting the substantial range or variation within each type. The several leaders identified show substantial ideological differences, although each would properly be described as a conservative-Parochial.

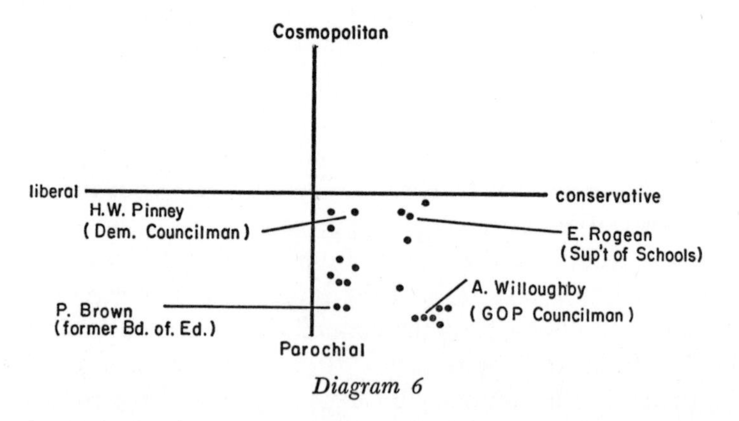

Diagram 6

Liberal-Parochialism is the least represented of the four ideological types in Bloomfield. We would expect it to be generated in the needs, interests, and cognitions of lower-class whites and Negroes, and these groups are not numerous in the suburb. Eight Bloomfield leaders were classified as liberal-Parochials, five Negroes and three whites (see Diagram 7). They have been active principally in race relations, supporting integration of neighborhoods and other measures permitting Negro Americans to share in a normal suburban existence. They have strongly backed measures to eliminate imbalance in Bloomfield schools. Nationally, they applauded the Johnson administration's civil rights policies, and were broadly supportive of the welfare programs of the Great Society. But they have little contextual grasp of politics beyond Bloomfield or Hartford's North End. Typically, they have richly-detailed information on racial problems in Bloomfield, but their perspectives are narrow. Lacking command of a body of technical expertise treating racial problems in suburbs and in the larger society, they have been forced to play a peripheral role, one of exhortation rather than innovation. Racial problems often are conceptualized in narrowly moralistic terms.

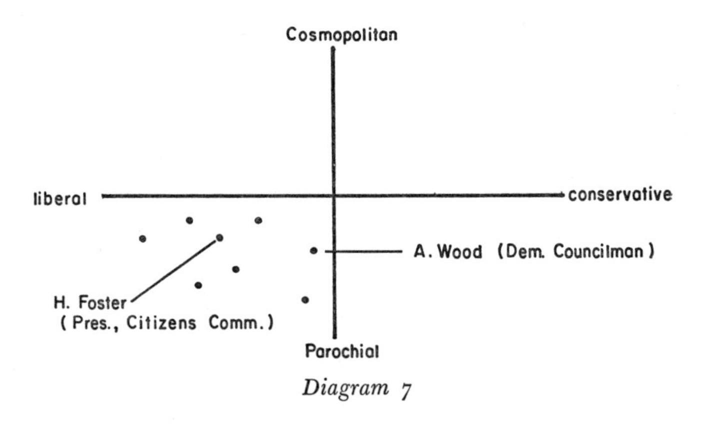

Diagram 7

Liberal-Cosmopolitanism is a major ideological position in the suburb. But though influential, the policy preferences of liberal-Cosmopolitans have not been ascendant or controlling. Eighteen of the ninety leaders interviewed were classified as liberal-Cosmopolitans. Fifteen are whites, three Negroes. All are college educated. All are relative newcomers to Bloomfield. Liberal-Cosmopolitans hold the major leadership positions in the BIC and the Citizens Committee. They have representation but are a distinct minority in the leadership of the suburb's Republican party. And they are a major block in the Democratic party and threatened in the late 1960's to seize control from the conservative-Parochials who had run the party since the early 1950's. Liberal-Cosmopolitans are oriented toward national political life, and they typically see local divisions linked to broader national ones. In 1965–67, when this research was conducted, the Johnson administration was praised for its beginnings in civil rights, antipoverty, urban redevelopment, and related dimensions of the Great Society. But it was strongly criticized for having faltered, principally due to commitments of money and psychic energy to the war in Vietnam. Liberal-Cosmopolitans reject anticommunism as a sufficient guiding principle for American foreign policy. The communist world in the 1960's is a highly disparate collection of state systems, each influenced by national interests more important to their foreign policies than communism. Liberal-Cosmopolitans with near unanimity opposed American involvement in Vietnam: "We are not fighting communism but rather Vietnamese nationalism." "Any threat which Chinese nationalism may pose is not being confronted." "It is at least questionable whether the people of South Vietnam would be better off under the regimes we have supported." "We have lost support in the world because of our Vietnam position, and have precluded further mitigation of the Cold War with the Soviet Union." "We have disturbed our body politic, fragmented the liberal alliance in Congress, and siphoned off national resources which could have built a better society domestically."

Liberal-Cosmopolitans are suburbanites, not small-towners. Their attachments are entirely to the new Bloomfield. Though many value the opportunities for participation which the small community provides, they are strongly committed by both their liberalism and their Cosmopolitanism to the region: "Local control is good, but in some cases it is a luxury we can't afford." Bloomfield is part of a rapidly expanding and problem-ridden region and while there is a real appeal to hiding behind suburban boundaries, there is no intellectual justification for doing so. Ways should be found to distribute part of the growing core-city Negro population throughout the suburban towns. Experimentation with regional solutions to racial imbalance in city schools should be encouraged. They want their community to grow, to welcome Negroes as long as it is in no danger of becoming largely Negro, and to integrate Negroes into community life. They see a Bloomfield increasingly committed to regional approaches, under federal and state sponsorship, to such problems as blight, unplanned growth and the isolation of the nonwhite poor, and are willing to give up at least a bit of their autonomy to regional institutions. Once again, the positions of our ideologues are more precisely located (see Diagram 8).

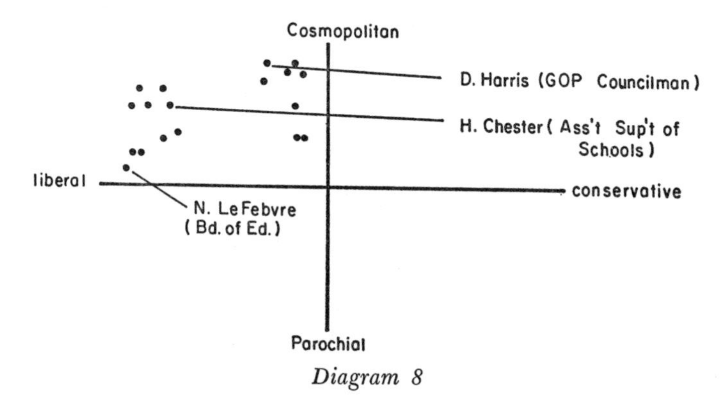

Diagram 8

When research was conducted, conservative-Cosmopolitans were running Bloomfield (see Diagram 9). Their strategies were followed, their goals implemented. Twenty-five of the ninety community leaders are conservative-Cosmopolitans. Yet their influence has been greater than numbers might suggest. In their ranks are the town manager, the chairman of the Council, and the chairman of the Board of Education, plus other key leaders in the political parties and a majority of the major business leaders. Conservative-Cosmopolitans have tried to balance the demands of liberal-Cosmopolitans and conservative-Parochials, and have been sufficiently successful to maintain working relations with both and to put through programs which many in both camps could accept.

They are ideally situated, ideologically, to act as mediators, sharing much of the "world view" of the liberal-Cosmopolitans. They have welcomed rather than feared the transformation of Bloomfield into a white-collar suburb, are at home in a big, bureaucratized, metropolitanized, industrial America. There is no nostalgia for a more personalized, localized, independent society. Conservative-Cosmopolitans understand and sympathize with the pressures toward regionalism. Their perspectives are cosmopolitan, not local. Of secure and ascendant status, they can afford, like liberal-Cosmopolitans, a tolerant posture to the demands of change-oriented, low-status groups. But their conservatism has made their approach far more acceptable to conservative-Parochials.

One conservative-Cosmopolitan, active in Republican politics in Bloomfield, revealed both dimensions of this position, what set him apart from conservative-Parochials and what made alliances with the latter possible in some circumstances.

I am both attracted and put off by the welfare programs of the Johnson administration. There is clearly a need for welfare programs like antipoverty, for urban renewal and redevelopment and the like. The object should be to help people who cannot by themselves remedy their situation, and in helping them strengthen the fabric of the entire society. But at the same time, you should not take action such as to blunt people's initiative and drive. And the Johnson administration's programs have done this to a certain extent. . . . There needs to be some arrangement whereby people are more encouraged to advance themselves. These things are hard to blend, aren't they? . . . I am attracted by [Medicare] and at the same time put off. Medical expenditures have increased fantastically, people are living longer, and the whole structure of families has changed, become more nuclear. Frankly, it will benefit me to have Medicare, because my parents are alive and that age, and they don't have the money to handle a major illness. I would have to pick it up. But still, I would like to see if we could not work out some private approach which would do the job. Maybe we can't, but I am not satisfied that we explored all of these alternatives as far as we might have [this was July, 1965].

Although committed to the same analysis of racial problems and the course of their resolution as liberal-Cosmopolitans, conservative-Cosmopolitans draw away from government action "to achieve arithmetical balance." And as liberal-Cosmopolitans operate from the premise that Bloomfield's failings in race relations demand direct confrontation and dramatization, conservative-Cosmopolitans value more highly accommodation, compromise, and adjustment for the maintenance of stability. More generally, the two groups of Cosmopolitans separate over relative receptivity to the demands of disadvantaged groups. When they look beyond our shores, both see communism as a many-splendored thing, continually evolving; still, on Vietnam they were sharply divided, conservative-Cosmopolitans generally supportive of the Johnson administration, liberal-Cosmopolitans uniformly critical.

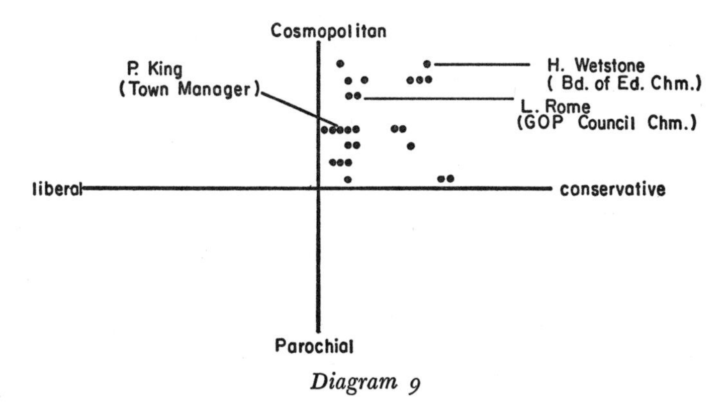

Diagram 9

Seventy-two of the ninety Bloomfield influentials interviewed were thus located in the typology. Eighteen do not appear, for one of two reasons. The ideational positions of twelve were insufficiently wide-ranging and constrained. They simply never saw conflict as other than highly immediate and specific, personal or group interests.[13] The remaining six adhered to coherent, extremely conservative or radical rightist positions, and thus, while ideologues, were outside our typology.

None of the liberal-Cosmopolitans are part of Old Bloomfield. Indeed, the longest term of residence in the suburb for any of this group was thirteen years (in 1966). All are college graduates and eleven of the eighteen hold professional degrees. They (or their spouses) are employed as clergymen, lawyers, educators, social workers. Seventeen of the eighteen are Democrats. Although all the major religious denominations and many different ethnic groups are represented, the largest number (seven) are Jewish. Liberal-Cosmopolitans are younger than other Bloomfield leaders. They are upwardly mobile, the children of such parents as storekeepers, service station operators, and tailors.

Although conservative-Cosmopolitans are not Old Bloomfield (only five of the twenty-five had lived in the suburb as long as three decades), they are older than the liberal-Cosmopolitans and have had a longer attachment to the community. In 1966, the median residence for conservative-Cosmopolitans was sixteen years, contrasting with six for the liberal-Cosmopolitans. Like the latter, they are well educated; twenty-three are college graduates and fourteen hold professional degrees. Like liberal-Cosmopolitans in Bloomfield, they typically attended a "prestige" eastern university: Wesleyan, Tufts, Harvard, Yale, the University of Pennsylvania, Oberlin, Trinity, Brandeis. Occupationally, conservative-Cosmopolitans are upper middle class: corporation executives, lawyers, professional government administrators, and doctors. Ethnically and religiously, WASPs and Jews are the predominant groups.

Since conservative-Parochials are drawn from two quite distinct groups, an old middle class and a new lower middle class,

[13] The line dividing an ideological from a nonideological view of politics in practice, though not in theory, is located in a quite arbitrary manner. But there are some activists who apply no overarching dimensions to order public life and thus reveal a bewildering scatter of responses.

aggregate biographical data in a sense is conflicting or contradictory. Still, their median length of residence in Bloomfield was twenty-seven years, substantially longer than for the other groups. Small business and lower white-collar positions are the most common occupations. Only six of the twenty-one are college graduates, and only one of these has a professional degree. All but four are WASPs or Italian and Irish Catholics. Conservative-Parochials show an even division in party affiliation—eleven Republicans and ten Democrats—but this conceals the clear Republican allegiance of Old Bloomfield and the Democratic ascendancy among the new middle class of eastern Bloomfield. Conservative-Parochials are of a distinctly lower SES position than either group of Cosmopolitans. These data are summarized in Table 33.

A Closer Look at Some Specific Sociopolitical Groups

In 1968, Negroes were approximately twelve and one-half per cent of the population of Bloomfield, numbering 2,400 in a community of 19,000. And, according to data supplied by town officials in late 1967, all but sixty to seventy of the more than six hundred Negro families lived in the southeastern corner bordering on Hartford.[14] Most of these Negro suburbanites are marginal-middle-class, with both husband and wife working to bring family income to a level where it can buy the most modest suburban living. Negroes are not the only Bloomfielders in this marginal position, but as a group they rank below the white suburbanites by various indicators of socioeconomic status (see Table 34). Bloomfield had a small Negro population for three decades before the large influx of the 1960's, and most of these neither made nor are now making waves. Invariably, the small group of activists drawn from these "old" families are spoken of warmly and with pride by community leaders as "our good responsible Negro leaders." In

[14] See Map 2 in Chapter 3 for a more complete description.

Table 33. Bloomfield, four ideological groups, by a set of personal biographical variables

Variable	Liberal-Cosmopolitans (n = 18)	Conservative-Cosmopolitans (n = 25)	Liberal-Parochials (n = 8)	Conservative-Parochials (n = 21)
Age (median)	37 yrs.	52 yrs.	54 yrs.	52 yrs.
Residence				
Three decades or longer in Bloomfield (as of 1966)	–	20	13	48
Less than 15 years in Bloomfield	100	48	50	29
Median years in Bloomfield	6	16	16	27
Occupations				
Professionals and salaried executives	100	92	25	14
Small business owners	–	8	–	38
Lower white-collar workers	–	–	50	38
Blue-collar workers	–	–	25	10
Sex				
Male	67	88	63	90
Female	33	12	38	10
Education				
Eighth grade or less	–	–	13	–
Some high school, high school graduate	–	8	50	71
Some college, college graduate	39	36	38	24
Professional degree	61	56	–	5
Ethnicity				
Anglo-Saxon	22	36	–	38
Irish	6	4	13	14
North European	–	20	13	5
Italian	11	–	–	29
Jewish	39	32	13	10
Negro	17	–	63	5
Other	–	8	–	–
Political party				
Republican	6	64	25	52
Democrat	94	36	75	48

Note: All figures are percentages of n unless otherwise indicated.

Table 34. Bloomfield Negroes and whites, by socioeconomic status variables, 1965 sample survey data

Variable	Bloomfield whites (n = 445)*	Bloomfield Negroes (n = 45)
Percentage of families earning over $10,000	46	15
Percentage college graduates	24	9
Percentage employed as white-collar professionals	36	8

* Number of respondents is lower for income and occupation variables.

1965–67, one Negro of long residence in Bloomfield was on the Council, and another was a selectman. Still, not all of Bloomfield's older Negro families consider past relations as exemplary as whites appear to. One Negro woman spoke of her experience in the late 1940's and early 1950's:

Well, until recently Bloomfield Negroes took all their social and economic activities into the North End of Hartford, and thus developed no personal ties or affections for the community. Many still do have most of their friends in the North End. It took me an awful long time to feel that I was accepted at all as part of the Bloomfield community, even though I had been active on committees in the community. . . . I was never invited into a fellow board member's home in all my years on that board. As a member of the Republican Town Committee I was treated so cruelly that often others on the committee wouldn't recognize me when they saw me on the street. I finally resigned from the Town Committee because I felt like a stranger.

In the late 1950's and 1960's, Bloomfield received a relatively large immigration of younger, marginal-middle-class Negroes from the North End. These Negro newcomers, docile by current Black Power standards, have shown considerable impatience with the older Negro activists. They speak out more forcefully, and the leadership which they are sustaining is somewhat less acceptable to most Bloomfield whites. Certainly, the relationship of whites to the new Negro leadership lacks the condescending intimacy possible with the old. The new Negroes confront the new whites as strangers, and their interactions are far more formal and impersonal. Again, the newer Negro leadership is middle-class leadership and its style is far removed from that of ghetto leadership. But it does insist on confronting more directly questions of discrimination or imbalance, and it pushes more for their resolution. Younger Negro leaders have been active principally through the biracial Intergroup Council and the largely Negro Citizens Committee.

The newer activists are slightly ahead of their constituents, and express unhappiness that Bloomfield Negroes are not more aggressive.

> You know, a fellow scrimps and saves for years and at last is able to buy a place in Bloomfield. He feels, "Now I've got it made." Well, that kind of a guy isn't going to rock the boat much. He has just gotten what he has been working for for a long time. . . . One of the big fears Negroes here in Bloomfield have is that this eastern corner will become a ghetto. They have just escaped a ghetto and they don't want this to turn into another one.

For many Bloomfield Negroes, escape from Hartford's North End and the purchase of a small house in the suburb has been an achievement, and they wish to rest a while on this plateau. Thus, their demands have been modest and quietly represented. But the Negro population continues to expand, and its base of supply in the city ghetto is not about to be exhausted. With greater numbers will come, almost certainly, heightened demands. A Bloomfield sharply bifurcated into a west and central portion of more affluent whites, and an eastern corner of marginal-middle-class Negroes remains the most likely future.

"Are you in favor of the Federal Government's antipoverty program?" (Responses are expressed as percentages of *n*.)

	Yes	*No*	*Undecided* and *Don't know*
Negroes (*n* = 45)	93	4	3
Whites (*n* = 445)	72	16	12

	"Some people favor our foreign aid program and others are critical of it. Do you, generally speaking, favor or oppose the program?"			"Some think we should relax our immigration quotas to allow more people from foreign countries to become citizens of our country. Do you agree or disagree?"		
	(Responses are expressed as percentages of *n*.)					
	Favor	*Oppose*	*Undecided* and *Don't know*	*Agree*	*Disagree*	*Undecided* and *Don't know*
Negroes ($n = 45$)	60	40	–	29	64	7
Whites ($n = 445$)	61	31	8	38	51	11

On matters dealing strictly with race, in Bloomfield or nationally, Negroes and whites are far apart. The former will continue to make demands for full entry into community life that a large segment of whites will resist. But outside immediate group interests, Negroes and whites in the suburb do not see the issues of public life very differently. Negroes were somewhat more supportive of federal welfare programs. But they were no more willing to share American abundance with others. Nor are they more tolerant of the civil liberties of other minorities.

"Should anyone who is a Communist be allowed to go about the country freely?" (Responses are expressed as percentages of *n*.)

	Yes	*No*	*Undecided* and *Don't know*
Negroes ($n = 45$)	33	67	0
Whites ($n = 445$)	40	51	9

Bloomfield Negroes generally respond, in short, as their economic position and educational level would suggest. One important exception, however, is in party preferences. Negroes are overwhelmingly Democratic, and the growth of the Negro population in the suburb can hardly be a source of comfort to Republican leaders.

"Generally speaking, do you consider yourself a Republican, a Democrat, or something else?" (Responses are expressed as percentages of *n*.)

	Rep.	*Dem.*	*Other (principally Independent)*
Negroes (n = 45)	0	91	9
Whites (n = 445)	28	35	37

In the 1960's, Bloomfield had a small collection of community activists whose ideational commitments fell outside the principal polarities. They are extreme conservatives or Radical Rightists. Six of the leaders interviewed were identified with the extreme Right. Four acknowledged membership in the John Birch Society. Economically, all are successes. They include a legal counsel to a major bank, leading insurance company executives, the president of a small but prospering corporation. All are college graduates. They are striking in their technical accomplishments. One, while being interviewed, calmly and in a matter-of-fact manner concluded a financial transaction involving millions of dollars. They are not, in short, out of touch with the new America, but creatures of it, men who are unusually well equipped to succeed within a big, bureaucratized industrial system. In each interview, we were impressed by the contrast between the modernity of their approach to economic life, their technical expertise, their sophistication and confidence in handling the complex tasks thrust on them by their occupations; and that curious blend of prescientific orthodoxies infused with passion which is their political philosophy.[15]

All seven Radical Rightists interviewed had strongly supported Goldwater's candidacy. All indicated they would welcome a conservative party in Connecticut, and all had backed the Republican Citizens Committee, a right wing splinter or-

[15] Although a careful examination of the sources of the Radical Right is beyond our purposes here, I did suggest some tentative explanations in another work. See "The Radical Right," *South Atlantic Quarterly*, LXV (Summer, 1966), 314–324.

ganization active in Connecticut between 1962 and 1966. They showed evidence of having read widely—though heavily in conservative journals and tracts—and had accumulated enormous quantities of information about American political life, even though, typically, this was distorted in strategic places. They spoke easily and confidently about public life, but with bitterness. Our interviewers were led through blow-by-blow accounts of the treacheries of American foreign policy since 1930 (lasting over two hours). It varied on specifics and in emphasis, but here was the standard cosmology of the Radical Right. America's difficulties had begun with Roosevelt who carried the country to socialism. Businessmen are penalized for their initiative. Graduated taxation is iniquitous. The real enemy is the increasing number of Americans who "think like Communists." There is a growing disrespect for law and order and the hands of the police are tied. The National Council of Churches is populated with "comsymps" and the United Nations is a Communist instrument. Somehow the trend to greater and greater federal usurpations must be stopped.

Several of the Bloomfield Radical Rightists attempted in times past to gain power in the local Republican party, but were rebuffed. In 1968, none held office in the suburb or position in either party. Though prosperous businessmen, they are unable to express freely their political views without inviting vituperative criticism. Little wonder, perhaps, they display symptoms of a kind of political paranoia! One told the interviewer, after nearly four hours, "You know, this is one of the few times I have ever had a chance to talk to a person who didn't share my views without having him attack me. I appreciate having the chance to express my ideas without your arguing with me." We are not suggesting that the Radical Rightists of Bloomfield deserve sympathy. But they are a somewhat anomalous group, mixing professional acumen and sophistication with a set of political views which exclude them from most community political life. Not since the budget battle in 1961 have they intervened actively and publicly in a major local dispute. Their inactivity, or at least the absence of overt activity, as Bloomfield's racial tensions increase is striking.

Many Bloomfield leaders speak of "both parties working together for the good of Bloomfield" and deny the existence of serious policy differences. In fact, sharp divisions exist within each party and are especially deep among the Democrats. Large numbers of Democrats moved to Bloomfield in the decade after 1957 and made Bloomfield a Democratic community in that Democrats now hold a substantial plurality over Republicans in party registration. But for the Democrats of Old Bloomfield, this new-found wealth in voters has been a mixed blessing. Old Bloomfield was a Republican community, but there were few policy differences between the Republican and Democratic leaders. Yankee Catholics such as H. Ward Pinney, a former state representative and in 1968 a member of the Town Council, and Phillips Brown, a florist who has held a number of positions in Bloomfield government, ran the Democratic party. These Democratic leaders of Old Bloomfield were conservative-Parochials, and they established without much difficulty an alliance with the Irish and Italian Democrats who moved into Bloomfield's east side in the 1940's and 1950's. But in the 1960's, a new group of Democrats began arriving in Bloomfield and promptly declared war on the established party leadership. The party was split, permitting the continued ascendancy of the now-minority Republicans.

The new Democrats are young well-educated professionals; many are Jews and Negroes. The new Democratic leaders are mostly liberal-Cosmopolitans. Thus, Bloomfield's Democracy has entered a real if undeclared war between liberal-Cosmopolitans and conservative-Parochials. And unlike the G.O.P., they have few conservative-Cosmopolitans to act as mediators. One of the first clear-cut manifestations of this conflict was the Democratic caucus in 1965. Phillips Brown, a conservative-Parochial, had been designated by the Democratic Town Committee for renomination to the Board of Education. But though Brown was a long-time member, the caucus rejected him, nominating instead a newcomer, Mrs. Norma LeFebvre, a young, bright, outspoken, and politically naive former Conecticut College coed. Mrs. LeFebvre was a liberal-Cosmopolitan, but for personality reasons proved an ineffective board member. She succeeded in alienating most who heard her. She was the "one" in a series of four-to-one decisions by the 1965–1967 Board, and repeatedly upbraided her colleagues for timidity in handling Bloomfield's racial problems.

In 1967, the Democratic Town Committee selected a "safe" slate of three for an expanded Board of Education. One was a four-term incumbent whose term was expiring, Oscar Coletta. Coletta had opposed any action by the board to meet *de facto* segregation, and had only reluctantly acceded to the compromise arranged in the spring of 1967. A second choice was Phillips Brown, the long-time incumbent who had lost his seat only two years before. The Democrats' third designee was Donald Harris, a Negro and a teacher at a Hartford high school. (The Republicans also nominated a Negro for one of the three slots open on the Board.) But only Harris survived the Democratic caucus. Liberal-Cosmopolitans were in control of the caucus, and the two conservative-Parochials were replaced. Incumbent Coletta was defeated by a young Hartford attorney, Paul Orth; and Phillips Brown was beaten again, by another young Hartford lawyer, Richard Turner. Turner's election campaign was an exceptionally vigorous one, and he was strongly supported by liberal-Cosmopolitans in the community. But in the election he and Orth were not challenging Parochials, whom they might well have defeated, but the conservative-Cosmopolitan, Republican leadership of the Board.

In the course of the campaign, one liberal-Cosmopolitan remarked to an interviewer: "You know, its funny about [Board of Education chairman Howard] Wetstone. Back around 1960 and 1961, we thought he was really great. But something has happened to him. He has changed a lot." We doubt that either

Wetstone or the respondent had changed much. It was the conflict situation which had changed. In 1961, Wetstone was spokesman for Cosmopolitans against the Parochial leadership of Old Bloomfield. He articulated the concerns which separated these two groups of ideologues. By 1967, the Parochials had been routed, and two groups of Cosmopolitans confronted each other in the school board election. Liberal-Cosmopolitans would have found much attracting them to the Republican conservative-Cosmopolitan nominees in 1967 had the latter been challenging Parochials over the shape of the suburb's school system. But the possibility of Parochial control of the Board had vanished. Turner, Orth, and Harris ran well behind their Republican opponents, with only Harris getting a place on the Board under Connecticut's minority representation law.

Liberal-Cosmopolitans will remain a major force, probably ascendant, in the Democratic party, bringing a more partisan tone to Bloomfield politics. They are little attracted by community consensus, and their model posits sharp party conflict. Their contempt for the conservative-Parochial old guard of local Democratic party is poorly disguised. One said of this old guard:

> They just don't know what is going on. They are committed to inactivity, to the *status quo*. They can't do the job, can't identify and respond to our problems. We must offer realistic alternatives to the programs of Rome and Wetstone. People like Brown and Coletta can't do this. They are small town types, completely out of it. The young professionals in town know this. They are the ones I look to.

In the late 1960's, conservative-Cosmopolitans were in complete control of the Bloomfield Republican party (see Table 35).

We noted in Chapter 6 that Putnam Republicans and Democrats closely resemble each other in their socioeconomic profiles. The only clear difference between these two groups of identifiers is in ethnic backgrounds. But Republicans and Democrats in Bloomfield differ sharply in social and economic position, with the G.O.P. the upper-status party. We can com-

Table 35. Bloomfield Republican and Democratic leaders, by ideological position (expressed as percentages of *n*)

Party	Liberal-Cosmopolitan	Conservative-Cosmopolitan	Liberal-Parochial	Conservative-Parochial
Republican (n = 30)	3	53	7	37
Democratic (n = 42)	41	21	14	24

pare Republican and Democratic adherents for level of family income and educational backgrounds. We can also approach this another way. Republican identification drops precipitously as we move from high- to low-status respondents.

	Bloomfield Republicans (n = 110)*	*Bloomfield Democrats* (n = 171)
Family income		
Under $5,000	12	15
$5,000 to $10,000	28	55
Over $10,000	60	30
Education	(n = 120)	(n = 189)
High school education or less	49	79
At least some college	51	21

* Data are expressed as percentages of *n*.

"Generally speaking, do you consider yourself a Republican, a Democrat, or something else?" (All responses are expressed as percentages of *n*.)

	Rep.	*Dem.*	*Other (principally Independent)*
High SES (n = 89)*	41	19	40
Medium SES (n = 113)	13	57	30
Low SES (n = 37)	0	41	59

* For purposes of analysis here, low SES was defined by family income of less than $5,000 per year and less than a high school education. Medium SES was defined by a family income of between $5,000 and $10,000 and a high school education; and high SES by family income of over $10,000 per year and a college education. Two hundred and thirty-nine of the 490 respondents in Bloomfield met one of these three sets of criteria.

Since Republicans and Democrats in the suburb differ significantly in socioeconomic position, we should not be surprised that they disagree in wide areas of policy choice. The "have-not" Republicans of Putnam swallowed their partisanship and endorsed the domestic welfare programs of the Great Society. Their more prosperous suburban brethren offered substantial opposition. Especially striking is the contrast in the responses of hard-core Republicans in the two communities.

	"Are you in favor of the Medicare program now before Congress?"			"Are you in favor of the Federal Government's antipoverty program?"		
	(Responses are expressed as percentages of *n*.)					
	Yes	*No*	*Undecided* and *Don't know*	*Yes*	*No*	*Undecided* and *Don't know*
All Republican identifiers (n = 120)	52	39	9	53	33	14
All Democratic identifiers (n = 191)	95	3	2	84	6	10
Hard-core Democrats (n = 83)	100	0	0	84	5	11
Hard-core Republicans (n = 69)	39	48	13	46	45	9
Hard-core Republicans in Putnam (n = 33)	70	21	9	73	27	0

In Bloomfield, conflict assumes greater scope than in Putnam as a more politically literate citizenry confronts a much more dynamic and expansive public sector. Bloomfield is a changing community in a rapidly changing metropolitan region. Though it prospers, struggles over the direction of change and its implications contribute a cutting edge of uneasiness to its politics. A less prosperous Putnam basks in relative community satisfaction. As political argument in the small town is of an older variety, rooted in personalities and patronage, in the suburb it is generated by the clashing service demands and status interests of different layers of the population. Putnam's ideational conflict is, like the larger community setting which nourished it, we think, a variety in decline. The concerns which divide Bloomfielders and the way they conceptualize these seem to point to patterns which will occur with greater frequency in community ideational systems.

8. Hartford: The Ideational Life of an American City

The task of describing political ideas and ideology in a big city, even a "little old" big city like Hartford, is a forbidding one. More than modesty requires that this be said. There is simply much more of everything, and analysis of ideational conflict for the city thus is less complete and exhaustive, and more skeletal and suggestive than for town and suburb. In addition, although the suburb is linked to the sociopolitical life of the metropolitan region, the city thoroughly merges with the region. One influential segment of the political leadership of Hartford—business and professional leaders—lives outside the city. And Hartford still serves as the region's economic and cultural heart. Our approach to the ideational life of Hartford will depart in a number of ways from Bloomfield's and Putnam's, with the differences resulting principally from the greater scope and complexity of the city's public life.

Conflict takes different forms in our three communities. Local government in Putnam has never been an instrument for social change, and the public sector there is not a battleground in which contending groups seek to impose their conflicting prescriptions for the course of change. Government is seen as an instrument for social change in both our city and our suburb. The contending claims to Bloomfield's future, though, are all middle-class: Negro middle class and white; marginal lower-middle and upper-middle; the farming and entrepreneurial old middle class of the small town and the professional and managerial new middle class of the suburb. In Hartford, the conflicting objectives and expectations are at once more sharply divergent and hotly disputed: those of a disadvantaged black lower class which is the latest entry into the urban melting pot; of white lower and lower-middle classes which in the last half century won political ascendancy in the city; of a business and professional elite who are disproportionately suburban dwellers but who have strong economic and cultural interests in the future of the city.

The public sectors of our three communities range from the minimal and limited of the small town to that of the central city dominated by the pressing domestic concerns of our times—racial conflict, poverty, congestion and blight, crime. Catalogs of urban "crises" have become commonplace, but this should not cause us to overlook the fact that conflict in the city is fundamentally set off from that of the town or the suburb by depth and urgency. The ideational life of Hartford reflects the intrusion of virtually the entire range of major domestic concerns. Hartford leaders cannot avoid responding to the big national domestic issues, and their conflicting assessments of the problems and varying prescriptions as to solution bear important implications for the future of the city.

As conflict assumes its narrowest, most limited, concrete, and personal dimensions in the small town, it takes on its broadest, most abstract, categoric, and impersonal configurations in the city. Hartford, Bloomfield, and Putnam are all "local communities," but they present divergent conflict situations, sustaining markedly different sets of issues and structures of political discourse.

I. THE TALK IN HARTFORD

What Are the Problems?

Race Relations. Race is never far below the surface in the talk in Hartford. Welded to status and economics, it intrudes in most of the difficult problems which preoccupy the city's elites. In Hartford as elsewhere, schools have been a focal point in race-linked controversies. The city of Hartford has operated with what is essentially a system of schools housing kindergarten through eighth grade, with pupil assignment on a neighborhood basis. This, coupled to the concentration of Negroes and Puerto Ricans in North Hartford, has produced sets of schools nearly all white in the South End and overwhelmingly nonwhite in the North End, with only a half dozen schools approaching the city-wide white/nonwhite ratio. In 1967–68, two North End schools, Arsenal and Clark, had between them seven white pupils, while two in the South End, Burr and Kennelly, together had but seventeen nonwhites. The white/nonwhite balance for the entire system is rapidly changing. White pupils declined from 55.2 per cent of the total in 1964 to 44.6 per cent in October, 1967.

The exodus of whites from city schools, the growth of the nonwhite school population, and *de facto* segregation form the core of a continuing series of controversies. There has been prolonged and bitter argument over school building programs, the location of schools, and the distribution of grades; over the future of neighborhood schools and intracity busing; over how, if at all, the metropolitan region should be involved in Hartford's school problems. Two massively distinct and conflicting positions have emerged. Many Negro leaders and some of their white allies feel that Hartford should make the removal of racial imbalance a principal objective. Most spokesmen for South End whites insist with equal firmness that nonwhite pupils not be brought into the schools of South Hartford or white pupils there transported out. Thus pressured, city administrators in the school system and outside it, portions of the business leadership, and some city-wide elected leaders have sought solutions.

One avenue explored was suburban busing. In 1965, the Harvard Graduate School of Education presented to the Hartford Board of Education a report which tried to suggest how an urban school system rapidly getting darker should respond over the next decade. One of the recommendations dealt with suburban busing, and when the Harvard consultants spoke of busing "poverty area" pupils they meant nonwhites. "We recommend that by 1974, 6,000 pupils be bused from the poverty areas of the city to the area surrounding the City of Hartford." [1]

This suburban busing recommendation of the Harvard Report was not received with unrestrained enthusiasm. Negro leaders whom we interviewed typically concurred on the desirability of busing, but none assumed the forefront of support for such a program. The Democratic political leadership of South Hartford, which might have been expected to strongly endorse a program costing them nothing and relieving pressure on South End schools, was distinctly unresponsive. Predictably, a cry of "Foul!" went up from some in the suburbs. But there were three main groups of supporters: the education establishment, including area superintendents of schools, officials of the state Department of Education and other professional educators; the business community of Hartford through the Greater Hartford Chamber of Commerce; and collections of "committed" suburbanites, including human relations commissions in the suburban towns.

In March, 1966, the Connecticut Department of Education formally proposed busing children from segregated city schools to the suburbs. Recognizing the potential for strong opposition, the Department underscored the "experimental" aspects of its program. It would be a pilot project, and there were no assumptions that it would naturally mature to the proportions envisioned by the Harvard consultants (6,000 children bused by 1974). This would be a two-year trial, fully financed by Federal monies, busing between two and three hundred Hartford Negroes each year. Four Hartford suburbs were suggested as likely participants.[2] This plan was given strong backing by the

[1] Harvard Graduate School of Education, *Schools for Hartford* (1965), pp. 10–11.

[2] The four were West Hartford, Glastonbury, Farmington, and Manchester. Bloomfield was expressly excluded in such planning because, as

Greater Hartford Chamber of Commerce. Actually, the Chamber had participated in its formulation. Its Education Committee prepared and sent to school officials in area suburbs a letter urging support.

But along with support, there was strong hostility in the designated suburbs. Meetings held to discuss participation drew big, angry crowds. A public hearing in the spring of 1966 in West Hartford, the most affluent of the Hartford suburbs, attracted 1,200 persons. One hostile white proclaimed that "I worked hard forty years so that I could live in West Hartford and have my children educated here. No one bused me in here." Still another insisted that "this busing plan will only cause hatred, as you can see here tonight. This should never have been placed in the hands of the Board of Education." He went on:

> I have a feeling that the Board of Education has already made up its mind on this matter and I fear the minority will prevail. The Negro should have to do it the hard way the same as I did. During the Depression, I was on welfare in this town and I have paid the Welfare Department back $1,500. I suggest that the Board of Education call a special election on this matter.

When a West Hartford Rabbi urged support for busing, he was booed and told "to take your congregation and go home."

A few days later, 1,200 Farmington residents packed their high school gymnasium in what was described as "the biggest town meeting in memory." The tone was the same as in West Hartford. One speaker felt that "these Hartford children have a place in the North End—let them stay there. Individual Negroes are friendly, but damn it, you get them together and you've got hell." Another observed that "living in Farmington is a reward, something we've all worked up to. You'll bring in a group that has not come up to this social standard. They'll feel as freaks, whereas in their own environment they'll feel

---

one Department of Education official put it, "they have enough problems of their own there."

very self-assured." And another argued that the Negroes of Hartford's North End "are not the higher element. If this is snobbery, let it be. But the educated Negro is not my complaint. What I complain about is the uneducated one who cries NAACP until I hear it ringing in my ears." But the meeting was told by a Negro mother from the North End to "look beyond the blackness of my skin, and you will find there the same concern for my children. We must prepare them to cope with life as it will be, and we live in a white society." And a student at the Farmington High School told his elders:

> I've seen an awful lot of prejudice and an awful lot of hate, but I never thought I would see it come to this town. . . . I cannot see why you people cannot set aside your prejudices and discuss whether this thing is socially and economically practical.

Similarly heated meetings were held in other Hartford suburbs.

When the shouting ended, five communities agreed to participate in the pilot program and accepted 265 Negro pupils. Busing started in September, 1966, and progressed to the satisfaction of the educators directing it. With the additional participation of five suburban Catholic schools, 350 Negro children were bused in the second year. Plans were formulated for the continuation and substantial expansion of busing, and such supporters as the Chamber of Commerce began, in late 1967, efforts to get the necessary suburban backing.

The proponents of suburban busing attempted throughout to keep the program an elite decision area, assuming strong popular opposition to the program. There appears to be ample basis for this assumption. The backers of busing in one participating suburb were soundly defeated in a subsequent town election, and most observers saw busing as the principal underlying issue. Attempts were made in a number of the participating suburbs to secure referenda on the program, but all of these were successfully opposed by the program's supporters.[3]

[3] Indeed, so anxious were supporters to avoid more extensive popular discussion of the program that they successfully resisted the initiation of

Suburban busing in Hartford was conceived, initiated, and executed by Cosmopolitans. It would not have succeeded in even the modest dimension in which it did without the consistent backing of the Cosmopolitans of the business and education "establishments." Parochial leaders in the city, whether whites in the South End or Negroes in the North End, remained at best mildly supportive.

In addition to suburban busing, the Harvard Report called for extensive busing of pupils within the city. Intracity busing was linked to a proposed reorganization of city schools in which the old K–8 units would be replaced by K–4 schols, servicing neighborhoods and presumably segregated, and middle schools (grades 5–8), constructed to avoid segregation and to require busing.[4] The Harvard plan also suggested the busing of Negro high school students from the North End to a new Bulkeley High School in south central Hartford. *Schools for Hartford,* in short, envisioned locating only a minimal number of schools, and all of these K–4, in North Hartford on the assumption that any school there would be wholly nonwhite. The intracity busing of nonwhite pupils thus would be central to the entire reorganization.

Predictably, intracity busing linked to a 4–4–4 school plan (primary schools: through grade 4; middle schools: grades 5–8; high schools: grades 9–12) generated extreme opposition in South Hartford. Virtually all political leaders based there expressed complete opposition. One city-wide leader who had his base of support in the South End told our interviewer:

Busing will not solve the problems of race. It has been tried in New York and it has been a failure, right? Whites in the South End will just never accept it. People in Hartford will never accept a Negro for mayor, nor will they ever allow a city official to appoint a

a study by social scientists at an area university of the politics of suburban busing. An architect of the program insisted that interviewing in participating communities could only serve to arouse more attention and controversy.

[4] *Schools for Hartford,* p. 17.

Negro as department head. It's not that the people in Hartford are any more prejudiced than those in any other city, it's just that they look at the number of Negroes on welfare in the North End, and see these people as being a great expense to the city. You've heard the stories. "They often spend their welfare checks on booze instead of food." . . . Actually, there is no sense to bus young children anyway. The problem of races doesn't come up until people reach an age where they can think about sex. They don't consider themselves boys and girls until they are about in the eighth grade. Then they start thinking of race. When a colored boy wants to go out with a white girl, then the idea of race becomes evident. . . . The race problem principally means that there are certain people in our society who are on relief, who generally cause a lot of problems. To end this cycle of relief, children should be taken away from the parents at an early age and then they would not inherit bad attitudes about jobs and work. This is the way to solve the race problem—not busing grade school children.

A series of eight public hearings held throughout Hartford in the fall of 1965 to discuss the future of city schools gave whites ample opportunity to express their displeasure at the busing recommendations. Most city leaders, whatever their persuasion, concluded that intracity busing was politically impossible, and school officials concentrated on putting together a school building package which aroused whites would support.

Hartford's public school plant, with the most minimal building and renovation, had steadily declined. By the mid-1960's, inadequacies had almost reached crisis proportions, but big hurdles stood in the way of any building program. First, the demands made on the limited dollar resources of Hartford—like other central cities—are severe. In 1965 Hartford spent more per capita from current revenue than did Bloomfield ($267.96 and $250.03) but the suburb spent nearly twice as much per capita for schools ($145.43 and $83.86). In addition Hartford has more voters currently not making claims on the public school system: a higher percentage of the elderly and unmarried adults than suburbs like Bloomfield, a higher proportion of parents sending their children to parochial and other private schools. Would these voters back tax hikes for schools they wouldn't use? And Negro families, who contribute heavily to the public school population, would not, many politicians believed, turn out in numbers in bond referenda. The Negro population of North Hartford is highly fluid and many of the newcomers have not been integrated into the political system.

In the reckoning of political leaders, in short, North Hartford could not be counted upon to support a new school building program in proportion to its numbers in the city or its stake in such a program. Also in the catalog of obstacles was the fact that South End schools were generally sounder physically and suffered less from overcrowding. South End voters would not feel the same sense of urgency. Further, while many urbanites support a strong school system, it was felt they do not have the same commitment to "good schools that can get our children into good colleges" as suburbanites and thus, typically, are less willing to sacrifice one value (tax dollars) for another (a better school plant). Finally, political leaders reasoned, any school building program which has as a prime component the achievement of further integration (as through the location of schools) would suffer massively at the hands of white voters who would see themselves being asked to build new schools which they would vacate as Negro pupils entered.

These assumptions, whether justified or not, had produced years of inactivity and, finally, the crisis situation of the mid-1960's. And into this setting were dropped the recommendations of the Harvard consultants, calling for a massive new building program linked intimately to the location of schools and the busing of pupils to achieve racial balance. The ensuing argument was extraordinarily complex and confused. But several major positions stand out. First, school officials and the business and professional leaders of Hartford—many of whom lived in the suburbs—agreed on the absolute necessity of completely rebuilding the school plant. And they decided for the short run to subordinate efforts to gain racial balance to the need to secure popular approval of the rebuilding program.

> We could not get voter approval for a building program based around the Harvard Report. It's as simple as that. We must have the schools. They are deplorable, especially in the North End, and terribly overcrowded. Our school population is rapidly increasing now, and we're already much too late. We simply had to make the necessary compromises in order to get voter approval for the 42 million dollar bond issue.

The compromises were reflected in the Board of Education's 1966 "renewal plan for Hartford schools" which outline a 6–2–4 system to replace the then existing 8–4.[5] The compromise 6–2–4 plan, if implemented, could only produce a situation in which schools in the northern and central districts would become largely Negro and Puerto Rican, while those in the southern third would stay white. The compromise promised South Hartford, in short, the prospect of a physically improved South End school system remaining white.

Once this basic concession to white voters had been made, the supporters of school renewal embarked on an energetic campaign to overcome other resistance. The Greater Hartford Chamber of Commerce went all out for the bond issue. The mass media kept up a steady barrage of proschools propaganda. The bond carried in November, 1966, only with the energetic support of the business and professional establishment. This support was given with the understanding that the 42-million-dollar bond being voted would meet less than half of the building needs over the next decade. Said one leader: "It is obvious and we must recognize that we face a school building program

[5] The Harvard consultants recommended a 4–4–4 arrangement, with busing to achieve integration in the middle schools, grades 5–8. In the School Board's proposal the middle schools would hold only two grades, 7 and 8, and school lines for these would be drawn in such a way that the middle school (and the high school) for school district C would service only the southern third of Hartford, and with no busing across school district lines both would remain overwhelmingly white.

that ultimately may reach . . . one hundred million. . . . We must be prepared for a four mill increase from the initial bonds and another mill from the second issue." [6]

Most South End leaders were either unenthusiastic about or actually opposed to the building program. A "Consumers Civic Economic Council" was formed, and one of its leaders argued that "the very people Hartford is interested in retaining in the city—the middle class, the homeowner—are going to leave if the bond issue is passed. . . . The problem of additional classrooms can be solved by adding to existing buildings." The appeal of the opponents was both economic and racial: economic when it stressed the added burdens to taxpayers which the bond issue would entail; racial as it implied that with passage of the bond issue "those in charge" might manipulate things to promote further integration of schools. We noted in Chapter 5 that the then mayor of Hartford, a South End Democrat, cautiously joined the vocal opposition two months before the bond issue was to be voted on. Fully aware of the years of controversy which had preceded bringing school renewal to a vote, he urged that the whole matter be delayed and, instead, that a modest sum be voted to plan the construction of new schools for city children in the suburbs. Civil rights leaders branded the Mayor's proposal a thinly veiled racial appeal to the South End, school officials reacted with horror, and the business and professional establishment jumped hard on the Mayor. The Hartford *Times* editorially labeled him a "champion of delay."

Mr. Kinsella's proposal is distasteful for its flavor of bland arrogance —a quality which the Mayor perhaps does not realize is tainting his public statements. No modern government, especially at the municipal level, can solve its problems by exile of the people who are involved in them. It would make as much sense—or as little— for the Mayor to propose that the white lower middle class in which

[6] In the plan envisioned by supporters of the building program, these two bond issues would provide about half the funds needed over the next decade.

fear of Negroes is most frequently found be moved to the suburbs. . . . We expect, as perhaps Mayor Kinsella does, that one day Hartford and its suburbs will be joined as a single metropolitan community. But that will take time to bring about; it well may be a decade before the move draws serious and enlightened discussion or action. . . . Mayor Kinsella must realize that his proposals cannot be accepted as anything other than tactics of delay.[7]

Things got too hot, and the Mayor backed off. The school plant was deplorable. The media stood ready to pillory anyone opposing renewal. Businessmen who did not use the city schools were not expressing opposition to paying the higher taxes which new schools would require. This was the position South End leaders found themselves in. But their opposition, though hard to justify publicly, was not without foundation. Tax pressures on lower-middle-class property owners in the city are severe. Affluent buinesses can much more readily afford tax increases. Neighborhoods undergo rapid ethnic transformation painful to long-time residents. The white working and lower-middle classes directly confront a burgeoning nonwhite population and are asked to do front-line fighting in redressing racial, and behind these, socioeconomic, injustices. They reject this role. Hartford's establishment—educators, government administrators, big businessmen, well-trained and well-heeled professionals active in various segments of community life—who attacked the Mayor's proposal as clumsy, "unknowing," unaware of the immediacy of the plight of city schools, could be faulted here as in other racial controversies for asking others to bear the heaviest burdens. But we are not looking for some moral calculus by which to assess the motives of the contenders. Our point is simply that a "progressive" proposal like the new school building program was carried through the support of such nonpopular forces as big business over the opposition or indifference of a substantial portion of the popular leadership of South Hartford.

[7] Hartford *Times,* August 10, 1966.

Conflict did not end with passage of the bond issue. The Hartford NAACP repeatedly voiced opposition to the compromise 6–2–4 plan for failure to extend integration. In June, 1967, it escalated its opposition by threatening to file suit in federal courts to stop the planned building program on grounds that it perpetuated *de facto* segregation. The NAACP's position was a difficult one. To force the Board of Education to redraw its master plan, it threatened court action that could keep pupils in makeshift classroom facilities while litigation was being acted out. The North End needed new schools badly. But to fail to challenge the building program would be to consent, *ipso facto,* to segregation in the schools.

The school administration at first offered half loaves, such as the slight juggling of school district lines and a formal endorsement of "quality integrated education" as a principal objective of the system. But then, in the late fall of 1967, it suggested plans in the next school construction phase for a twenty-two-million-dollar "education park" in northwest Hartford adjacent to and cooperating with the University of Hartford. The Board of Education promptly accepted these plans and the business leadership applauded them. Slipped in with these plans for a park that could become the "envy of the nation" were suggestions that school district lines be redrawn substantially, that the number of middle schools be increased, and that the grade levels of middle schools be changed to make them, in effect, the 5–8 school the Harvard consultants had recommended. This would achieve an approximately equal ethnic composition throughout the city. It was kept vague, and all school officials wanted to talk about was the new education park, but no one was fooled. Here was an attempt to reverse the victory won by integration opponents two years earlier.

South End councilmen retaliated in January, 1968, by stopping the first phase of the renewal program, approved by the voters in 1966 and well in progress. If proponents of integration were guilty of trying to hide their objectives, opponents led by Thomas Corrigan, chairman of the education committee of the Common Council, were no more straightforward. Said the Hartford *Times* editorially:

Simply put, neither party in the debate says what it means or means what it says. Predictably then, neither party believes the other. Behind a smokescreen of talk about renewal credits, the need for flexibility in planning, poor timing and the future of present schools, each party is really concerned about the future of integration in Hartford schools.

So the battle goes on between South End Democratic leaders as prime opponents of integration and the business, professional, and school leaders who, together with Civil Rights spokesmen, are integration's principal backers.

Behind the various controversies over race in the schools, the broad outline of the Cosmopolitan-Parochial division can be seen. Cosmopolitans agree that the city's public school system is severely troubled and agree further on the sources of its difficulties and on the directions in which solutions lie. The basic problems are not the fault of any group: they cannot be ignored or wished away but are inherent in the role the city has been asked to play. Hartford is taking in large numbers of disadvantaged newcomers who probably should be receiving school services more costly to provide than those suburban children typically require.[8] Each year city schools are asked to handle a larger proportion of disadvantaged children—children with more education problems reflected in lower levels of achievement, serious language disabilities, and general ad-

[8] A survey conducted in 1964 showed that 4,622 Hartford pupils, more than one of every four in the elementary school population, came from a broken home. An additional 603 children were not living with either parent. In 1967, in Hartford's twenty-four elementary school districts there were nearly 10,000 school-age children whose families were on state welfare and an additional 2,000 from families receiving city welfare payments. Although Hartford's school enrollment is but 4.4% of the public school enrollment in the state, the number of children in city schools from families receiving aid to dependent children (ADC) represents more than 27% of all ADC cases in Connecticut.

justment problems. The president of the city Board of Education observed that "the run-down areas and the substandard crowded dwellings into which the families move do not provide the proper environment for educational growth. The children inevitably reflect the hopelessness of the parental outlook." Financial resources have not expanded as rapidly as demands on the school system.[9] Thus, greater state and federal assumption of school costs is essential. Essential too, if racial imbalance in the city's schools is to be overcome, is some regionalization of education.[10] Liberal-Cosmopolitans and conservative-Cosmopolitans divided at times—as in Bloomfield—over the relative priority of ending racial imbalance (against such competing values as securing more funds for education and minimizing racial antagonisms). But they were generally able to work together.

Opposing them were the varieties of white Parochials who insisted that schools should remain neighborhood facilities and expenses be kept at a minimum. Like Bloomfield Parochials, they resented and resisted steps toward a dual transformation of the schools: the tremendous expansion of services (and expenditures), and the use of schools as an instrument in race advancement. They had little interest in the regionalization of education. Their model for schools was one ascendant through most of our public school experience: that is, schools perform-

[9] The public school population in the city increased by 36% between 1950 and 1967 while the total population was declining by 10%. In that same decade and a half, the city's property tax rate went up drastically. Despite this and increasing federal and state aid, the city stood in 1965 lowest among the twenty-nine communities of Greater Hartford in per capita expenditures for schools.

[10] Hartford's School Superintendent issued such an appeal for regionalization in an August 1967 report. He suggested that the State Board of Education seriously consider eliminating all local school systems, perhaps setting up in their place big, regional school districts ("Report to the Hartford Board of Education," by Superintendent of Schools Medill Bair, August 22, 1967).

ing fairly limited teaching and, where necessary, Americanizing functions, and operating as the instruments of communities.

Racial tensions and conflict extend well beyond the school yard. But in each substantive area, the same basic positions can be found. White Parochials have resisted the demands of nonwhites citing past practices and older orthodoxies: "We always went to neighborhood schools and didn't see anything wrong with it." "We lived in neighborhoods with our own kind and didn't expect to be bused out." "We were poor, but the opportunity was—and is—there to work hard and get ahead." Their principal role in the racial struggle in the 1960's is "saying no" to the demands of nonwhites. Cosmopolitans, in contrast, accept the contemporary scientific orthodoxy on race and a bundle of prescriptions following from it. Though priorities vary from "racial justice" to "maintaining a stable social order," they look to an expansive and innovating role for government.

The Physical City: Housing and Redevelopment. Increasing attention has been directed by scholars, businessmen, labor leaders, and professional urbanists to the plight of the physical city. One senses here both shadow and substance, real commitment and superficial rhetoric, continuing concern and fad. But students of ideology continually confront the problem of distinguishing between substance and smoke screen. It does seem symptomatic of a major change in the ideational orientation of certain sociopolitical groups in the United States that so diverse a collection as that which comprised the Emergency Convocation of the Urban Coalition in the summer of 1967—big city mayors, civil rights leaders, presidents and board chairmen of big corporations, labor leaders and academics—could find fundamental agreement in an analysis of American urban problems and prescriptions as to how to deal with them. The same is manifested by other organizations now dotting the urban landscape, such as the New Detroit Committee on which Henry Ford II and Walter Reuther serve. It is evident, too, in Hartford.

The elites of Hartford do not argue about the legitimacy or desirability of large-scale programs financed primarily by the federal government for rebuilding the city. No important political interest in the city has shown any ideological objections to going to Washington—as Hartford repeatedly has in the last decade—for funds for housing, redevelopment, the war on poverty, and to get designation as a "model city."

Where, then, has conflict occurred over rebuilding the city? There have been three distinct conflict loci. Differences have arisen over priorities, between the claims of commercial and business renewal on the one hand and residential redevelopment on the other. There has been conflict around efforts to couple renewal with the dismantling of the ghetto, distributing Negroes throughout Hartford and indeed throughout the region. And there has been a deep and continuing division between those who have looked to the new federal-urban programs as vehicles for significantly changing the urban environment and those who have construed such programs in terms of an older, entrepreneurial view of politics.

The first redevelopment program in Hartford was for the central business district and culminated in the 1964 completion of the much-acclaimed Constitution Plaza. Businessmen were not the only ones to gain from completion of the Plaza. Few benefit when a core city dies economically, and in 1957 Hartford was in trouble. A big insurance company, Connecticut General, had moved its home offices out of the city that year; the Phoenix Mutual Life Insurance Company was similarly inclined, and there were dark suggestions that Travelers too might move. As a result, business and civic leaders came together and initiated the renewal projects which produced Constitution Plaza. But if many benefited, this was essentially the flexing of business muscle for a business project. Moreover, the next set of redevelopment objectives further renewed the business center. It yielded principally office, parking, and industrial facilities and only a little housing and not of the type to benefit slum families. Not until the mid-1960's was a phase of the redevelopment program begun with a primary commitment to the needs of slum families. In sum, Hartford's big business leaders have strongly endorsed commercial and residential redevelopment of the city and have been active throughout, initiating and lobbying for projects. But it is commercial renewal or "economically sound" residential renewal which has received priority. The party leadership has deferred to business, and the renewal of slum areas has lagged.

Urban renewal and public housing offer possibilities for achieving at least some dispersion of the nonwhite population, in addition to replacing deteriorating housing. But efforts to build low-cost housing in the South End of Hartford or in the suburbs, where it must be built if racial integration is to be promoted, have been successfully resisted. Most of the small nonwhite population of South Hartford lives in the public housing complexes located there, and further public housing is strongly opposed. In 1967, for example, a federal grant of just under one million dollars to build a "campus style" project for housing of the elderly had gone unused for more than half a decade, although there were nearly 500 applicants on the waiting list of the Hartford Housing Authority (HHA), and the number was growing. The HHA discovered in 1960 a ten-acre lot in the Hyland Park section of South Hartford that was vacant and zoned for the type of housing they wished to build. A resolution was introduced in the City Council to deed four acres to the HHA. Within four days a South End Councilman introduced a counterresolution to dedicate the entire ten acres permanently to park use. Area residents deluged a public hearing with pleas for park and playground expansion, and the Park Department responded by outlining ambitious recreational plans for the area. The resolution to make this a site for elderly housing was withdrawn.

A year later the HHA took an option on a four-acre lot a few blocks away and sought a zoning change to accommodate the project. Neighborhood opposition was again organized and vocal, and the HHA could not collect sufficient Council votes for rezoning. In 1965 the HHA tried once more on a site near Colt Park in the South End. This too failed. Again in 1966 the Housing Authority sought approval of another unused South End tract. Once again opposition developed, and South End Democrats recommended that the city try to buy land for future playground development. In each case, the source of the opposition was the fear that some of the elderly tenants would be Negroes or Puerto Ricans.[11] The Hartford Democratic leadership has continually acceded to demands for the maintenance of residential segregation. The South End has said no to more low-cost housing and thus far has made this stick.

The leaders of Hartford's Democratic party have not approached the problems of the physical city as liberals or conservatives, consistently supporting or opposing activity in housing and redevelopment on behalf of the little against the big. These leaders have tried to tailor programs to patronage and organization-maintenance needs rather than to social change. And as a result, there has been continuing controversy between them and those who have made a prime commitment to substantial change in the urban environment. We must be careful here, for the distinction is not between selfishness and altruism. We cannot imagine any set of community leaders approaching a major spending program with blithe disregard for their own interests, financial and otherwise. We are not suggesting greater selfishness in the majority party elite, then, but commitment to a political orthodoxy in which a dimension of social change has little place.

A good example is the conflict surrounding Hartford's entry into the Model Cities program. Hartford was designated for Model City funds in 1967 amidst much hoop-la and bold claims.

[11] In fact, such fears were groundless. Only four of fifty tenants at an existing elderly project (1966) were nonwhites, and only twenty-eight of four hundred and fifty-six then on a waiting list for elderly housing were either Negroes or Puerto Ricans. But if the opposition were this intense to so limited a venture, it is not hard to understand why more ambitious low-cost housing projects have not been attempted in South Hartford.

The staff of the city manager's office began meeting with representatives of neighborhoods to be included, and one neighborhood organization, the "Council of Twelve," appeared to be especially effective. Redevelopment-area residents were promised a voice in planning the program. Then in January, 1968, without consultations outside party circles, the Democrats introduced and rushed through the Council a resolution designating the Council—on which they had a 6–3 majority—the "interim" Model Cities agency. "City Hall vs. the poor" has become a prominent theme in the acting out of federal-urban programs, of course, but there were some interesting wrinkles here. Any permanent Model Cities agency would have had to be set up by ordinance and the city manager would have selected its director; under the city charter, the manager picks department heads and the staff is selected with the help of the personnel department. But under the interim arrangement, the manager was bypassed, and control of the Model Cities staff was kept with the Council, that is, with the Democratic majority on the Council.

When they rushed their resolution through, the Democrats had already selected a director and other personnel for the program. Few observers doubted the party had any other objective in its action than keeping control of mammoth patronage possibilities. Dozens of meetings had been held to plan for participation by neighborhood representatives, and those who had been involved in these meetings reacted angrily. The High Noon club, a Negro organization, called for a cut-off of funds unless the Council action was rescinded. Chamber of Commerce officials charged a profound setback in communications between city officials and the residents of the areas requiring Model Cities aid, and threatened to seek an injunction against the Democrats' interim agency. And the Hartford *Times* proclaimed editorially that the "Democratic machine runs over the poor." At the very least, further delays were caused by the Democrats' action, and groups already profoundly suspicious about the good faith of the power structure were made more so. Our interviews with Democratic leaders make it clear that their actions in Model Cities and in similar though less dramatic situations resulted not from some peculiar contempt for or opposition to the poor, but from a conceptualization of politics in which social change has little place, in which patronage and organization-maintenance are the natural and overriding objectives.

The City and the Region. The question of the relationships between the city and its problems and the metropolitan region occupies an increasingly prominent place in the talk in Hartford. Regional initiatives are defended on grounds of efficiency and rationality: since metropolitan regions exist, government units equipped to deal with problems which are region-wide should be established. They are defended for reasons of economics, as when a businessman notes that the labor he hopes to attract measures the desirability of the entire region, not one narrow component of it. They are defended for essentially humanitarian values, as in the argument that many cities cannot provide integrated education but a region-wide school system could. And they are defended in terms of the requirements of the "good society" in an age of affluence: our metropolitan environment can be made more humane and more attractive if fratricidal struggling is ended and region-wide planning is assured, if problems and resources are matched.

Similarly, regionalism is opposed from habit and familiarity: the existing town governments have been around a long time and are comfortable. It is opposed, too, on the grounds that it is unnecessary, that local government as presently constructed is well-equipped to deal with the problems before it. It is opposed as a threat to the continued influence of certain local leaders. And it is opposed as a vehicle for denying towns the capacity to keep undesirables and/or problems out. The struggle over regionalism in Hartford, in sum, pits against each other elites of Cosmopolitan and Parochial perspectives and, of course, interests which sustain the ideological polarity.

Any ideological position grows out of the interests and

broader life situation of substantial and relatively enduring sociopolitical groups. From this perspective, why are Cosmopolitans at least sympathetic to various regional initiatives, and why do Parochials show disinterest if not displeasure? A Hartford insurance executive, a Cosmopolitan, revealed some of these interests and concerns:

> My perspective is that of a businessman looking at the city in a somewhat different context: the city as a marketable commodity—for which the citizen of the future will shop, just as he shops today for the family automobile. . . . When we . . . find a man, either inside or outside our organization, whom we want to locate in Hartford, we bring him—and often his wife as well—to take a look at our city. . . . Then they look at Hartford, not just the core city, but the region in which they will live. . . . Once we view the Greater Hartford region as a product which people will consider along with a number of other regions, we become aware of two facts: first, who our true competitors are, and second, the degree to which our efforts involve our own self-interest. We become aware that the competition is not between the core city and Newington, or between East Hartford and Simsbury. Our whole region is competing with San Francisco, Phoenix, Milwaukee and Miami not only for economic success, but for the most important resource of all—people.

Is the rhetoric a bit tired? Yes, we have heard it all before as businessmen have discovered regionalism. But familiarity should not obfuscate the change to which it speaks. Part of America is beginning to have local attachments—insofar as they have them at all—to metropolitan regions rather than individual communities. Their backgrounds—education, physical mobility—sustain and support this.

But there are other concerns as well. This businessman and others like him feel they have an important economic stake in what happens to the core city, and they want the region to help bail the city out:

> And the final question is: "Can people afford this product?" Cities like other products must have a cost-value balance. An attractive

city will fail if its costs—either in taxes, living expense or inconvenience—are prohibitive. Here we, as businessmen, should make sure the taxes and other costs are distributed equitably. . . . With higher levels of government recognizing regional entities and goals, the state using its taxing powers and returning a large part of the revenues to the region and its communities for their use, a more equitable balance would be established. If there is any state or community that can afford such a revision in revenue distribution, it is the state of Connecticut and the communities that make up the Greater Hartford region.[12]

Big business in an age of affluence can afford, and to a degree will pay for, the more attractive metropolitan regions it desires.

One objective of Hartford's conservative-Cosmopolitan business elite which is seldom discussed publicly but freely acknowledged is avoidance of a situation in which a black lower class dominates the city, the base of their economic activity.

I will be very frank with you on this. Do you think that Hartford business looks forward with relish to a situation in which a bunch of lower-class people, angry and embittered at a society which they believe is doing them in, has firm political control in the city? We meet this two ways by metropolitan approaches: We serve to better integrate Negroes into the life of the society, thus blunting hostility. And, it must be noted, we change the balance of political power by bringing the white suburbs in.

There is fear time may be running out.

Look, Negroes are still a minority in Hartford today, and perhaps can be convinced to support metropolitan approaches. There is the appeal, after all, of opening up the suburbs. But let them become 55% and gain real political power here. Do you think, then, they will be willing to give up that power, to subordinate it to some

[12] The preceding quotations are from a speech made to the annual meeting of the Greater Hartford Chamber of Commerce in May, 1967, by Sterling T. Tooker, President, The Travelers Insurance Company. He concluded by proclaiming that "July 4, 1976, would be a totally appropriate date for the member communities of the Greater Hartford region to enact their own 'declaration of interdependence.' "

political authority in which white suburbanites have the upper hand? I was talking a few weeks ago to Cecil Moore [then President of the Philadelphia NAACP]. Do you think he is interested in seeing Philadelphia incorporated in some metropolitan government agency? Not on your life. He believes Negroes have the prospect in the near future of dominating Philadelphia politics and he wants that.

It is better, this conservative-Cosmopolitan might have said, to reside in a suburb in which a few Negroes live or go to school, than to work in a city which Negroes control.

Liberally-inclined Cosmopolitans, of course, are more attracted by the possibilities of achieving through regional efforts certain social values like integration to which they are committed. But regionalism in Hartford in the 1960's is primarily a Cosmopolitan, not a liberal, interest. There is a well-trained and scientifically literate, upper-status group of metropolitan area dwellers who see local problems in regional terms, whose attachments are to an area not to a town, who believe present local government arrangements make little sense and that in certain areas new regional entities will do a better job, who see the city in trouble and want to marshall area resources to help bail it out, who have a strong interest in an attractive and stable metropolitan region, and who are not likely to lose status or influence as a result of regional initiatives as in housing and education. Thus drawn to regionalism, conservative- and liberal-Cosmopolitans find in it a vehicle for pursuing some distinct and even antagonistic objectives.

In 1967, a bill was introduced in the Connecticut General Assembly to bring Hartford and six surrounding suburbs under one public housing agency. The measure was supported as a means of dismantling the ghetto: the new authority would be able to build low-cost public housing in the member suburbs. The bill was opposed, predictably, by many suburban government officials as "an erosion of local government." But the controversy over a regional housing authority was not a straightforward self-interest struggle in which suburbanites saw it in their interest to leave with the city the burden of the nonwhite poor, while city leaders were working to somehow dump their poor nonwhites on the suburbs. The measure was not supported by the South Hartford legislative delegation. And most of the support which it received came from suburbanites—newspaper editors, lawyers, area business executives, and other professionals.

Neither this measure nor others with similar intent have been urged by the Parochials of the city. The Hartford Democratic organization, for example, has not initiated regional government approaches. One councilman was summing up the views of many of his colleagues when he told us:

> Generally, everything should be done to take care of the problems Hartford has in Hartford. . . . The problems in the North End can be solved by building more and better recreational facilities and schools there. And the people have to pitch in themselves. . . . Busing is a ridiculous idea, and that goes as much for busing to the suburbs as busing to the South End. I grew up in my school district and that's where everyone in the district went, including at least one or two Negroes and they didn't make any difference. There was no trouble. Besides, haven't all Negroes decided to settle together in the North End? So why shouldn't they attend their neighborhood schools? It's ridiculous to think about busing them beyond the city, and besides to say that it isn't costing anything is wrong because in the long run it is the taxpayer who will get hit for the bill.

And these party politicians in the city see in regional institutions a threat to their authority and influence. Hartford has problems, but now, at least, they are *their* problems.[13]

[13] Pressure for a regional housing authority has continued, with much the same "pro-con" alignment. In 1967, the Governmental Functions Committee of the Capitol Region Planning Agency proposed a Hartford Regional Federation with powers in the field of housing and sanitation. The latter caused little controversy but the former much: as proposed, the federation would have powers of condemnation and would be able to place low and moderate income public housing in the various towns of the Capitol Region.

The debate over regional government institutions in Hartford is being stepped up, and their proponents continue to nibble away. In the wake of the Greater Hartford Conference on Metropolitan Cooperation and Development, sponsored by the Chamber of Commerce in 1964, several new regional discussion groups were set up. In 1965, the General Assembly adopted a public act authorizing towns in any planning region to form a council of elected officials. Under this umbrella, the Capitol Region Council of Elected Officials (CRCEO) was established.[14] Also created as a direct result of the 1964 conference was the Regional Advisory Committee (RAC), a private group of area leaders brought together to discuss regional cooperation. And an education discussion group was spawned, to weigh questions of education policy affecting the region. The Capitol Region Education Council (CREC) draws its membership from the school boards of twenty-seven area towns.[15]

Change and the Shape of Hartford's Future. The people who reside in this Connecticut valley city in 1968 are of lower socioeconomic status than those who lived here a decade and a half earlier, and there is every prospect that future inhabitants will be still more disadvantaged, in relation to the regional or statewide population. This is one meaning change has for the city. With 30 per cent of the families in the region in 1960, Hartford had 52 per cent of those earning under $3,000 a year

[14] Similar regional councils of elected officials have, recently, been spawned around the country. This really started in 1954 in the Detroit area with the Inter-County Committee of Supervisors. It was estimated in 1966 that some 500 local governments were participating in various regional councils of elected officials ("Regional Councils of Elected Officials in Connecticut," *Connecticut Urban Research Reports,* No. 11 [Institute for Urban Research, University of Connecticut], December, 1966).

[15] These joined three existing regional agencies: (1) the Hartford Metropolitan District (MDC), a water and sewerage district comprising Hartford and six suburbs; (2) the Capitol Region Planning Agency, just what its name suggests; and (3) METRO, the Metropolitan Effort Toward Regional Opportunity, a vehicle for requesting funds for regional education experiments.

but only 18 per cent of those earning over $10,000. Hartford's population shrinks as the metropolitan area population rapidly expands, and in the mid-1960's only one in five area residents lived in the core where one in two had lived three decades earlier. But with one-fifth of the region's population, Hartford was home to nearly 90 per cent of its nonwhites. This nonwhite population is disproportionately poor and concentrated in the northern third of the city. Simply put, what was until recently a middle-class city is becoming a lower-class one: Hartford has a new role to play, new problems, and, inevitably, a new style of politics.

The talk in Hartford centers on change and decline, how to channel, resist, process, and alter them. Just what is the future of the city? Will it become a black core surrounded by white rings? Who will hold political power in the new Hartford? And for what objectives will power be wielded? Have the big sociopolitical changes in city and region made untenable the historic political boundaries? What kinds of local political institutions are called for in the problem-burdened city? What political coalitions will the new Hartford breed?

Perhaps the most pressing question resulting from the changes Hartford has felt involve government services: where will the tax dollars be found to meet the growing demands for services? And what level of services are now required? On the former there is one firm area of agreement: that the property tax in the city has been pushed as far as it should be and that alternate sources must be tapped more liberally. Hartford's tax rate was increased by 2.4 mills in fiscal year 1966–67 and 2.5 mills the next. And in 1968 the city manager proposed a budget which would require an additional 8.5 mill increase, this coming despite a $24.8 million jump in the city's grand list and substantial increases in state aid. All parties clamored for the state legislature to provide more dollars and to reduce the city's dependence on the property tax. The manager observed that

> the property tax is particularly agonizing for older core cities like Hartford. Increases in that tax touch off a vicious cycle. Higher

taxes produce higher rents and financial burden on Hartford's growing percentage of elderly and poor. . . . Rent is the major factor in the welfare assistance budget; the higher it goes the more difficult the job of getting families off relief.

And officials of the Chamber of Commerce urged the governor to set up a task force to prepare a revenue program bringing fiscal relief to Connecticut cities. "The plain fact is that the cost of city government has outrun the city's fiscal capacity."

But while wishing for outside relief, city elites had to choose between demands for higher services and demands to minimize tax increases. In 1968 the contending coalitions here were clearly defined. In favor of higher levels of services were Negro leaders, the professional administrators of the school system and other branches of city government, the mass media, and the leadership of the business community. The Hartford Chamber strongly backed the manager's 8.5 mill increase, declaring there was little alternative to it. Again, the prosperous executives of affluent corporations were responding differently than their scarcity-minded brethren of three and four decades earlier. Insisting on cuts in the budget were most South End party leaders. This line of battle appears again and again in argument over Hartford's response to socioeconomic change.

The Use and Comprehension of Abstract Conceptual Dimensions (A.C.D.)

City elites generally resemble those of the suburb in their use of abstract conceptual dimensions for ordering political divisions. The public sector in the city is still larger and more problem-laden. More local controversies are linked directly to national political arguments, as over poverty, race, and redevelopment. A larger flow of local problems, therefore, permits packaging. Only partially contradicting these influences in the setting toward a more ideologized view of conflict is the background and training of a substantial segment of the party leadership. The leaders of the party organizations in Hartford make somewhat less frequent use of A.C.D. than do other groups of community leaders, apparently because of less formal education and their "schooling" in machine politics. We compared party and business leaders in Hartford, the entire leadership sample in the city, and the Bloomfield sample for use of A.C.D., and specifically for their comprehension of the Conventional Dichotomy.

	*Hartford party leaders** (n = 58)	*Hartford business leaders* (n = 57)	*Hartford leadership sample* (n = 210)	*Bloomfield leadership sample* (n = 90)
Does not use A.C.D.; no comprehension of the C.D. or any other†	22	0	10	7
Does not use A.C.D.; construed the C.D. with minimal rigor and coherence	10	12	8	7
Limited use of A.C.D.; rudimentary but fully coherent constructions of the C.D.	41	46	47	53
Frequent use of A.C.D.; a widely-integrating construction of the C.D.	26	42	35	33

* The selection and composition of party leaders and business leaders is described below, in footnotes 18 and 27.

† Data are expressed as percentages of *n*.

We have suggested that the level of use and comprehension of A.C.D. is related both to the amount of formal education—as a means of accustoming individuals to abstract ideas—and the conflict setting itself. Data from our Hartford mass sample offer further confirmation of this. In educational background, Hartford and Putnam residents resemble each other and are clearly distinguished from the better-educated Bloomfielders.

But when we compare respondents in the three communities for their familiarity with A.C.D., we find Hartford residents substantially more at home with such dimensions than Putnamites. In Chapter 7, Bloomfield and Putnam respondents were compared for their ability to use the C.D. to describe or

	Sample 1965				Census 1960			
	0–8 yrs. school	*9–11 yrs. school*	*H.S. grad.*	*At least some coll.*	*0–8 yrs. school*	*9–11 yrs. school*	*H.S. grad.*	*At least some coll.*
Hartford (n = 736)*	39	21	27	13	46	20	22	13
Putnam (n = 335)	45	21	25	10	58	18	16	9
Bloomfield (n = 490)	15	15	35	36	26	16	30	28

* Data are expressed as percentages of n.

locate the positions of five prominent leaders and organizations. Hartford respondents can now be added.[16]

	Correctly located, 5 of 5	*Correctly located, 4 of 5*	*Correctly located, 3 of 5*	*Correctly located, 2 of 5*	*Correctly located, 1 of 5*	*Correctly located, none*
Hartford (n = 736)*	3	5	13	22	44	13
Putnam (n = 335)	1	2	10	12	61	14
Bloomfield (n = 490)	6	11	20	34	25	4

* Data are expressed as percentages of n.

The same thing is revealed when respondents are invited to "pick their own" liberals and conservatives, to suggest leaders at the local or national level whose positions they would describe in terms of the C.D. The precise construction of each of the five strata in which respondents were located and the survey items

[16] See Note 11 in Chapter 7. The five leaders and organizations are:

31. Former Senator Barry Goldwater?
35. Mr. John Lupton?
40. The National Association of Manufacturers?
41. The Americans for Democratic Action?
43. The American Medical Association?

All respondents were asked, "Now, I am going to mention names of people [organizations] active in politics nationally. I would like you to tell me whether you consider them to be conservative(s)."

used in placing them are described in the previous chapter, pages 254–255. Respondents in the first stratum are those able to correctly locate at least five leaders in the C.D. and to justify these categorizations in terms of a wide-ranging construction of the C.D. By the time we reach stratum V, we have respondents with no comprehension of the Conventional Dichotomy whatsoever and unable, then, to use it to distinguish the positions of any group of leaders (see Table 36). Hartford respondents at

Table 36. Use and comprehension of the C.D., Hartford, Bloomfield, and Putnam samples (expressed as percentages of *n*)

Stratum	Hartford (n = 736)	Putnam (n = 335)	Bloomfield (n = 488)
I	3	1	8
II	6	2	14
III	29	9	52
IV	41	50	21
V	21	39	5

every level of education demonstrated greater comprehension of this abstract dimension that did their Putnam counterparts. City residents have been exposed to a setting in which conflict is broader and more categoric than in small towns. Presumably those interested in political life are thus "taught" to rely on abstract dimensions to order the conflict around them (see Table 37).

II. POLITICAL GROUPS AND POLITICAL IDEAS

The shape of conflict in the city has been generally described, and we can now look more closely at several groups of community leaders assigned especially important roles in decision making. One is a government group, the Hartford Common Council, whose members preside over virtually the entire range of major community problems. The leadership of the political

Table 37. Use and comprehension of the C.D., Hartford and Putnam samples, by educational background (expressed as percentages of n)

	Hartford				Putnam			
Stratum	0–8 yrs. school (n = 287)	9–11 yrs. school (n = 155)	H.S. grad. (n = 199)	At least some coll. (n = 95)	0–8 yrs. school (n = 150)	9–11 yrs. school (n = 70)	H.S. grad. (n = 82)	At least some coll. (n = 33)
I	0	2	3	14	0	0	1	9
II	1	5	6	24	0	0	2	13
III	14	31	36	57	1	3	14	48
IV	47	43	47	5	46	61	57	21
V	38	19	8	0	53	36	26	9

parties is another. We have already made reference to the ideational orientations of the Democratic politicians, but the "machine" is so important to governing the city that the ways in which its members conceptualize their roles and see the problems of the city need more careful examination. The same is true for the business leadership, a principal opponent of the machine. Finally, some comment must be made on the ideology of Hartford Negro leaders, although the subject is too large to handle in a satisfactory way here. The policy role of a leadership group is the product of a number of pressures and constraints, the ideology of group members being one of these. While we cannot untangle the precise relationship of ideology to action, we can be certain that the configuration of ideological positions in a leadership group is an important indicator of the way it will respond to the problems before it.

The Hartford Common Council

The Hartford Common Council as constituted between December, 1965, and December, 1967, had nine members—five Democrats and four Republicans. The councilman with the most votes in the November 1965 election, George Kinsella, became Mayor, a position which conferred little beyond title and gavel. The Mayor, like the other councilmen, was unsalaried, and he had virtually no administrative or appointive powers. Eight members of this Council, elected at large, were whites, one a Negro. Six were residents of the South End of Hartford and had their political base there. One lived in North Hartford and two in the West End (see Table 38).

The ideological position of each of the nine councilmen has been plotted on both the Cosmopolitan-Parochial and liberal-conservative axes (see Diagram 10). This gives us a more precise description than the four ideal type categories permit. Although elements other than ideology shape the responses of political leaders in specific decision situations—a leader may give in one area to get in another, there are the demands of party loyalty, and the electoral consequences of commitments must be meas-

Table 38. Selected biographical data, Hartford Common Council, 1965–1967

Councilman	Occupation			Ethnicity					Party		Residence		
	Lawyer	Small business operator	Middle level white-collar	Irish	Italian	WASP	Jewish	Negro	Rep.	Dem.	North End	South End	West End
Corrigan	X			X						X		X	
DeLucco		X			X					X		X	
DeLorenzo	X				X				X			X	
Kinsella		X		X						X		X	
Ritter	X						X			X			X
Uccello			X		X				X			X	
Bennett		X						X	X		X		
Kelly			X	X						X		X	
Ladd			X			X			X				X

ured—the Council's liberal-Cosmopolitans, Ritter and Bennett, have played a sharply different role than such conservative-Parochials as Kelly and Uccello.

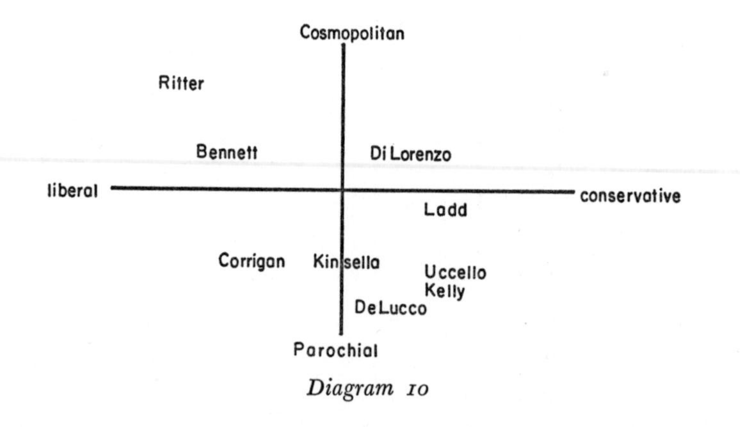

Diagram 10

The councilmen divide over the desirability of regional initiatives. Ritter has consistently supported steps toward regional cooperation in housing and education; Kelly, to take his polar opposite on the Council, has seen little merit in these. He dismissed suburban busing:

Quite frankly, I'm opposed to busing. I don't think it has proved anything educationally, culturally or intellectually. It's unrealistic. If the State Department of Education hadn't stepped in, there probably wouldn't be any busing at all. I'm afraid that once the novelty wears off, the absenteeism will start and there will be trouble. Why the other day, I was going to work and I saw one of those poor little kids [one of the Negro pupils being bused to a suburban school system] waiting at a bus stop and she was shivering from the cold, because she wasn't dressed warmly enough.

Beyond specific policy questions, the Hartford councilmen conceptualize their roles and the role of government differently. The Parochials are wedded to the old entrepreneurial view of politics: parties exist to gain control of government, and this control or power is used properly to disperse jobs and favors, helping friends and maintaining the organization. One Parochial councilman philosophized:

Politics is being able to do favors for others. My father's success is that he was able to do little things for people, maybe for 3,000 people, and he was respected for this. . . . Appointments and other controls on departments should be in the hands of the Council. As it is, the Council has no power over the behavior of the department heads. For example, a friend called me up a little while ago to ask me to help have suspended a health ordinance requiring rain gutters to drain into rather than on top of the ground. The ordinance is to prevent the collection of stagnant waters. But the way things worked out, if the ordinance were enforced he would have to build things differently for his new restaurant and it would cost him an awful lot of dough. Now, you can read that ordinance in at least three ways, but we have no control over it. When I called ———, he refused to do this favor for my friend. Now, things have to be all done over because we don't have any power over the administrators.

He practices the organic politics of O'Connor's "Skeffington." [17] Hartford, he feels, should be governed the way it has been over the last half century. The politicians he most admires are those party regulars who have worked their way up, who eschew issues, who faithfully reward their friends. He once challenged the Democratic organization, but he did so only because jobs and other favors to which he and his friends were "entitled" had been denied.

The Council Cosmopolitans look at politics differently: government must harness resources to order and direct social change; jobs must be parceled out to workers at times, and favors done, but an organization which exists solely for such objectives is anachronistic and at odds with the people's interest. Conflict management, efficiency, expertise, and innovation become the golden words. Here are two widely divergent conceptions of the role of government in urban America in the 1960's. According to one, government should be invoked

[17] Edwin O'Connor, *The Last Hurrah* (Boston: Little, Brown, 1956).

to marshal the resources of the society, to move it in directions which technology and affluence make possible. The other broadly accepts the older entrepreneurial or organic construction of politics.

Six of the nine Council members in Hartford in the period of research were Parochials, three Cosmopolitans. The majority were conservatives, though committed to positions that in the larger context of American politics tend to be centrist. Thus, power on the Council itself was with conservative/centrist–Parochials. But the Council was bombarded by conflicting pressures. Business and professional men, supported by the media, urged Cosmopolitan commitments upon it. The regulars of the party organizations thrust demands typically Parochial. Short-run alliances were made for specific objectives, and votes were cast on various questions in directions not implied by the position of the Councilmen on our ideological map. But the principal responses of the Hartford Common Council in 1965–67 reflect the conservative/centrist–Parochial orientations of its majority. It resisted a politics that was more innovative, more clearly committed to social change, and more designed to meet the needs of the nonwhite poor.

Political Party Leadership

The Democratic party in Hartford is the home base of Democratic State and National Chairman John Bailey. Forty-seven of its leaders were interviewed (and many reinterviewed) between July 1, 1965 and December 1, 1967.[18] This is a predomi-

[18] The forty-seven Democratic leaders were thus selected: (1) all Democrats on the Common Council as of May 1, 1966; (2) the five officers of the Democratic Town Committee, as of May 1, 1966; (3) ten members of the Democratic Town Committee (as constituted May 1, 1966), one from each of the ten Assembly Districts; (4) those Democrats nominated for the ten legislative seats which Hartford has in the lower house of the General Assembly for the November 1966 election (all were elected); (5) the Democratic nominees from Hartford's two Senatorial Districts for the State Senate elected in November, 1966 (both were elected); (6) the six Hartford Democrats on the Democratic State Central Committee, as of May 1, 1966;

nantly Irish and Italian elite, though Negro representation is increasing, of long-time residents of the city, of small business and locally-oriented prefessional men.

The Hartford Democracy is dominated by conservative/centrist–Parochials (see Diagram 11).[19] Most of the leaders are

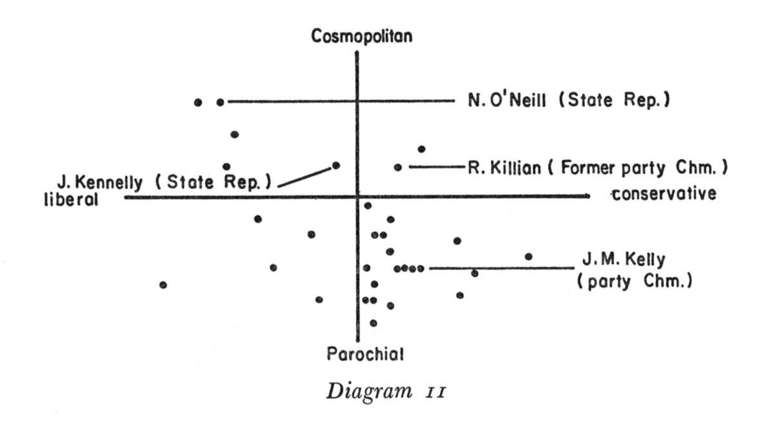

Diagram 11

locals in Merton's sense: they have gained influence through long residence in the city, through personal associations, through diligent labor on behalf of the party. Their resources are friendships and personal ties. They are well informed, but only of the immediate events and personalities of Hartford politics. The drama being acted out on the national and international stages occupies them much less than that in the districts of Hartford.

As a group, Hartford Democrats have succeeded in a politics based on party regularity, ethnic loyalties, and friendships, and

---

and (7) thirteen additional Democrats holding other positions of influence, such as Democratic club presidents, and several not holding any formal party leadership position but reputed to be important district or city-wide party influentials.

[19] Of the forty-seven Democratic leaders interviewed, only thirty-one have been located in our ideological polarities. The remaining sixteen leaders did not hold sufficiently constrained positions. In the section below, only eight of the eleven Republican leaders interviewed were located in the ideological polarities.

they are, not surprisingly, little attracted to a politics based on efficiency and expertise. Predominantly lower-middle-class, they still value the jobs and recognition which the organization can bestow in a way that prosperous businessmen could not possibly value these.

Banfield and Wilson talked about the ideology of such men in terms of a "private-regarding, lower-class immigrant ethos." It is not "private regarding" simply because these are men of typically modest means who cannot afford to treat political jobs and petty favors with disdain and certainly not because they are somehow more selfish than their "public-regarding" brethren. Instead, their orthodoxies, their ways of conceptualizing public life and its problems are the older ones: principally, they simply do not conceive of government as an instrument through which resources are channeled to control, shape, and direct the massive transformations which the urban scene is now experiencing.

The Hartford Democracy lacks the social base for a reform movement. But it does contain a small cadre whose social background and ideological orientations correspond to those of reform Democrats in other cities. Seven of the Democratic leaders interviewed, the above diagram shows, are Cosmopolitans. Though only one of these has formally challenged the inner circle, others probably would have if they believed they had prospect of success. These Cosmopolitans are professionals in their thirties and forties, well educated, economically successful. They see themselves separated from many of the regulars by socioeconomic status and ideology. The "machine" is led by people who do not comprehend the needs of the city. It is "old style." The Cosmopolitans are national Democrats, and their main interests are in national political debate and local politics as it is an extension of the national. On the peripheries of real power in the organization, the Democratic Cosmopolitans generally have chosen to cooperate with the organization rather than to challenge it. Their skills, expertise, and attractiveness to middle-class voters make them useful to the organization. Power in the party remains with lower-middle-class whites of Italian and Irish ancestry living in the South End.

The Republican party in Hartford is weaker than the outcome of Council elections would indicate.[20] Only 17 per cent of the registered voters in the city are Republicans, and the sixth assembly district in the West End is the only one of ten in which Republicans and Independents exceed Democrats: 32 per cent of the registrants are Independents, 25 per cent Republicans and 43 per cent Democrats. And this district is the only one in Hartford in which the Republican candidate for the state legislature in 1966 received as many as one third of the votes cast. Republican Councilman Roger Ladd polled 48 per cent of the votes in this middle-class district which is home to the only appreciable number of WASPs in the city.

Because of its weakness, the Republican organization was not examined in detail, and direct comparisons between it and the Democratic party cannot be made.[21] Moreover, the Hartford Republican organization stands in a quite different relationship to Republican leaders from the surrounding towns than does the city Democratic party to suburban Democratic leadership: the city Democrats are a power center in the state Democratic party, but Hartford Republicans are not influential, and the party is subject to strong "guidance" from Republican leaders in the Greater Hartford area. We did plot the ideological posi-

[20] There were four Republicans on the nine-man Council elected in November, 1965, and three on the Council elected two years later, including the leading vote-getter (and hence the mayor) Ann Uccello. But the Republicans here benefited from the absence of party labels on the ballot, and from internal feuding in the Democratic party encouraged by the structure of the electoral arrangements.

[21] Eleven city-wide Republican leaders were selected as part of our leadership sample. These include the four Republicans on the Council, the chairman and the two immediate past chairmen of the Republican town committee, and four other Hartford residents long active in the politics of the organization.

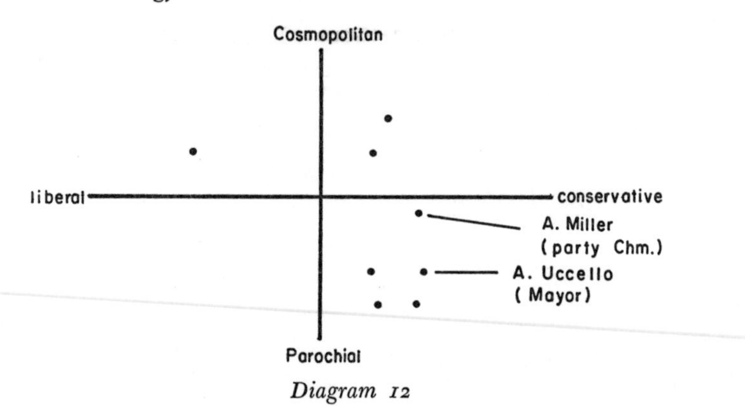

Diagram 12

tions of eight city Republican leaders interviewed (see Diagram 12). Five are conservative-Parochials.

"Generally speaking, do you consider yourself a Republican, a Democrat, or something else?" (Data are expressed as percentages of *n*.)

	Republican	*Democrat*	*Other (principally Independent)*
All respondents (*n* = 736)	14	61	25
Education			
Eleven years or less (*n* = 440)	14	69	17
At least some college (*n* = 90)	18	48	34
Income			
Under $5,000 (*n* = 202)	17	64	19
Over $10,000 (*n* = 110)	8	55	37
SES index			
High SES (*n* = 39)	4	50	46
Low SES (*n* = 147)	15	78	7

In Hartford, like Putnam but unlike Bloomfield, the Democratic party is the choice of a large majority of the middle class, and the proportion of respondents of higher SES identifying with the G.O.P. is no larger than those of lower status. Hartford Republican identifiers closely resemble Putnam Republicans in socioeconomic position, and both are sharply distinguished from their higher-status Bloomfield counterparts. We can compare Republican and Democratic adherents in the three communities for level of family income and educational background.

	Hartford		Putnam		Bloomfield	
	Rep.	*Dem.*	*Rep.*	*Dem.*	*Rep.*	*Dem.*
	(*n* = 68)*	(*n* = 348)	(*n* = 77)	(*n* = 161)	(*n* = 110)	(*n* = 171)
Family income						
Under $5,000	50	32	47	38	12	15
$5,000 to $10,000	37	49	39	50	28	55
Over $10,000	13	19	14	12	60	30
Education	(*n* = 94)	(*n* = 414)	(*n* = 82)	(*n* = 182)	(*n* = 120)	(*n* = 189)
High school or less	88	87	86	88	49	79
At least some college	12	13	14	12	51	21

* Data are expressed as percentages of *n*.

What we find is this: The middle class of the suburb is large and gives strong support to the Republican party. It is much smaller in both the city and the small town, as would be expected, but what there is supports the Democratic party at about the same level as does the entire population. And only a small minority of Republican identifiers in city and town are of high SES. This pattern is not substantially changed when religion-ethnicity is entered as a control. Among Jewish and Catholic Bloomfielders, for example, support for the Republican party increases as SES increases, to approximately the same degree as it does for Protestant Bloomfielders, though it is higher for the latter at all levels. In Hartford and Putnam, however, the proportion of Protestants supporting the G.O.P. is about the same for those earning under $5,000 as it is for those earning over $10,000 and about the same for those with less than a high school education as for those who are college graduates. This suggests that the association between socioeconomic status and party identification may be modified by the relative prestige, standing, strength, and persistence of the two political parties in the local community. The Republican parties of Putnam and Hartford have little standing. They are losers and have been for decades. Their leaders are men of modest position. They have no muscle, no future. The Bloomfield Republican party, in contrast, has high standing, both in terms of its membership and of its promise. It appears to be a "natural" home for successful men. Have Putnam residents of substantial income been dissuaded from identifying with the G.O.P., to which their economic interests might incline them, by the picture drawn from the local experience of the party as a bedraggled loser, an organization wholly lacking in prestige?

	"Are you in favor of the Medicare Program now before Congress?"			"Are you in favor of the Federal Government's antipoverty program?"		
	(Responses are expressed as percentages of *n*.)					
	Yes	*No*	*Undecided* and *Don't know*	*Yes*	*No*	*Undecided* and *Don't know*
All Republican identifiers ($n = 93$)	61	24	15	74	4	22
All Democratic identifiers ($n = 418$)	88	8	4	82	5	13
Hard-core Democrats ($n = 148$)	91	4	5	89	3	8
Hard-core Republicans ($n = 16$)	75	13	12	75	13	12
Hard-core Republicans in Putnam ($n = 33$)	70	21	9	73	27	0
Hard-core Republicans in Bloomfield ($n = 69$)	39	48	13	46	45	9

In Hartford as in Putnam, Republican identifiers were principally from lower-status groups and gave strong endorsement to the spending programs of the Great Society. The contrast between the responses of hard-core Republicans in Bloomfield on the one hand and in Putnam and Hartford on the other to Medicare and the antipoverty program in the summer of 1965 when both were widely debated is striking.

The Business Community

The economy of Greater Hartford is dominated by two sets of industries: insurance companies, and manufacturing firms intimately linked to defense spending. The big home-office firms of Hartford have intervened actively in the sociopolitical life of the city, and, although most of their leaders reside outside, there can be little doubt that any assessment of the ideology of Hartford decision makers requires attention to the ideological positions of the business leadership. This analysis focuses heavily on the leadership of one business organization, the Greater Hartford Chamber of Commerce. The roles played by local chambers, the extent of their activity, and what types of business they speak for appear to vary substantially from community to community. In Hartford, the Chamber of Commerce is the instrument of the biggest corporations of the area and the principal vehicle through which these corporations move and act politically. On the Chamber's Board of Directors sit leading officers of all major area businesses. The Chamber is handsomely financed and staffed by a large and able cadre of full-time administrative aides. It intervenes vigorously in all areas of the political decision-making process in Hartford and is rarely challenged frontally. That the Chamber has become the main instrument for political action by Hartford big business is the result of the exceptionally vigorous leadership of the man appointed its executive vice president in 1956, Arthur Lumsden. A decade later, the Chamber took the unusual step of giving Lumsden, its full-time administrative head, the title of president.

The literature describing American business ideologies in terms of historical patterns and current developments makes several things clear. Businessmen today talk differently than did their 1895 or 1935 counterparts, and probably think differently. Few today could say with the innocent sincerity of John D. Rockefeller: "God gave me my money." There is no such thing as "the ideology of American business," but rather a set of business ideologies reflecting the quite different interests and cognitions of various strata of business.[22] Differences in the

[22] The competing versions of capitalist ideology are variously described as "classical business ideology" (the National Association of Manufacturers), "managerial ideology" (*Fortune* and General Motors) and "small business ideology." See, for such distinctions, R. Joseph Monsen, Jr., and Mark W. Cannon, *The Makers of Public Policy* (New York: McGraw-Hill, 1965), pp. 24–63; and Francis Sutton *et al.*, *The American Business Creed* (Cambridge, Mass.: Harvard University Press, 1956), *passim.*

ideological orientations of the salaried managers of our biggest national corporations and the entrepreneurs who have built their own businesses appear sharp. Geographic variations in business ideology seem to be substantial as well: contrast, for example, big business in Detroit with big business in Dallas.[23]

In discussing business ideology in Hartford we are treating principally managerial ideology, the ideological commitments of paid managers of big corporations. This is managerial ideology in a middle-sized northeastern city, of managers for whom struggle such as took place in the 1930's over the legitimacy of "big government" is almost wholly dead. There is no suggestion that the patterns located here are common to the various American business communities. They should be reasonably representative of the orientations of corporation managers in the Northeast and the North Central States.

In the 1950's and 1960's, American big business has increasingly adopted the "gospel of social responsibility." "Never before," Earl Cheit has written, "have corporate officials so openly acknowledged the responsibilities of business to society, and never before have they spent so much time discussing them." [24] Business leaders and their spokesmen have labored hard to convey a sharp break between the old harsh, exploitative capitalism and a new responsible, socially aware business professionalism: ". . . the manager is becoming a professional in the sense that like all professional men he has a responsibility to the society as a whole." [25]

The "gospel of social responsibility" has not been received with uncritical acclaim. It is variously argued that the rhetoric

[23] Witness *Fortune* spanking the business community of Dallas for failing to seize "the greatest opportunity on earth," for being remiss in executing the dictates of the gospel of social responsibility. (Richard Austin Smith, "How Business Failed Dallas," *Fortune,* LXX [July, 1964], 157+).

[24] Cheit, "The New Place of Business: Why Managers Cultivate Social Responsibility," in Earl F. Cheit (ed.), *The Business Establishment* (New York: John Wiley & Sons, 1964), p. 155.

[25] The Editors of *Fortune, The Permanent Revolution* (New York: Prentice-Hall, 1951), p. 159.

of responsibility is largely a smoke screen, concealing drives toward new and greater profits, that the concept of "corporate conscience" fails in its mission to fill the gap between a lost world where competition was a true brake and the present one in which managers are able increasingly to act free of restraint, and that the great public problems of our day are better attacked by that instrument which is responsible to the people—government—than by nonresponsible corporate managers.[26] It is not surprising that emphasis by business on its responsibility to eradicate slums, eliminate poverty, and improve education meets skepticism in those who remember that the business of business is dollar-making. In the analysis which follows, we hope to clarify what business in one American metropolitan area is now committed to ideologically. And, hopefully, the analysis will not be taken as a paean to new business virtues or a criticism of business failings: the ideological orientation of Hartford business is testimony to neither vice nor virtue, but to the position in which one socioeconomic group finds itself at this point in time.

Few leaders of the Hartford business community are moved by questions of "big government." [27] Decentralizing govern-

[26] Michael Harrington, "The Social Industrial Complex," *Harpers,* CCXXXV (November, 1967), 55–60; Bernard Nossiter, "The Troubled Conscience of American Business," *Harpers,* CCXXVII (September, 1963), 37–43; Andrew Hacker, "When Big Business Makes Gifts (Tax-deductible)," New York *Times* magazine, November 12, 1967, pp. 34+.

[27] The fifty-seven business leaders interviewed were thus selected: (1) all directors and officers of the Greater Hartford Chamber of Commerce as of May 1, 1966; this group included the president of Phoenix Mutual Life Insurance Company, the publisher of the Hartford *Times,* the president of the Hartford Federal Savings and Loan Association, the president of the Hartford Electric Light Company, the president of Heublein, Inc., a senior vice president and secretary for Aetna, the president of Travelers, the executive vice President of Colt, the vice president of Hartford National Bank and Trust Company, the chairman of Emhart, the president of Connecticut General Life Insurance Company, the president of the Mechanics Savings Bank, the senior vice president of the Phoenix Mutual Life Insurance Company, the president of the United Aircraft, the chair-

ment, "revitalizing" federalism, sharing new tax plans between national and state governments—none of these elicited enthusiasm from Hartford businessmen. Indeed, it became clear that such were rarely thought of or discussed.

Look, my business is such where we come into contact with both state and federal administrators. It has been my experience that the federal administrators typically are better informed, better trained, more on top of things. . . . This is an age of bigness, and the national government is generally better able to give the direction and supervision needed.

The level of urban services needs to be continually expanded. More expenditures for education in the central city, more construction of low-cost and middle-income housing, more (and regional) efforts to break down the ghetto, generally greater attention to the attractiveness and "livability" of the urban setting are required.

Business in Hartford sees itself as a socially progressive and responsible force; it is widely recognized as such and obviously values this recognition. A 1967 publication of the Greater Hartford Chamber of Commerce begins by modestly acknowledging that the Chamber has been characterized as "*the* organization for progress" in the area. The Chamber has been a principal mover of suburban busing. It energetically supported the busing proposals of the Harvard Report; then it backed the pilot busing program initiated in 1966 as "Project Concern"

man of the board of Hartford Electric Light Company, the chairman of the board of The Security Insurance Group of Hartford, the executive vice president of the Connecticut Bank and Trust Company, the president of the Mutual Insurance Company of Hartford, and other area business leaders whose institutional positions are less formidable; (2) area business leaders serving on all major boards and commissions which are part of the formal public policy-making structure of Hartford, including the Community Renewal Team (the antipoverty agency), and the Development Commission; (3) the officers of special area business groups, such as the Greater Hartford Board of Realtors; (4) eight additional business executives not included from the above, but noted to be especially active politically.

and in 1967 called for the "expansion of the program of busing North Hartford children to suburban schools and adding new communities to the list of those currently cooperating."[28] The Chamber has consistently backed bigger education budgets for the city of Hartford. Early in 1966, for example, it urged that several hundred thousand dollars cut from the school budget by the city manager be restored by the City Council.

> We urged the Hartford City Council to give school officials more than the City Manager provided for. Things like this confuse the City Council. Here is the Chamber of Commerce urging bigger appropriations for the city schools. The City Council was certainly surprised to see the Chamber advocating a four mill tax increase, and backing a bond issue of fifty million dollars to build new schools under the school board plan.

The Chamber applied pressure to advance the mammoth rebuilding of the city's school plant. It has played a primary role in the entire post-1957 rebuilding and redevelopment program. Here, its first love has been the renewal of the city center—the business district. But it has backed redevelopment projects in both the North and the South End and organized the Greater Hartford Housing Development Fund to provide "seed money" for the development of housing in the city. The Chamber has encouraged businesses to stress an "open door" policy in hiring and promoting employees and to expedite the upgrading of underemployed individuals.

Interestingly, Hartford business has anticipated the question, "What's in it for you?" and spends perhaps inordinate time constructing an answer. It is, of course, "enlightened self-interest":

> While the scope of the Chamber's activity is broad, it all is firmly based on the simple economic fact that business thrives best in a healthy, friendly climate. Thus, to the question "what's in it for me?" the hundreds of men and women voluntarily working on

[28] The expansion envisioned was substantial, to 1,500 or more Negro and Puerto Rican students a year.

committees and with Chamber affiliates to accomplish the Chamber's objectives, and the individuals and firms who voluntarily provide the Chamber's financial support, find an overriding answer founded in enlightened self-interest: my present and future prosperity.[29]

This fortunate congruence of self-interest and social responsibility was emphasized repeatedly in interviews with business leaders. It is as though corporate officials were simultaneously trying to persuade their less sympathetic brethren that they could back the building of new schools which raises taxes on their business properties and still be good businessmen, trying to convince themselves that their commitment to the gospel of social responsibility is real and well founded, and attempting to satisfy an at least quizzical audience that it is possible to trust business in the new enterprise of responsibility without a leap of faith—believing that businessmen have moved beyond self-interest.

Although business in Hartford has been fairly unified in local political struggles, its leaders differ in their assessment of national problems and policies. Goldwater's candidacy is a case in point. Twenty-one per cent of Hartford's business leaders strongly supported Goldwater, another 35 per cent voted for him but preferred some other Republican, and 44 per cent voted for Johnson. For the business leaders who defected to Johnson, Goldwater was anathema.[30] ("He was out of step with the whole flow of American life.") But a majority of the Hartford business community managed to vote for him, though many described him as "a poor candidate," and "not big enough for the job."

For one group of Hartford executives, principally those under fifty, the domestic welfare programs of the Great Society

[29] Greater Hartford Chamber of Commerce, "Highlights of Action, 1966–67."

[30] "Defected" is legitimate because only six of the fifty-seven businessmen included in this sample described themselves as Democrats.

are either supported, or criticized largely for administrative failings.

I'm basically sympathetic to the objectives of the Johnson Administration's poverty, medicare and related programs. . . . There is a need for a major, ambitious federal program to help eliminate poverty. We are a wealthy society, and there is no need for the bottom fifth of our population to live as they now do. My objections to the antipoverty program are largely administrative. In moving as it has, some serious dislocations have resulted. It is virtually impossible, for example, for any private welfare organization today to get adequate staffing. The federal government is tying up, in its antipoverty program, so many welfare workers, social workers and others that it becomes exceedingly difficult for private organizations like the Urban League to operate. The federal antipoverty program is building up an enormous and overlapping welfare establishment. Admittedly, many of the private welfare organizations were not doing an adequate job in the past, were not speaking the right language. But I think it would have been possible for the federal government to have moved in, using a threat to cut off funds as its lever, and to help transform existing welfare organizations into the kind of organizations they should be. Impose on them uniform and adequate standards. It might have been better for the federal government to come in via a United Fund organization in Hartford, and to say "follow these standards and we will give you matching grants up to a specified level."

For these leaders, in short, there is no problem in federal intervention. The objections are to inefficiency in administrative arrangements.

Only from a small group of Hartford business leaders—and these all in their late fifties and sixties—is the rhetoric of the 1930's still heard.

I grew up believing, and I still believe that the best arrangement is one where people are permitted to work as hard as they want to and then to keep in their entirety the fruits of their labor. Socialism is a bad thing, robbing people of their initiative and in a sense, by taking from them what they legitimately earned through hard work and initiative, robs them of their freedom. I strongly opposed the administration and policies of Franklin Roosevelt. Though I know that many people consider Roosevelt the very greatest of American Presidents, I didn't at the time he was in office nor do I so consider him such today. A whole set of Socialist schemes were developed under his leadership. . . . Oh, I guess I do think that we need Social Security today, but when it came into effect I can tell you that I was very strongly opposed to it.

The contrast is striking. Among the leaders of Hartford's largest corporations a few were still using "socialist" to describe the welfare programs of the New Deal and post-New Deal Democratic administrations, while many others were assigning government a major role in eliminating poverty:

We could, realistically, wipe out poverty here in this country and elsewhere in the world, wipe out inequality and all the agonies and antagonisms that go with both of these conditions of man. . . . This invites a continuing partnership of government and the private sectors. . . . The advances of technology . . . should not and cannot be confined within the borders of one nation or even one sector of the world. Increasingly, Americans and other members of the so-called "have" nations are aware, concerned and even alarmed about the disparity . . . between the per capita income of people in developed nations and those in developing nations.

The ideological center for Hartford business leaders lies with conservative-Cosmopolitans (see Diagram 13). The typical business leader is prosperous and wants to maintain a position which insures that prosperity. He finds businessmen most fit to lead and considers the expansive political role of business in Greater Hartford no more than what business talent invites. He is not strongly committed to a more popular distribution of values, and his "progressivism" in the contemporary urban setting is a function of his Cosmopolitan orientations, not of a miraculous conversion to liberalism.[31]

[31] Fifty of the fifty-seven Hartford business leaders have been located on our ideological polarities. Seven did not see politics ideologically.

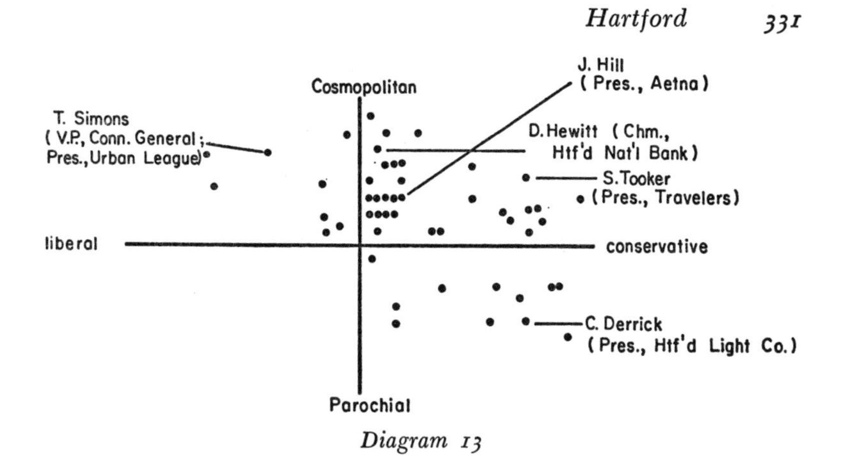

Diagram 13

Negro Leaders

The Negro subcommunity, about one-fifth of the city population in 1967 and growing, is a recent addition to Hartford politics.[32] There were only 12,000 Negroes in a population of 177,000 in 1950. Political power in the subcommunity is enormously fragmented, and the reasons for this are clear and probably affect most Negro subcommunities across the country. Race leadership is issue leadership. The issue is race advancement. Involved are the most vital political interests of Negro Americans. This type of leadership stands or falls on its success in gaining support for its definition of how race should be advanced. And since it cannot solve the big problems which are uniquely the lot of Negroes, it is ever vulnerable to challenges. Achievement lags far behind expectations, and the touchstone of politics is discontent. Political involvement for many white Americans is often relatively casual, especially at the local level. It is anything but casual for Negroes, and Negro leaders thus lack the security, the cushion which the more relaxed nature of white middle-class politics provides. Needs are so pressing,

[32] It is estimated that about 32,000 Negroes were living in Hartford in 1967. There were also 8,000 Puerto Ricans. The nonwhite population thus was slightly more than a quarter of the total.

and the whole structure of race relations so dynamic and changing that earlier achievements of a leader count little. The vulnerability of Hartford Negro leaders is further increased by certain structural characteristics of this leadership. Most operate from weak institutional and status positions. They have modest resources and possess few sanctions. Since there is little which they can do for their followers that someone else cannot do, there is little which they can threaten not to do.[33]

In short, it is easy to *become* a Negro leader in Hartford, but hard to *retain* substantial influence. An issue sufficient to attract popular attention is never absent, as it often is in white communities. Incumbent influentials cannot easily claim adequacy of performance: too much remains that is unsatisfactory. And when, in addition, incumbents possess few resources and hold institutional positions which are modest and confer little that they can use to maintain their influence, they can be challenged by rival organizations set up quite literally overnight, by persons hitherto unknown to the subcommunity.[34] On two occasions between 1963 and 1967, the incumbent Negro influentials in Hartford were pushed aside by new protest organizations: in 1963–64 NECAP, the North End Community Action Project, was started under the wings of the Northern Student Movement and patterned on the youthful biracial protest movements, of which SNCC was the most prominent example; in 1967 the new group was the Black Caucus, an all-

[33] In a few Negro subcommunities such as Chicago's, a political machine, a well-integrated organization which is a prime component of a city-wide party apparatus, provides a firm base of power and influence for a group of Negro politicians, provides resources which they can use to reward friends and punish enemies, and provides sanctions they can apply. The Negro Democratic organization in Hartford has modest resources and is badly fractured; there is no William Dawson, not even a scaled-down version.

[34] I have discussed the extreme vulnerability and fluidity of race leadership elsewhere. See my *Negro Political Leadership in the South* (Ithaca, N.Y.: Cornell University Press, 1966), esp. ch. 3; and "Agony of the Negro Leader," *The Nation,* September 7, 1964, pp. 88–91.

Negro movement whose rhetoric was in the Black Power tradition then coming into vogue.

Thirty-seven Negro leaders in Hartford were interviewed, and we have located thirty of them in our ideological polarities (see Diagram 14).[35] They are change-oriented. Even the more conservative among them cluster on the liberal side of the polarity in the entire sample of city leaders. The domestic programs of the Great Society are supported or criticized for not going far enough, for being "too little, too late." But most of

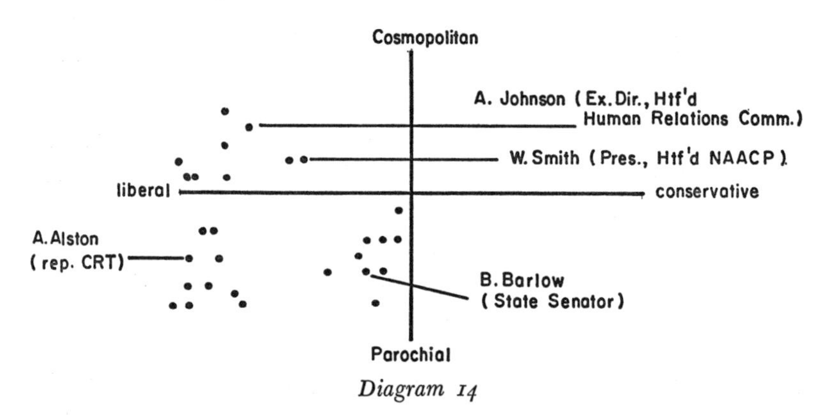

Diagram 14

these leaders are Parochials. Just as the typical big business leader is a conservative-Cosmopolitan and most party influentials conservative-Parochials, a majority of Negro leaders in Hartford are liberal-Parochials. The liberal-Parochial Negroes

[35] The race leadership sample was compiled to include: (1) all Negroes holding elective office or high administrative positions in Hartford; (2) the principal officers of all organizations active in race advancement, specifically the Hartford NAACP, the Hartford Interracial Council, the Hartford Urban League, the High Noon club (an association of Negro business and civic notables), the Hartford Ministerial Alliance (approximately thirty ministers, all Negroes), the Black Caucus, two very active Negro neighborhood associations (South Arsenal Neighborhood Association and North Arsenal Neighborhood Association), the Negro Democratic Club, and the Hartford Human Relations Council; and (3) six Negroes not drawn from the above but reputed to be influential and known to be active in some phase of community political life.

are locally oriented, their perspectives are narrow, they are unfamiliar with bodies of expert knowledge treating major public problems. Though they want things changed and thus back "more government," they conceptualize the role of government much as white Parochials do—essentially as a distributor of jobs, patronage and favors.

The Irish and Italians have had their turn. Now it is ours. . . . I'm not worried about Hartford becoming a black city. I've always wanted to be Mayor. I mean it seriously; then we can have our turn. [What would you do with political control in Hartford if you had it?] Hell, you know! What they have done, of course. The jobs would be *ours* then.

Theirs is a Parochial response, or a set of Parochial responses. Outside of race-linked concerns, white and Negro Parochials differ little. But we cannot, of course, confine ourselves to issues outside of race-linked concerns. Race is too central. There can be no alliance between white and nonwhite Parochials as long as racial concerns have the sovereignty they now enjoy.

And given the ascendancy of race, the inadequacy of this treatment of the ideology of Negro leaders is obvious: the C.D. and the Cosmopolitan-Parochial polarity were not designed to yield racial leadership typologies. They do not permit us to contrast the approaches to race advancement of Negro leaders, and it is precisely the differences of approach to race advancement narrowly construed which matter, which occupy the attention of Negroes and whites alike. Though any systematic construction of a continuum of race leadership styles lies well beyond our objectives or capabilities here, data were collected which permit us to suggest the form such a continuum would probably assume for Hartford in the late 1960's.[36]

[36] We have defined *style of leadership* as the identifying public face of a category of leaders: goals pursued, means through which they are pursued, and rhetoric—the language and symbols with which objectives are described. In another publication, we suggested that styles of race leadership are shaped and defined by prevailing patterns of race relations: "For our part, then, we insist that there is nothing inherently militant (moderate,

There are three principal styles of race leadership in this old New England city, which we will call moderate, militant, and radical. Moderates hold positions in the Democratic party organization in Hartford, in the Urban League, the Human Relations Commission, and in agencies of the antipoverty program. They occupy places, in short, which require that they be acceptable to whites, although the standards of "acceptability" of white leaders in Hartford in 1967 are quite different from those of whites in Winston-Salem in 1962, and bear no resemblance to those of Birmingham whites in 1948. Still, rhetoric, in particular, must not exceed the boundary of offensiveness. The goals pursued are the conventional ones shared by liberal whites—more jobs, better housing, improvement of welfare services. The resources which their institutional positions provide them are the principal ones utilized in promoting these goals. Access to white leaders is seen as an important resource.

The militant style in Hartford is pursued by leaders of the established protest organizations such as the NAACP and the Ministerial Alliance. Militants play a role long associated with the civil rights movement, demanding action in the most sensitive areas of Negro-white relations. They focus upon specific and visible issues where shortcomings in community response are most notable; they dramatize these and marshal resources for their resolution. An example here is the challenge by the Hartford NAACP in 1967 to the school construction program outlined by the Board of Education on the grounds that it perpetuated *de facto* segregation. Typically, Militants are not restricted or restrained by positions in organizations dominated

---

conservative, etc.) about a given leadership style. Instead the limits are determined by the prevailing pattern of race relations which varies with time and geography. Because of this the composite of goals, means, and rhetoric that in one period would be called conservative or accommodating leadership might not even be on the continuum in a later period" (Ladd, *Negro Political Leadership in the South,* p. 151). The content of the moderate style in Hartford in 1967 is vastly different from the moderate style as we described it for Winston-Salem in the early 1960's.

by whites. They operate from without rather than from within, and see themselves as prods to the "power structure." But though Militants push the community in sensitive areas, their thrust is *within* the system. White leaders distinguish them from the Radicals, see them as system-sustaining if annoying. And Militants themselves recognize that their commitment is a continuing one within the institutional framework of a continuing political system.

We're concentrating on long-range accomplishments. We were around before they [the Black Caucus] got there, we have remained, and will be here when they go. . . . These *ad hoc* committees come on the scene, make a lot of noise for awhile, and then they disappear. You don't solve problems that way. We're on the scene all the time, continuing to apply the prod, the needle.

NECAP and the Black Caucus have been the most prominent organizational manifestations of the third, the radical, style. Radicals have worked principally through direct action demonstrations, picketing, and marches. But more significantly, they have started from the premise that the "power structure" specifically, the white community generally, cannot be persuaded and must be compelled to take action, and that discussion within normal channels is an exercise in hypocrisy. Thus, rhetoric is designed to rally the subcommunity, and no effort is made to build bridges to the white leadership. If whites are "offended," nothing is lost for nothing will be done without compulsion anyway.

You simply can't trust whitey! That has been proved often enough. He won't give us anything. We must take what is ours. We don't want to kill white men. But if they do not respond soon, you can be sure of one thing, white men will be killed.

While some Negroes may have responded to radical movements simply as a more dramatic form of protest, getting some satisfaction in "twisting whitey's tail," the leadership has shown a profound alienation from the system. Radicals linked their condemnation of the actions of white America domestically to what they believed to be a white American effort to dominate peoples of color in other countries. The Vietnam policy of the Johnson administration was opposed as an exercise in racial imperialism. "Black Power," in short, was a way of saying: "Black men have no future within the system."

The black underclass of Hartford appears curiously ambivalent in the struggle for influence among Moderates, Militants, and Radicals. Negoes are conscious of themselves as a deprived, shabbily-treated group; and give support, at times grudging, to Radicals who, as the leadership group least acceptable to whites, lay claim to the strongest expression of bitterness and frustration. We repeatedly encountered, in our survey work and in observation of various meetings, older Negroes "turned off" by the style of the younger Radicals, yet at the same time drawn by the raw power of their ethnocentric appeal. Radicals probably are most severely disadvantaged in working with the black underclass by their wide-ranging ideological critique of the iniquities of white America. We found again and again at political meetings members of the underclass expressing overriding concern with highly immediate needs: how awful it is to live in run-down houses filled with roaches and rats; how terrible it is to live in neighborhoods where one is constantly preyed upon, where it is often a hopeless struggle to keep your sons away from crime and drugs, your daughters from early pregnancies; how humiliating it is to be lectured as a fifty-year-old woman, by a twenty-three-year-old case worker; how painful it is to see your children continually denied the bright baubles which TV displays to them. Radicals, in their ideological critique of the racist society at home and in its foreign policy manifestations, and in their concern with bringing "the system" down, are talking another language. The underclass not so much disagrees with the critique of the Radicals as considers it less relevant; it is on a different wave length, and their receivers really cannot pick it up. The underclass is not at all hostile to Moderates and Militants who appear to be really attending to the day-to-day problems of the ghetto.

Table 39. Hartford, four ideological groups, by a set of personal biographical variables

Variable	Conservative-Cosmopolitans (n = 43)	Liberal-Cosmopolitans (n = 27)	Conservative-Parochials (n = 72)	Liberal-Parochials (n = 30)
Age (median)	53 yrs.	41 yrs.	52 yrs.	47 yrs.
Occupations				
Professionals and salaried executives	91	78	15	17
Small business owners	–	7	33	23
Lower white-collar workers	9	15	39	40
Blue-collar workers	–	–	13	20
Sex				
Male	91	74	92	83
Female	9	26	8	17
Education				
Eighth grade or less	–	–	9	16
Some high school, high school graduate	7	–	56	47
Some college, college graduate	74	37	29	27
Professional degree	19	63	6	10
Ethnicity				
Anglo-Saxon	40	15	15	3
Irish	16	15	38	10
North European	12	7	3	–
Italian	7	7	29	7
Jewish	16	30	6	7
Negro	5	22	–	73
Other	4	4	9	–
Political party				
Republican	74	11	21	10
Democrat	16	74	74	83
Independent	10	15	5	7

Note: All figures are percentages of n unless otherwise indicated.

Leaders identified with the ideological postures described in this study are rather clearly differentiated in social group terms. But the relevant social categories are not, as we have often observed, those defined simply by economics, by sources and amounts of income. Cosmopolitans and Parochials in Hartford, as in Bloomfield, are separated by a wide chasm in social status, as the data in Table 39 indicate. The typical Cosmopolitan is college-educated, at least modestly affluent, employed as a government administrator, a business executive, a lawyer, or some other professional. Parochials, in contrast, are drawn from the lower-middle class. In Hartford, a large majority are small businessmen and lower white-collar workers. Only one in three has attended college. Parochials are city dwellers (while Cosmopolitans are suburbanites), and their associations and contacts are narrowly local.

Here are two sharply differentiated status groups. Their contrasting educational backgrounds and career lines have exposed them to different bodies of knowledge and different ways of conceptualizing the public problems of this technological society. The Cosmopolitans are the managers of the new society. Their technical expertise assures them high social status. The new society, more complexly technical, interdependent, and nationalized, is one they find congenial for, in a sense, it has made them. Demands for change typically are not seen as threatening. Things are quite different for the white lower-middle-class leaders of the city who are asked to bear the brunt of change. Not at odds with the new order as a peasant might be in an industrial society, they nevertheless are somewhat bewildered by and resentful of its demands, its style, its orthodoxies. Conservative-Parochialism is the principal ideological statement of their resistance and resentment.

Conclusion: Social Change and Ideational Change

Two levels of analysis, distinct yet tightly related, are contained in this study, and its findings can best be related to them.

I

At the loftier level, the study has explored the response in political ideas and ideology to the massive social and economic changes which have bathed and buffeted this society. One commentator recently noted that while "ages" used to be measured in centuries, we now are inclined to see a different age each decade.[1] This may speak to our conceit, but it probably testifies as well to a telescoping bred of the rapidity and extent of contemporary change. Political ideas are a primary source of data on the political response to social change. After all, we would expect any far-reaching political development to express itself in an alteration of the political dialogue of a system. To cite an example from this study: the fact that big business in an age of American affluence no longer sees itself seriously threatened by demands for a popular distribution of economic values (in part because the working class has been caught up in the affluence and is no longer making very bold demands, in part because both business and businessmen are wealthy and secure enough to be willing and able to make certain concessions), manifests itself in the diminished comprehension of the Conventional Dichotomy. It no longer makes much sense to describe the ideological confrontation as one between "conservative" businessmen and "liberal" labor leaders.

[1] Midge Decter, "Anti-Americanism in America," *Harpers*, CCXXXVI (May, 1968), pp. 39–48.

There is wide agreement that the structure of political debate in the West has been transformed in the postwar period. The ideological struggles which consumed European policies after the birth of modern politics in the eighteenth century simply have lost their former intensity: nationalization is only slightly more appealing to the new managers of the Labor party in Great Britain than to the Conservatives; the old arguments between socialism and capitalism seem quaint, indeed largely irrelevant. There is less agreement on how this "something" which is happening in ideas and ideology in the West should be described. Bell and Lipset are among those who have addressed this in terms of the "end of ideology." [2] Others, and I am among them, distrust this catchy phrase; we believe that it confuses rather than clarifies, that it draws attention from transformation of ideological conflict which is the proper focus of attention. As long as men live together, there will be conflict, and some will systematically articulate what they see to be the points at issue between them and other men. But the shape of this conflict in ideas and ideology will certainly change as societies change, and we should not be surprised that systems of ideas generated by the early and middle phases of the egalitarian and industrial revolutions—for example, by the enormous deprivations attendant upon the building of a factory system—do not survive unmodified in the technologically developed, post-industrial, and affluent society.

What are the principal features of political ideology in contemporary America? Apter writes of science as an ideology in a *civilisation technicienne* and finds the division between a scientific elite and the scientifically illiterate a primary one. Along this line, Robert Lane refers to ours as the "knowledgeable society," one in which social knowledge is "creating its own attitudinal disequilibrium." On a somewhat different tack, Lowi writes that "the liberal-conservative dialogue made sense only up until, but not after, the establishment of positive government," and sees the "end of liberalism." Beer finds that the

[2] See Note 2 in the Introduction to this study.

C.D. spoke to the ideological conflict of the 1930's, not of the early 1900's and not of the 1960's.[3] We could go on here. All such efforts are designed to help reconceptualize conflict in the new society. The present study set out to explore this further through different data. My focus has been not the West or the country as a whole, but three Connecticut communities. The close-cropped empirical data gathered on the ideological divisions among community elites in metropolitan Hartford indicates clearly, I think, an ideological response to social change closely paralleling in important regards that suggested by many of the above-mentioned observers.

The polarity described here as *Cosmopolitan-Parochial* explains or accounts for the principal ideological conflict in Greater Hartford in the late 1960's. The Conventional Dichotomy does not. What has changed the shape of conflict over the last three decades? For one thing, affluence, which has shrunk the number who consider themselves to be aggrieved economic "have-nots" and freed many of the more prosperous from worries about their continued high prosperity. For another, the massive development of status politics, in which new collections of individuals find threats in demands for popular change. And finally, among the principal causes, the rapid growth, maturation, and extension of a scientific culture—both a way of conceptualizing major public problems and a body of technical expertise necessary to their effective solution—which generates prescriptive positions sharply at odds with the products of prescientific orthodoxies.

I dwelled upon the Cosmopolitan orientations of big business leaders because it seemed to point out rather dramatically

[3] David Apter, "Ideology and Discontent," in David Apter (ed.) *Ideology and Discontent* (New York: Free Press of Glencoe, 1964), pp. 15–46; Robert Lane, "The Decline of Politics and Ideology in a Knowledgeable Society," *American Sociological Review,* XXXI (October, 1966) 649–662; Theodore Lowi, "The Public Philosophy: Interest-Group Liberalism," *American Political Science Review,* LXI (March, 1967), 5–24, and *The End of Liberalism* (New York: W. W. Norton, 1969); and Samuel Beer, "Liberalism and the National Idea," *The Public Interest* (Fall, 1966), 70–82.

the commitment of an elite to new political roles. Business in Hartford today often acts as a socially progressive force. The Negro subcommunity of North Hartford will find the response of most whites unsatisfactory, but almost certainly it will more often find support over the next decade, as it has in the last decade, among the heads of business corporations than among the leaders of the local Democratic party. To equate businessman and conservative, labor leader or urban Democratic politician and liberal, probably was never very satisfactory. But it seems certain that both are far less satisfactory today than three decades ago.

There will be a strong temptation to draw from my construction a picture of Parochials as the bad guys of the new ideological struggle. This is not intended. The response of Parochials probably is as "reasonable," given their sociopolitical position, as is that of Cosmopolitans in light of theirs. What I have tried to suggest is that however humanely inclined they may be as individuals, Hartford Parochials are fundamentally "reactionary," reacting against a new orthodoxy, a new expertise, a new complexity, and for them a new and diminished status. Parochialism is a "reactionary" ideology in a *civilisation technicienne,* one that has muffled traditional economic tensions, accumulated scientific knowledge about the agonizing social problems, and acquired a staggering body of technical expertise. Parochialism is a reactive, as well as a reactionary, ideology. Indeed, it could be called anti-Cosmopolitanism for it has been forced into coherence by the new orthodoxy. Cosmopolitanism and Parochialism together appear as ideologies of our "overdeveloped" society, the one positive and "progressive," the other reactive and "reactionary," both contributing to the changing face of American political ideology.

This ideological conflict may prove disappointing to some observers. It is rather prosaic, after all, when compared to the grand struggles which consumed European elites in the 1930's. Some, indeed, may feel cheated, may be inclined to dismiss the American versions as "small potatoes," altogether unworthy of attention. I am tempted to respond like the anxious suitor, "I may not be much, but I am all I have." It is a simple fact that ideational conflict in the United States—and increasingly throughout the West—does not invite ringing slogans. The enemies cannot be painted nearly so darkly, are not nearly as threatening. We are not going to be propelled to the barricades by the ideational positions detected here.

But of course, American political ideas and ideology never did send men to the barricades. We were spun off from Europe just as aristocratic society was being torn asunder. A middle-class fragment—in Hartz's phrase—settled territory in which the existing society was so far less developed that it could be swept completely away. The fragment became the whole, and unlike its continental counterpart did not have to contend with the prime enemy of Liberalism, the old aristocratic order. The great physical resources of the New World, the suitability of the population for exploiting these resources, and the birth of our regime at the very time technological and economic changes were beginning to make possible enormous expansions of the wealth of nations—all served to endow the new regime with the aura of success. Naturally, its institutions and processes were soon smartly attired in legitimacy. Of course we have had little conflict extending to the very fabric of the regime, to the basic constitutional order and procedures. Ideological conflict today for the most part is not regime-reaching, then, but neither was it in 1815. This has been a continuing feature throughout our several agendas of politics. Still, ideational conflict as we have known it reflects the key dimensions of the American sociopolitical setting as faithfully as more intensely fractured forms do other political systems, and is as worthy of attention.

II

At a more modest level, this study has treated comparatively the fabric of political ideas and ideology, of ideational conflict, in one central city, one white-collar suburb, and one small town. In doing this, it has, of course, continually referred back to the utility of the trichotomy of city, suburb, and rural town which has figured so prominently in discussions of sociopolitical settings in the United States, a utility which was accepted in the hypotheses on which the inquiry was based. What differences distinguish the ideational systems of the places of the trichotomy? How imposing are these? And what do they add to our picture of towns, suburbs, and cities as three Americas?

Political and economic power in this century has ebbed away from small towns, which is to say from the elites who remain ascendant in small towns. This means, principally, members of the old middle class. Small towns have become backwaters in contemporary American society, continually robbed of their more ambitious children, moved along by the flow of a nationalized socioeconomic system, but away from the mainstream. Such developments so readily lend themselves to an overstatement which must be avoided, for there is in fact little real disaffection in Putnam, and, it seems, in other towns. So many of the changes which collectively have spelled decline and loss of independence for the town have been in many regards munificent. The response, then, appears not so much to be alienation as a quiet withdrawal. Politics in Putnam is overwhelmingly parochial, despite the advanced state of communications and transportation and the pervasive impact of national decisions. Putnam elites, operating in the backwaters of the new society, are little involved intellectually in its great problems.

The scope of local government remains modest in Putnam and really is not debated. Little happens in the public sector which matters much to any group of residents. Moreover, the matters with which government in the town deals are not linked to the great national controversies, a situation common enough historically but at odds with contemporary experience in metropolitan regions. Local conflict, then, is limited, and since community elites are little involved intellectually in problems which lie beyond the town's boundaries, the whole structure of political discussion is narrow.

The small town experience commonly is described in terms of an intense personalization of political life, and certainly this is true of Putnam. How could it be otherwise when a small group of community activists, in close and regular contact in a public sector distinguished by a lack of differentiation and minimal specialization, deals almost exclusively with matters which are narrow, immediate, and concrete? The ideational life of Putnam is defined by an absence of impersonality and abstraction, the stuff of ideology. Almost any issue is immediately personalized.

Politics in Putnam lacks heat. Those divisions which three decades ago might have been counted upon to generate real tensions no longer matter much. Ethnic and religious distinctions among white Americans, for example, in Putnam as throughout the country, move few to anger today. At the same time, Putnam has been little touched by those developments which are sustaining sharp ideological conflict in metropolitan America. There is nothing comparable to the clash in Greater Hartford among upper-middle-class businessmen and professionals, marginal-middle-class whites, and lower-class Negroes over the future shape of the metropolitan region. There are no proposals which promise substantial changes in the modes of living of any group. There is no radical Right or radical Left seriously challenging some feature of the recent flow of political life.

In Putnam we find a nonideological politics, an old-style community politics: personalities not issues; narrow local concerns, not an intrusion of wide-ranging national problems; a politics devoid of argument about the uses of government to effect social change. Curiously, the troubles of the "troubled small town" are not politicized, and its ideational life bears few marks of conflict.

Joseph Lyford noticed this in Vandalia, his troubled Illinois small town, and remarked that political life there was completely devoid of the stormy controversies which have rocked Westport, an affluent commuter suburb in southern Connecticut.[4] The same comparison can be made between Putnam and Bloomfield. The ideational life of our Hartford suburb contrasts strikingly with that of the small town, and the differences appear to follow from the primary feature of suburbanness: position in a metropolitan region outside the core. As a piece of the Hartford region, Bloomfield has been inundated by newcomers. Thus, it has had conflict among different generations of residents—generations defined not only by time of arrival but by social and economic position as well—and especially among the old middle class of Bloomfield the small town, the new-middle-class professionals who have entered after World War II, and the lower-middle-class Negroes who have arrived, for the most part, in the 1960's. As a piece of the region, Bloomfield has been caught up in regional problems, of which race is only the most prominent. The public sector is thus much larger than in Putnam, and elites find themselves confronting local statements of what are major national problems. Community politics in Bloomfield is much more outward-looking, less parochial. As a part of the region, Bloomfield has a population whose associations and perspectives tend more to be area-wide than local. Politics, then, is less intimate, less mired in personalities.

Other characteristics of Bloomfield politics generally, and ideational life specifically, result from the kind of suburb it is. White-collar professionals are ascendant, and their vision of Bloomfield's future has been controlling, though not unchallenged. The agenda has reflected their new-middle-class service demands, in the level of public spending, as to the shape of the school system, over the physical appearance of the suburb. The occupational attachments and educational backgrounds of these professionals give them more cosmopolitan perspectives, an orientation to national affairs, and the intellectual tools needed to comprehend them.

[4] Lyford, *The Talk in Vandalia* (New York: Harper & Row, 1965).

Politics in this suburb is ideological: the public sector is large enough, the issues are more remote enough, the divisions are sufficiently categoric, and enough citizens are inclined and able to see conflict in abstract terms. What happens in the public sector in Bloomfield matters much more to its residents than do developments in the public life of Putnam to those who live in that small town. But the residents of Hartford are still more vitally affected by local decisions. Some principal differences in the shape of conflict in suburb and city result from this: the outcome of the local political struggle has deeper implications for Hartford's future and for the position of the groups which comprise the city's population.

But there are other differences. The resources of Cosmopolitans and Parochials contrasts sharply in city and suburb. A majority of the Cosmopolitan leaders of Hartford do not live in the city, and the entire electoral process is firmly controlled by Parochials. In Bloomfield, Cosmopolitans operate within political party leadership and control of elective offices. But the Hartford Cosmopolitans do have impressive resources: their economic power, their control of the mass media, their technical expertise, and their access to state and national officials with whom Hartford must deal.

The patterns of alliances also vary between the two communities. In Bloomfield, during the transition from small town to suburb, liberal- and conservative-Cosmopolitans worked together against the incumbent Parochial leadership. But since the early 1960's their ascendancy has been so clear that liberal- and conservative-Cosmopolitans have been able to indulge their less substantial disagreements. Conservative-Parochials have mostly followed the lead of conservative-Cosmopolitans. In Hartford, the continued strength of conservative-Parochials has not only kept together a fairly effective alliance of Cosmopolitans—despite some sharp differences in the demands of their institutional positions, as between those of a Chamber of Commerce officer and a liberal-Cosmopolitan Democratic representative—but it has forced an unstable alliance of Cosmopolitans and race leaders. These two groups of leaders do not share a common conceptualization of the problems of the city, and they certainly do not have the same interests in its future. But they have found through alternate routes a common enemy in conservative-Parochials, and their *de facto* alliance is a principal instrument in the politics of Hartford's present, and, it appears, its future.

Here in this "little old" big city, this white-collar suburb built on land where before World War II cattle grazed and tobacco grew, and this tired French-Canadian mill town, we do find three Americans, blown on different courses by the winds of sociopolitical change in the twentieth century. Here are different varieties and magnitudes of public problems, different patterns of political conflict. The old-fashioned, nonideological, "friends-and-neighbors" politics of the small town contrasts with the wide-ranging ideological politics of city and suburb. The struggles of the middle classes of Bloomfield contrast with the less easily reconciled conflict among lower-class Negroes, lower-class and lower-middle-class whites, and upper-middle-class whites in the city. The response to change and decline in Putnam is not politicized, in contrast to the highly politicized reactions to change and decline in Hartford; and the elites of an ascendant Bloomfield appear more anxious for their community's future than the leaders of a "troubled" Putnam do for theirs.

Appendix: Methods of Study

Extensive socioeconomic and political background data on Hartford, Bloomfield, and Putnam were gathered at the beginning of the study. Files on political issues, on persons active in various phases of community life, and on the major events and developments in the recent history of each community were prepared. Local newspapers were carefully surveyed for the period from January, 1950, to April, 1965; and after April, 1965, a detailed clipping file, arranged chronologically by subject area, was maintained. Four newspapers—the Hartford *Times* and the Hartford *Courant* for Hartford and Bloomfield, and the Worcester *Evening Gazette* and the Windham County *Observer*/Putnam *Patriot* (the latter a weekly paper) for Putnam—were the sources. Newspapermen and other informed observers in each community were interviewed at various times throughout the study to secure more extensive and detailed information. Members of the project staff were present, as well, at numerous local meetings, formal and informal.

Unfortunately for those who find the community study an important vehicle for exploring American social and political life, the writing of local history has all but vanished in the twentieth century. Historical background for the eighteenth and nineteenth centuries was culled from memorial and county histories; but for 1900–1950 we had to rely upon a variety of fragmentary sources including scrapbooks of newspaper clippings, letters, and other documents in the collections of local historical associations and libraries, and the modest collection of pamphlets and clippings for each town in the Connecticut State Library.

Economic and demographic data for the contemporary period

were perhaps unusually complete. Along with the usual published materials such as U.S. Census reports, we had free access in Hartford to the extensive data collections of the City Clerk, the Registrar of Voters, the Commission on the City Plan, the Board of Education and Superintendent's office, the Manager's office, the Community Renewal Team (antipoverty agency) and the Housing Authority; in Bloomfield to the Board of Education and Superintendent's office, the Manager's office, the Town Clerk and Registrar of Voters; and in Putnam to the Housing Authority and Renewal Agency, the Town and City Clerks, the office of the Superintendent of Schools and the Registrar of Voters. The same support was given by state departments and agencies including the Secretary of State, the Development Commission, the Labor Department, and the State Library. Finally, the extensive data collections of certain private organizations were opened to us. Especially valuable were those of the Greater Hartford Chamber of Commerce, the Putnam Chamber of Commerce, the Connecticut Public Expenditure Council and the Southern New England Telephone Company.

In sum, before we began interviewing in Hartford, Bloomfield, and Putnam, we had gathered rather complete data on the historical development, political life, and the social and economic structure of each community. And these data collections were continually supplemented and updated as the research progressed. Behind this, of course, was our very strong commitment to examining the three community ideational systems in the richest possible contextual setting. A principal advantage of the community-study approach is the opportunity it provides for treating the subject with maximal depth and continuity.

THE ELITE SAMPLE

Because we were principally interested in the ideational responses of the various groups of community influentials and were not systematically exploring power relationships, the more rigorous selection or sampling procedures of power studies were not followed. We wanted and obtained a broadly representative cross section of those actively involved in the public life of Hartford, Bloomfield, and Putnam. The background information surveys described above permitted us to make the two essential determinations: "What is the scope of public life in each community?" and "Who have been prominently engaged in it?" We did not wish to describe in any precise, arithmetical sense what proportion of the "leadership" of each community adhered to a particular ideational position. We did want to locate *the principal positions among community elites,* to describe these in depth and with precision, and to explore their relationship to community decision making. In all, 210 community activists were interviewed in Hartford, 90 in Bloomfield and 55 in Putnam. Included were all principal officeholders and government administrators, the leaders of the local political parties, the heads of major local businesses and the officers of businessmen's organizations, the directors of the local mass media, and the officers of the other politically interested groups, including trade unions, civil rights organizations, political clubs, "good government" groups such as the League of Women Voters, certain church groups like Hartford's Catholic Interracial Council, and *ad hoc* organizations formed around specific issues. Some additional persons often referred to as active and influential in our interviews and in newspaper accounts were also included. More detailed information on the selection of the community elites to be interviewed and the composition of the samples will be found in Chapters 6, 7, and 8. The reader is referred specifically to footnotes 18, 27, and 35, in Chapter 8.

Those selected for interviewing were sent introductory letters which were followed by telephone requests for interview appointments. Only one person in the three communities refused. The interviews with community elites were loosely structured by the interview guide reprinted below. They ranged in length from forty-five minutes to four hours, with the average length approximately two hours. About 30 per cent of the sample were reinterviewed for one of three reasons: (1) a failure to go through all items in the guide in the first interview (about 25 per cent of the reinterviews); (2) interest in exploring specific questions at greater length (40 per cent); and (3) a desire to clarify aspects of the respondent's position in view of the flow of events subsequent to the initial interview (35 per cent).

MASS SAMPLES

The sampling procedure used in this study is one variety of probability sampling variously called *quasi-random* and *systematic sampling from lists.* The most recent (1965 for Hartford and Bloomfield, 1964 for Putnam) city directories provided complete lists of all dwelling units in each community, arranged by street (listed alphabetically) and by dwelling unit number (lowest to highest) on each street. The directories also supplied data on all adults living in each dwelling unit and on the occupations of those employed.

After calculating the desired sampling fraction for each community (let $k = N/n$), we selected every kth dwelling throughout the list of all dwelling units, starting with a random number chosen between 1 and k. A card, with a carbon, was then drawn up on the adult residents in each selected unit.

Decision as to sample size (n) was made after surveying our resources and after computing what numbers were needed for the various subgroups anticipated in the analysis to furnish the desired precision. It was decided to draw about 900 dwelling units in the three towns, and to select every 15th in Putnam and Bloomfield, every 120th in Hartford. This yielded 178 households in the town, 273 in the suburb and 455 in the city.[1]

[1] In June, 1965, there were approximately 4,100 households in Bloomfield, 2,700 in Putnam, and 54,600 in Hartford. In drawing the sample, if a dwelling was listed as vacant, the next listed was selected. If the family indicated in the directory no longer lived at the given address, if the designated respondent was no longer alive, too ill to be interviewed, away on an

Each community was divided into a number of interview districts and the sample dwellings sorted accordingly. Then, before our interviewers went into the field, the one adult in each unit to be interviewed was designated. Once designated, no substitution in the field was permitted. If the respondent was unavailable for the reasons discussed in footnote 1, the project director made a substitution. Otherwise, the selected respondent was either interviewed or recorded as a sample mortality. Each adult in the units selected was numbered in the manner described by Leslie Kish, and determination of which one was to be interviewed was made through recourse to tables which were a modification of those suggested by Kish.[2] The great advantages of designating the adult to be interviewed before sending the interviewers into the field are obvious: it frees the interviewer from having to make the determination after calling on the residence, and it eliminates error by the interviewer. We did rely heavily upon the city directories, of course, for several pieces of information vital to the selection procedure. But preliminary to drawing the sample, we undertook a spot assessment of the accuracy of the directories and found it to be very high. This accuracy was enhanced by their recent publication, less than five months before our survey for two of the three and only 10 months for the third.

Again following the technique suggested by Kish and used by, among others, Robert Presthus (*Men at the Top*), after each interview was coded and punched on cards it was "weighted," which is to say reproduced according to the number of adults

---

extended trip (more than three months), or unable to speak English, a substitute dwelling unit was selected at random from a special list as a replacement.

[2] Leslie Kish, "A Procedure for Objective Respondent Selection Within the Household," *Journal of the American Statistical Association,* XLIV (September, 1949), 380–387. All adult males were listed first, from oldest to youngest; then adult females in the same order. In a limited number of cases, the directories did not permit such listing (chiefly when an adult who was not related to the head of household as parent or child was listed for the unit), and in these cases a preliminary call was made.

in the household. Thus, a sample of households was translated into a sample of the adult population. It is widely agreed that multiple interviews in a single household is undesirable.

The sample mortality in each community is given below. The refusal rate was substantially higher in Bloomfield, and the cause of this was evident. In the months before the survey, Bloomfield had been besieged by sales persons posing as a variety of things which they were not, including as interviewers. Though we had considerable success in overcoming the suspicion that our interviewers were salesmen in disguise, we could not eliminate this completely.[3]

Sample mortality	*Hartford**	*Bloomfield*	*Putnam*
Interview terminated	2	1	1
Refusal	3	6	3
Respondent not reached	4	3	3
Total	9	10	7

* All data expressed as percentages.

Up to four "call backs" were made and the "respondent not reached" figure was thus reduced to modest proportions. The question of bias through nonresponse was carefully considered, but we felt able to dismiss it because the total mortality was not large in view of the uses to which we were to put the data. The only systematic comparison of respondents and nonrespondents was for sex.

[3] Each interviewer carried credentials, including a letter of introduction from the widely known and respected town manager. In addition, the project director and his staff were shown on local television and the director discussed his study in general terms on the radio. Favorable news stories were carried by local papers. In general, though, we never achieved the community rapport which we established in Putnam. News travels fast in the small town and after the project director had gone on a local radio station to answer telephone questions about the project and after he had spoken before such local groups as Rotary, the interviewers with few exceptions were warmly received. The status element in "our town's being selected" was real. It was nearly nonexistent in the suburb and completely absent in the city.

Sex	*Hartford**	*Bloomfield*	*Putnam*
Respondents			
Males	46	50	47
Females	54	50	53
Nonrespondents			
Males	48	45	50
Females	52	55	50

* All data expressed as percentages.

When weighted by the number of adults in the dwelling, a sample of 1,561 was obtained: 335 in Putnam, 490 in Bloomfield, and 736 in Hartford. A comparison of the samples and the total population as revealed through 1960 Census data, although the latter was five years old at the time the survey was conducted, gives us some further confidence in the sample's representativeness.

	Hartford*		Bloomfield		Putnam	
	1965 Survey	*1960 Census*	*1965 Survey*	*1960 Census*	*1965 Survey*	*1960 Census*
Sex						
Males	46	48	50	51	47	47
Females	54	52	50	49	53	53
Education						
0–8 years	39	46	14	26	45	58
9–11 years	21	20	15	16	21	18
H.S. grad.	27	21	35	30	24	15
Some college	13	13	36	28	10	9

* All data expressed as percentages.

The mass sample interviews were conducted in the summer and early fall of 1965 by a team of interviewers composed of senior graduate students in the social sciences at the University of Connecticut. The interviews took approximately one hour to complete, and the schedule is reproduced below.

In the summer of 1966, two senior graduate students in political science with extensive interviewing experience reinterviewed a 10 per cent subset of the original sample, chosen randomly. The reinterviews, loosely structured, were conducted for a number of purposes, some not relevant to this publication.

The principal objective, so far as this study is concerned, was to determine whether the picture yielded by the structured interviews of the use and comprehension of abstract conceptual dimensions was fully precise and valid. It was found to be. In virtually all cases, the classification of respondents made from the structured interviews was confirmed by the loosely structured data. The subset interviews covered the same areas as the original structured interviews, but did so almost entirely with open-ended questions. Each subset interview was set up by a letter followed by a telephone call, and the respondents were asked to devote approximately two hours.

INTERVIEW SCHEDULE

(Mass Samples)

Part I

I am (   ) from the University of Connecticut. We are here in (this community) studying public opinion on various political issues. We hope as a result of this study to understand better how the American democratic system works. We would like to have your opinions. I can assure you that your opinions will be kept in complete confidence.

We are mainly interested in questions such as these:

1. What would you say is the single most important problem facing (this community) today?

2. Who would you say are the three most important leaders in this community; that is, people who have the most say about the way things are run here?

   1. ______ 2. ______ 3. ______ 4. DK*
   5. NA†

3. Have you ever talked with any of these people you just mentioned about some problems you are interested in?
   1. Yes 2. No 3. Don't remember 4. NA

4. Are you a registered voter?
   1. Yes 2. No 3. Don't remember 4. NA

5. Generally speaking, do you consider yourself a Republican, a Democrat, or something else?
   1. Republican 2. Democrat 3. Independent 4. Other
   5. NA

   6. (Ask of Republicans and Democrats) Why do you favor the (preferred) party?

* Don't know.
† No answer.

7. (Ask of Republicans and Democrats) What do you dislike about the (opposed) party?

8. You may remember that Goldwater ran against Johnson for President. How much interest would you say you had in that presidential election—a great deal, quite a lot, not very much, or none at all?
1. A great deal 2. Quite a lot 3. Not very much
4. None at all 5. NA

9. Whom did you vote for?
1. Goldwater 2. Johnson 3. Did not vote 4. Other
5. NA

10. (If *did not vote*) Whom did you favor?
1. Goldwater 2. Johnson 3. No opinion 4. Other
5. NA

11. What do you think was the most important issue raised during the whole campaign between Johnson and Goldwater?

12. Thinking back to 1960, do you recall whether you favored Nixon or Kennedy? (If necessary: *which one?*)
1. Nixon 2. Kennedy 3. Don't remember 4. Other
5. NA

13. Thinking back to 1956, do you recall whether you favored Eisenhower or Stevenson? (If necessary: *which one?*)
1. Eisenhower 2. Stevenson 3. Don't remember
4. Other 5. Too Young 6. NA

14. (To be asked only of *Eisenhower-Johnson* supporters) Now you have said you favored Eisenhower in 1956 but not Goldwater in 1964. Since Eisenhower and Goldwater are both Republicans, how would you say Goldwater differed from Eisenhower?

15. (To be asked only of *Goldwater* supporters) Did you agree with most of the positions taken by Senator Goldwater in the 1964 campaign?
1. Yes 2. Agreed with some 3. Agreed with few or none 4. DK 5. NA

16. (To be asked only of *Goldwater* supporters) What did you like most about Senator Goldwater?

17. (To be asked of *everyone else*) What if anything did you dislike about Senator Goldwater's position on the various issues in the 1964 presidential election?

18. Why do you think Senator Goldwater was so badly defeated in the 1964 presidential election?

19. People often use labels like "liberal" and "conservative" to identify the political leanings of others. Using terms such as these, how would you describe your own political views? (If unclear, probe: *Do you consider yourself a liberal? a conservative? or what?*)

20. What is the basic difference between a liberal and a conservative, anyway, in terms of their political beliefs?

21. Are there any leaders in (this community) whom you would call conservatives? (If necessary: *Who are they? Can you give me their names?*)
1. Yes (and names) 2. No 3. DK 4. NA

____

____

____

22. (If *yes*) What is it that they do or don't do that leads you to call them conservatives?

23. Are there any leaders in (this community) whom you would call liberals? (Again: *Who are they? Names?*)
1. Yes (and names) 2. No 3. DK 4. NA

____

____

____

24. (If *yes*) What is it that they do or don't do that leads you to call them liberals?

25. Are there any national leaders whom you would call conservatives? (If necessary: *Who are they? Can you give me their names?*)
    1. Yes (and names) 2. No 3. DK 4. NA

    ____
    ____
    ____

26. Are there any national leaders whom you would call liberals? (If necessary: *Who are they? Can you give me their names?*)
    1. Yes (and names) 2. No 3. DK 4. NA

    ____
    ____
    ____

Part II

Now, I am going to mention some names of people active in politics nationally. You may or may not recognize some of these names. Of those you do recognize, would you tell me whether you consider them to be conservatives?

27. Former President Eisenhower?
    1. Yes 2. No 3. Undecided 4. DK 5. NA
28. Former Vice-President Richard M. Nixon?
    1. Yes 2. No 3. Undecided 4. DK 5. NA
29. Former President Harry Truman?
    1. Yes 2. No 3. Undecided 4. DK 5. NA
30. Senator Thomas Dodd?
    1. Yes 2. No 3. Undecided 4. DK 5. NA
31. Former Senator Barry Goldwater?
    1. Yes 2. No 3. Undecided 4. DK 5. NA
32. Governor John Dempsey?
    1. Yes 2. No 3. Undecided 4. DK 5. NA
33. Senator Strom Thurmond?
    1. Yes 2. No 3. Undecided 4. DK 5. NA
34. Mr. Robert Welch?
    1. Yes 2. No 3. Undecided 4. DK 5. NA

35. Mr. John Lupton?
    1. Yes 2. No 3. Undecided 4. DK 5. NA

36. Mr. Robert Shelton?
    1. Yes 2. No 3. Undecided 4. DK 5. NA

37. Mr. A. Searle Pinney?
    1. Yes 2. No 3. Undecided 4. DK 5. NA

And what about these organizations? Are any of them what you would call conservative political groups?

38. The American Legion?
    1. Yes 2. No 3. Undecided 4. DK 5. NA

39. The Ku Klux Klan?
    1. Yes 2. No 3. Undecided 4. DK 5. NA

40. The National Association of Manufacturers?
    1. Yes 2. No 3. Undecided 4. DK 5. NA

41. The Americans for Democratic Action?
    1. Yes 2. No 3. Undecided 4. DK 5. NA

42. The Republican Party?
    1. Yes 2. No 3. Undecided 4. DK 5. NA

43. The American Medical Association?
    1. Yes 2. No 3. Undecided 4. DK 5. NA

44. The AFL-CIO?
    1. Yes 2. No 3. Undecided 4. DK 5. NA

45. The John Birch Society?
    1. Yes 2. No 3. Undecided 4. DK 5. NA

Part III

Now I would like to ask you a few questions about some important issues confronting all of us.

46. Are you in favor of the Medicare Program now before Congress?
    1. Yes 2. No 3. Undecided 4. DK 5. NA

47. Are you in favor of the Federal Government's antipoverty program?
    1. Yes 2. No 3. Undecided 4. DK 5. NA

48. Some people favor our foreign aid program and others are critical of it. Do you, generally speaking, favor or oppose the program?
    1. Favor 2. Oppose 3. Undecided 4. DK 5. NA

49. The recently adjourned session of the Connecticut state legislature increased spending on a number of state programs. Do you generally favor or oppose such actions taken by the legislature?
    1. Favor 2. Oppose 3. Undecided 4. DK 5. NA

50. Connecticut is in the process of reapportioning its legislature following the Supreme Court decision that legislative districts must be equal in population. Some people say that this is bad, that the Court had no business interfering in state apportionment. How do you feel about this?
    1. Bad: Court had no business 2. Good: Court did right thing 3. Undecided 4. DK 5. Other 6. NA

51. From what you have heard about the matter, do you think that reapportionment here in Connecticut will make for better government, or will have generally bad effects?
    1. Better government 2. Bad effects 3. Undecided 4. DK 5. NA

52. Now the civil rights movement all over the country has been very active during the last few years. Have Negro Americans been asking for too much, too fast?
    1. Yes 2. No 3. Undecided 4. DK 5. NA

53. Some, like Alabama Governor George Wallace, insist that the civil rights movement is Communist dominated, or at least has Communists in it in positions of influence. Do you agree or disagree?
    1. Agree 2. Disagree 3. Undecided 4. DK 5. NA

54. Do you think there are many Communists in the United States?
    1. Yes, many 2. Yes, some 3. No 4. Undecided 5. DK 6. NA

55. Have you ever known any one whom you suspected of being a Communist?
    1. Yes 2. No 3. Undecided 4. DK 5. NA

56. (If *yes*, ask:) Could you tell me what it was that he did or said that made you think he was a Communist?

57. Some people think that it may well be possible for the United States and the Soviet Union to talk out many of the pressing international problems. Do you agree or disagree?
1. Agree 2. Disagree 3. Undecided 4. DK 5. NA

58. Should we spend more than we presently are spending for defense, about the same, or less?
1. More 2. About the same 3. Less 4. Undecided
5. DK 6. NA

59. Some maintain that we should be working for a negotiated settlement in Vietnam. Others think we should be prepared to fight on to a military victory, while still others favor a holding action. How do you feel about this?
1. Negotiated settlement 2. Fight on 3. Holding action
4. Undecided 5. DK 6. Other 7. NA

60. Some think we should relax our immigration quotas to allow more people from foreign countries to become citizens of our country. Do you agree or disagree?
1. Agree 2. Disagree 3. Undecided 4. DK 5. NA

61. There are those who maintain that most poor people in this country are poor because they don't want to work or because they spend their money wastefully. Do you agree or disagree with this?
1. Agree 2. Disagree 3. Undecided 4. DK 5. NA

62. Should anyone who is a Communist be allowed to go about the country freely?
1. Yes 2. No 3. Undecided 4. DK 5. NA

63. Some people feel that Negro leaders pressing for full equality for Negroes at once have in fact hurt their cause by frightening responsible white leaders in the South. Do you think that this is correct?
1. Yes 2. No 3. Undecided 4. DK 5. NA

Part IV

Now I would like to ask you just a few questions about these changing times in which we live. There has been so much change so fast over the last half century.

64. On balance, are we better off today than we used to be, or aren't things as good?
    1. Better off   2. Not as good   3. About the same
    4. Undecided   5. DK   6. NA

65. Have we lost anything in all this change? (If necessary: *What have we lost?*)

66. Do you think things are changing too fast?
    1. Yes   2. No   3. Undecided   4. DK   5. NA

67. What about (this community)? Do you think things will be better, about the same, or not as good ten years from now as they are now?
    1. Better   2. About the same   3. Not as good
    4. Undecided   5. DK   6. NA

68. About how many times have you moved from town to town in the last 10 years?
    1. None   2. 1   3. 2–3   4. 4–6   5. 7 or more
    6. Don't remember   7. NA

    69. (To be asked of those who have moved *two or more times.*) Could you tell me the reasons for those moves?

    70. (To be asked of those who have moved *two or more times.*) Some people do not mind moving; others find moving an unpleasant task. How do you feel about this?

71. Fifty years ago, our population was smaller; our government, business, and labor organizations were smaller; we had only a very small army and we were not actively involved in foreign affairs. On balance, was America better off then or are we better off today?
    1. Better off then   2. Better off now   3. About the same
    4. Undecided   5. DK   6. NA

Part V

Finally, I would like to ask you a few questions about yourself.

72. How long have you lived in (this community)?
    1. Less than a year 2. 1–5 years 3. 6–10 years
    4. 11–20 years 5. Over 20 years 6. All my life 7. NA

    73. (If other than *all my life*) Where were you born?
    City State Country

    74. (If other than *all my life*) How many other (in addition to this) communities have you lived in?
    1. One 2. Two 3. Three 4. Four
    5. Five or more 6. NA

75. How old are you?
    1. 21–30 2. 31–40 3. 41–50 4. 51–65 5. Over 65
    6. NA

76. Do you rent or own your present home?
    1. Rent 2. Own 3. Other 4. NA

77. How many grades of school did you complete?
    1. None 2. 1–5 3. 6–8 4. 9–11 5. High school graduate 6. Some college 7. College graduate 8. Advanced degrees 9. NA

78. Was your education (for those with at least some college add: *up to college*) in public or private schools, or did it include both?
    1. Public 2. Private 3. Mixed 4. NA

    79. (If *private* or *mixed*) Who operated the private school?
    1. Catholic 2. Protestant 3. Jewish
    4. Nonsectarian 5. Other 6. NA

80. What is your present occupation? (Be certain to determine company and nature of work if employed by someone else, type of business if self-employed.)

    81. (If other than head of household, ask) What is (head of household's) present occupation? (Again, be certain to determine company and nature of work if employed by someone else, type of business if self-employed.)

82. What is your religious affiliation?
    1. Catholic 2. Protestant 3. Jewish 4. Other
    5. None 6. NA

83. If people asked you your nationality or descent, how would you identify yourself? For example, French, Irish, English, or something else?

84. (Hand respondent card) Would you look at this card and tell me the number that corresponds to your family's total income from all sources last year, 1964, before taxes.
    1. Under $1,000 2. $1,000–2,999 3. $3,000–4,999
    4. $5,000–6,999 5. $7,000–9,999 6. $10,000–20,000
    7. Over $20,000 8. NA

Thank you very much

(Complete *following* interview)

85. Name of respondent
86. Address
87. Sex
    1. Male 2. Female
88. Interviewer
89. Date of interview
90. Approximate length of interview
91. General comments by interviewer

INTERVIEW GUIDE

(Elites Samples)

I. *General Biographical Data on Respondent.*

II. *Major Problems Facing America.*
What does the respondent consider to be the biggest problems facing this country today? What should government seek to do about them?

III. *Major Problems Facing the Local Community.*
What does the respondent consider to be the biggest problems facing his community today? What should be done about them?

IV. *National and State Policy Areas Not Covered In Item II.*
Here follows a series of specific questions asking "How do you feel about . . . ?" national civil rights developments? the domestic welfare program of the Johnson Administration? the general foreign policy commitments of the United States today? the war in Vietnam? negotiations with Communist nations? foreign aid? government spending and "big government"? reapportionment in Connecticut and the state constitutional convention?

V. *Local Community Policy Areas Not Covered In Item III.*
For the metropolitan communities, especially, questions relating to the entrance of nonwhites; crime and delinquency; possible regional solutions to municipal problems; transportation; urban renewal; the role of government in meeting basic urban problems. For the small town, especially, questions relating to the broad economic and political decline of small-town America. Is there a sense of decline? Are the "villains" identified? What should national government do for the small town?

VI. *Civil Liberties.*
Respondent's views on civil liberties explored through a series of questions set against immediate and specific developments: for example, reclassification of students protesting the Vietnam war.

VII. *Evaluation of Local, State, and National Political Leaders.*
Which leaders (national, state, and local) does the respondent most admire, and why? How does the respondent describe the political position of the leader being discussed? How does he describe his support or opposition, his agreement or disagreement with the leader's position? Would the respondent normally use abstract conceptual dimensions like *liberal* and *conservative* in reference to the positions of political leaders?

VIII. *Description of Political Conflict.*
How does the respondent see and describe political conflict, national, state, and local? At which level is most conflict seen occurring? What values does the respondent see at stake in political conflict? How are the contending forces in political conflict seen and described?

IX. *Use and Understanding of Abstract Conceptual Dimensions.*
For the respondent, what is liberalism? conservatism? What leaders are liberals? conservatives? What is it that they do or do not do that demands the label? Would the respondent use any A.C.D. in describing the political positions of competing elites, local or national? with what understanding? Would the respondent describe himself as a liberal? a conservative? If not, would he use any such A.C.D.? with what understanding?

X. *Attitudes Toward Social and Economic Change.*
Does the respondent see the society of today as better, worse, or about the same as [e.g.] 4 decades ago? Have things changed too fast? Have any values been sacrificed in this change? What, principally, has been gained? To what extent is the degree of change understood and a part of the respondent's consciousness? What about the respondent's own community? Does he think things will be better, about the same, or not as good 10 years hence? What of the community's capacity to meet its major problems? Does the respondent see problems in the interdependence of society? in the increasing size and complexity? in the increasing mobility? in new balances of political power? in new value systems? in new attitudes toward work and leisure? What areas of change does the respondent find the most frustrating? the most welcome?

XI. *Localism vs. Cosmopolitanism.*

To what extent is the respondent aware of and interested in a wide range of political matters beyond his community? To what extent does he see politics in terms of local personalities, local problems? To what extent are his political thoughts caught up in the immediacy of personal and/or local events? To what extent can he extract meaning from less personalized conflicts which are the essence of the national political struggle?

Index